THE
ULTIMATE
BOOK OF

PAINT
EFFECTS

THE
ULTIMATE
BOOK OF

PAINT
EFFECTS

TIME
LIFE
BOOKS

Alexandria, Virginia

Time-Life Books is a division of Time Life Inc.

TIME LIFE INC.
Chairman and CEO   Jim Nelson
President and COO   Steven L. Janas

TIME-LIFE TRADE PUBLISHING
Vice President and Publisher   Neil Levin
Senior Director of Acquisitions and Editorial Resources   Jennifer Pearce
Director of New Product Development   Carolyn Clark
Director of Marketing   Inger Forland
Director of New Product Development   Teresa Graham
Director of Trade Sales   Dana Hobson
Director of Custom Publishing   John Lalor
Director of Special Markets   Robert Lombardi
Director of Design   Kate L. McConnell

THE ULTIMATE BOOK OF PAINT EFFECTS
Editor for Special Markets   Anna Burgard
Technical Specialist   Monika Lynde

Color separation by Colourscan in Singapore
Printed in Singapore by Imago
10 9 8 7 6 5 4 3 2 1

TIME-LIFE is a trademark of Time Warner Inc. and affiliated companies.

ISBN 0-7370-0322-7

CIP data available upon application:
Librarian, Time Life Books
2000 Duke Street
Alexandria, VA 22314
Books produced by Time-Life Trade Publishing are available at a special bulk discount
for promotional and premium use. Custom adaptations can also be created to meet
your specific marketing goals. Call 1-800-323-5255.

SAFETY GUIDELINES

Children's rooms

When working on projects for children's rooms, make sure that all materials, especially paints and varnishes, are nontoxic, and do not put anything that has small or loose parts within the reach of a baby. Always keep your equipment and materials, together with any unfinished projects, in a locked cupboard and out of the reach of children.

Cutting equipment

When working with a utility or craft knife, use a cutting mat or piece of thick cardboard to protect the work surface. Always cut away from your body in case the knife slips, and do not place your other hand in the path of the blade.

Protective gloves

Wear protective gloves when using paint and varnish strippers, because both are caustic and should not come in contact with the skin. If you find ordinary household rubber gloves cumbersome, try lightweight surgical gloves. However, do not wear rubber gloves when working with a heat source.

Step ladders

When using a ladder, make sure that the base is level and stable so that it will not slide or move when you are on it. Never stand on the top platform. Rather than leaning or stretching to reach difficult areas, move the ladder. Remove any paint or tools from the platform before moving the ladder.

Heat strippers

When using a heat gun protect your eyes with safety goggles and consider using cotton gloves. Do not wear loose-fitting clothing that could get in the way of the heat source, and tie back long hair. Make sure that the work area is free of anything that could catch fire, such as bedding or curtains, and never cover the floor with newspaper. Protect glass and plastic with a heat deflector when working near them with a heat gun.

Ventilation

When using oil- and solvent-based adhesives, paints, and varnishes, work in a well-ventilated area and do not allow open flames or cigarettes nearby. Always wear a face mask to protect you from fumes and dust, even when working outdoors.

Safety goggles

Always wear safety goggles when you are doing any job that could produce dust or flying debris, such as paint stripping, sanding, sawing, or hammering.

Electricity

Before plugging in a power tool, check for damaged cords and loose connections. Always use a 3-prong outlet and do not use extension cords. If you have problems with a power tool, always unplug it before attempting to fix it. Keep power tools away from water. Before working on an electrical fitting or appliance, turn off the current either by unplugging the appliance or shutting off the power at the main box.

ACKNOWLEDGMENTS

Authors: Salli Brand, Julie Collins, Catherine Cumming, Tricia Greening, Katrina Hall, Frances Halliday, Clare Louise Hunt, Joanna Jones, Laurence Llewelyn Bowen, Julie London, Merópe Mills, Maggie Philo, Fiona Robinson, Frances Robinson, Tony Robinson.

Photographers: Graeme Ainscough, Dominic Blackmore, Jon Bouchier, Anna Hodgson, Tim Imrie, Andre Martin, Lucinda Symons, Dai Williams.

Illustrator: Stephen Pollitt.

Contents

Introduction

PAINT EFFECTS ARE NOT A MODERN DISCOVERY. As long ago as prehistoric times, cave dwellers used natural pigments on rock faces to record their activities. For many centuries, paint-effect techniques were the secret of craftsmen but now this information is available to everyone. Today, painting is one of the simplest and most versatile ways of decorating your house. Not restricted to variations in color, paint can be manipulated and textured to produce a host of different finishes. A "paint effect" is any technique that goes beyond simple solid-color painting. It may involve painting a base of solid color and then applying a glaze—a slippery medium that enables you to move paint around on the surface. Or it may involve using some other piece of equipment such as a stencil or a stamp to enhance your design.

With the help of this book, you will soon be able to fill your home with a variety of paint finishes to suit any room or any object, large or small. "Getting Started" outlines the essential preparatory work and "Basic Paint Effects" introduces you to paint and its uses. With the chart on pages 26–9, you will be able to select the best paint for your purpose and using the tips on tool choice and color selection will help you to put your plans into practice. The introduction to paint and glaze techniques will give you a grounding in the fundamental principles of basic paint effects. Once you have mastered these you can move onto more complicated skills in "Advanced Paint Effects." Broken-color, or crazing, techniques are the key to many faux finishes—the imitation of a substance other than that on which you are painting. You could, for example, make plaster look like mahogany or wood look like marble. These methods are illustrated and explained in a clear and easy-to-understand way. Similarly, specialist paint techniques such as stenciling, gilding, and stamping are covered in detail. The "Inspirations" chapter will fuel your imagination and enable you to plan and design your decorative scheme. The special photography will show you how you can gather ideas from subjects as various as architecture, stone, wood, flowers, foliage, and fabrics.

Once you are equipped with the skills and have found the inspiration for your design, you will be ready to put them into practice. The rest of the book is devoted to step-by-step projects, which will give you the chance to do just that. Each is given a difficulty rating of one to five (indicated by the paintbrushes next to the title), which will act as a quick reference for helping you to decide which projects you might like to attempt. A difficulty rating of one means that you will be able to try your hand at it, achieve great results, and exert the minimum amount of effort; a rating of five means that your skills will be more tested and that perfect results may take time and patience.

With the techniques, inspiration, and practical ideas in this book, you will be ready to take on any paint challenge. Once you have tried them, you may find that paint effects become a lifelong hobby and you will be able to use them alone or together to give your home a truly unique and individual decorative scheme.

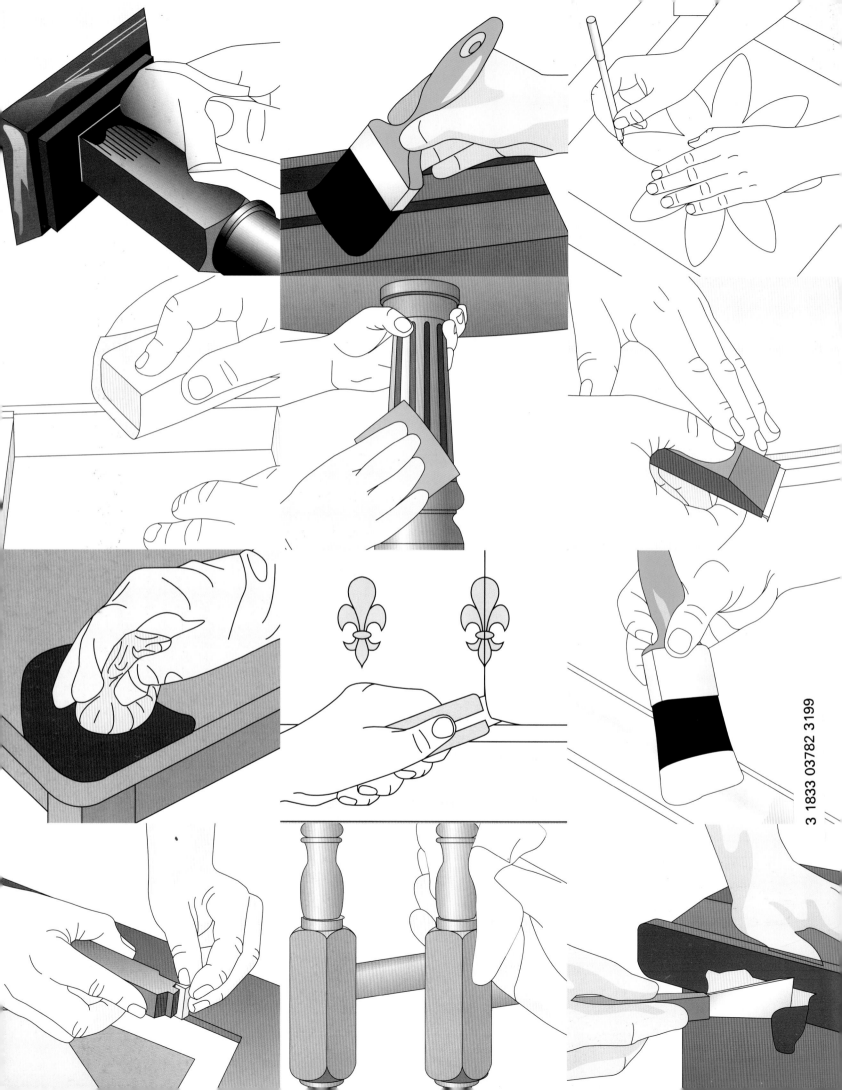

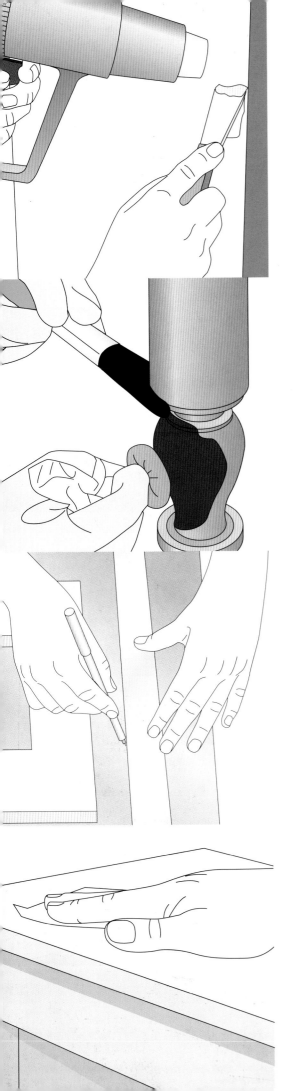

PAINT EFFECTS CAN BE CARRIED OUT ON ALMOST ANY SURFACE BUT EACH TYPE OF SURFACE NEEDS DIFFERENT PREPARATION BEFORE YOU CAN START. THE SUCCESS OF ANY PROJECT DEPENDS ON HOW MUCH THOUGHT AND PLANNING HAS GONE INTO IT BEFOREHAND. IT MAY SEEM THE MOST TEDIOUS PART OF THE WHOLE PROCESS BUT IT IS ALWAYS WELL WORTH THE EFFORT.

Getting Started

Preparing the surface

ALL PAINT EFFECTS, no matter how simple or complicated they are, require a well-prepared surface. Although sometimes boring and labor-intensive, thoroughly preparing your wall or piece of furniture will help to avoid unwanted peeling and cracking, and prevent your painstaking, dedicated work from going to waste. The next few pages provide a basic list of equipment that you might need, together with some guidance on how to perform these simple tasks to your best advantage. Many are ordinary household items, although others, such as masks and goggles, are vital investments for achieving the right finish—both successfully and safely. Remember that the value of good preparation can never be overestimated.

CLEANING

Cleaning is essential before you start to create your paint effects. Unwanted dust or grease could ruin the finish and threaten to destroy all your hard work.

WASHING EQUIPMENT

If possible, it is best to perform this task outside where making a mess will not be so much of a problem. Always have plenty of rinsing water at hand and make sure that you protect your clothes with a waterproof apron. Use a spare bowl, household sponge and/or scouring pad, together with a detergent solution for greasy surfaces. Some items will need more time and perseverance than others, but revealing the true surface beneath the dirt can be truly rewarding.

CLOTHS

Always set aside any old cotton shirts and sheets that you have for use as soft, lint-free cloths. It is amazing how quickly rags and cloths need to be replaced, so before embarking on a cleaning project, make sure that there are plenty at hand. It is also sometimes worthwhile investing in a few speciality cloths, particularly ones that can be used while performing decorative skills and techniques.

• CHEESECLOTH OR STOCINETTE: These are available from the majority of home-improvement stores and are used for polishing or general mopping up. This type of cloth can also be handy for decorative techniques, creating stipple-like textures on painted surfaces, or eliminating brush marks.

• TACK CLOTHS: Small, versatile and long-lasting, these oily cloths are ideal for cleaning wood, metal, plaster, or any other surface (except glass). They will pick up and hold dust and dirt, leaving a completely clean surface to work on. Tack cloths are used in most projects in this book.

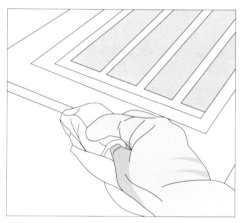
▲ Wear rubber gloves when applying chemicals.

DETERGENTS

A range of commercially available detergents and similar products are good for cutting through dirt and grease deposits, when applied with steel wool or cloths. Check with the chart on page 21 to find out what type of product is effective for the surface that you are using and always wear protective rubber gloves. Methylated and mineral spirits can be used to remove grease and grime, but always follow the manufacturer's guidelines with regard to storage and use.

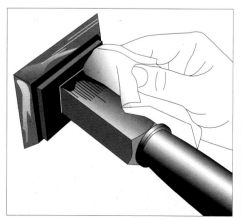
▲ Wipe all surfaces, edges, and corners.

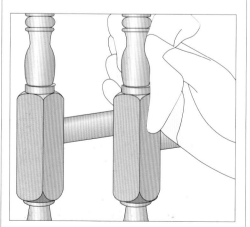
▲ Use a tack cloth to remove dust and dirt.

SAFETY ADVICE: Equipment

Always wear goggles and a mask whenever you are rubbing down surfaces. Gloves and protective clothes are especially important when using chemical products such as paint strippers or methylated spirits. Ear plugs are also a good idea for work with electrical equipment such as sanders. Protect all nearby surfaces with a suitable covering and always provide plenty of ventilation for dust and fumes.

RUBBING DOWN

Some items will require more rubbing down than others. In certain cases, you may have to get rid of a few loose flakes of paint and in others, you might have to remove several layers of varnish or paint in order to get back to the original surface. Metal, in particular, needs a thorough rubbing down because any rust left will invariably recur, spoiling the finished effect. The size of the piece, the type of surface, and the desired finish will help to determine what equipment should be used for the project.

SANDPAPER

Available in paint and hardware stores, sandpaper can be used to sand down a surface, distress paint, and smooth paint and varnish finishes. Most are graded as either coarse, medium, or fine, depending on the amount and spacing of the grit used—the higher the number, the finer and more compact the grit. Some can be fitted to electric drills or sanders, while others are designed to be handheld. Many people use a sanding block, or wrap the paper around a block of cork or wood for easy handling.

Bear in mind that some surfaces suit different types of paper more than others. For example, softwoods may need more abrasion than hardwoods.

Sanding down a surface takes patience and will often require two or more different types of paper. Use a coarse- or medium-coarse- (depending on the roughness of the surface) grit paper to remove most of the jaggedness before finishing off the surface with a fine-grit paper.

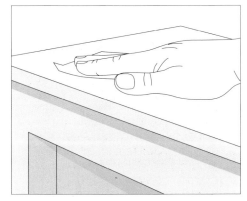

▲ Use sandpaper for rubbing down.

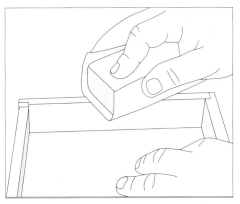

▲ Sandpaper can be wrapped around cork.

Remember always to wear a mask when using sandpaper, in order to avoid inhaling dust particles. It is also a good idea to follow the grain of the wood to help prevent surface damage and scratches.

• GLASSPAPER: This is a soft, abrasive paper containing small particles of glass, and is suitable for the first stages of sanding.

• GARNET PAPER: Often reddish in color, this paper is quite rough. However, it is more durable than glasspaper, making it ideal for hardwood furniture.

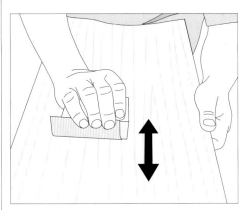

▲ Follow the direction of the grain.

• WET AND DRY OR SILICON CARBIDE PAPER: As its name suggests, this paper can be used wet or dry, and is good for fine-smoothing painted surfaces. It is also particularly good for distressing stencils or hand-painted designs, although in these cases the grit should be very fine. For best results, keep the paper dry, which will prevent black smudges on the decorative finish.

• A SANDING STICK: There is a very helpful product on the market known as a "sanding stick," on which you attach a piece of sandpaper. The stick has a swivel joint on the end of it, which means that you can reach up to sand and turn the sandpaper as you go without the aid of a ladder. A brisk run over a latex-painted wall with a sanding stick before painting will eliminate the orange-peel effect and create a quick, smooth surface on which to begin.

STEEL BRUSHES & STEEL WOOL

Relatively inexpensive and available from hardware stores, steel brushes are particularly good for large pieces of metal with flaking paint or rust. Although intricate areas are best treated with handheld brushes, it is possible to buy electric drills with steel-brush attachments for large surfaces.

Steel wool comes in various grades of coarseness and can be used for rubbing down wood, metal, and glass, as well as applying wax and distressing painted surfaces. It can also be used to apply paint and varnish removers, or be soaked in mineral spirits for cleaning wood furniture. If it is used gently, fine steel wool does not scratch or mark surfaces and it helps to create a very clean, smooth finish. However, the wool is made of fine steel filaments, which can be inhaled when loosened, so always wear a mask.

SCRAPERS

There are a variety of scrapers available that can be used to remove surface coatings, either alone or in conjunction with a paint stripper or heat gun. The main types are:

• BROAD SCRAPER: Wooden-handled with a wide metal blade, this is designed to glide between the surface and coating.

• SHAVEHOOK: This is either completely triangular or has a combination of curved and straight blades, designed to scrape in awkward surfaces such as curves and grooves.

• SKARSTEN SCRAPER: A scraper with disposable, hooked blades that clip into a wooden handle. Use on flat surfaces, on curves, and in difficult grooves.

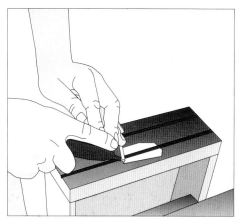

▲ Pull the scraper in the direction of the grain.

USING A SKARSTEN SCRAPER

1 Remove any hinges and handles from the object. Starting with flat areas, hold the scraper firmly and pull it toward you, following the grain of the wood. If the surface becomes bumpy, turn the scraper 45 degrees and scrape in the direction of the grain.

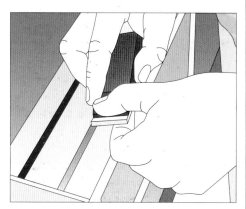

▲ Apply pressure close to the blade for grooves.

2 Only push the scraper away from you in exceptional cases, such as when cleaning out grooves, as this can gouge the wood. In these instances, hold the skarsten scraper firmly and close to the blade, so that you can control the pressure.

3 Fit a serrated blade into the scraper if you are tackling a particularly stubborn surface. However, this will scratch flat surfaces so be sure to remove it after use.

HEAT GUNS

Paint can be softened prior to scraping by using a heat gun. Much safer than a conventional blowtorch, which has a naked flame, the heat gun produces blasts of warm air, similar to those produced by a hair dryer. This causes

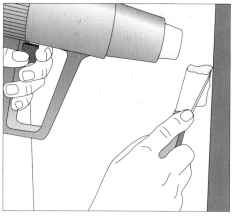

▲ Scrape away the paint as it peels under heat.

the paint to soften and bubble, making it easy for you to insert a scraper underneath and gently lift it off. Heat guns can also be fitted with various attachments that either disperse or concentrate the heat emitted.

1 Hold the nozzle about 2 to 4in (5 to 10cm) away from the surface so that the paint starts to bubble and blister, without actually burning.

2 As the paint layer begins to rise, insert a paint scraper underneath and lift it away carefully. Continue in this way until most of the paint has been removed.

3 Sand down the surface with medium- and then fine-grit sandpaper, then wipe it with a tack cloth in order to remove any paint or dust residue.

PAINT STRIPPERS

There are numerous paint strippers readily available for removing both paint and varnish. However, chemical strippers can burn if they touch the skin so always wear protective clothes and gloves when using them. Also, be sure there is plenty of ventilation for unpleasant fumes. If the task of completely removing old paint is too

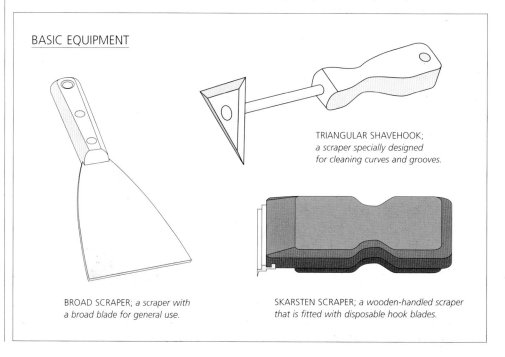

BASIC EQUIPMENT

TRIANGULAR SHAVEHOOK;
a scraper specially designed for cleaning curves and grooves.

BROAD SCRAPER; *a scraper with a broad blade for general use.*

SKARSTEN SCRAPER; *a wooden-handled scraper that is fitted with disposable hook blades.*

daunting, rub it down as well as possible and fill any deep indents where the paint has completely come away with decorator's caulk, using a damp cloth to wipe the caulk over the edge of the old paint, thus smoothing out the ridges.

STRIPPING PAINT

1 Remove any handles or hinges on the object. Then scrape off loose paint and wipe down the surface.

2 Using an old paintbrush, apply paint stripper to the piece, a section at a time. Wear heavy-duty waterproof gloves and work with the window open at all times.

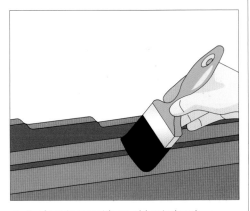

▲ Apply stripper with an old paintbrush.

3 Scrape off all the loose and soft paint with a scraper. Use a skarsten scraper for grooves and tight areas. Remove excess stripper with mineral spirits, as instructed. (Avoid using water on wood as this may cause damage.)

4 When the bare surface is dry, use medium- and then fine-grit sandpaper to sand it down. Finally, wipe the surface with a tack cloth to remove any residue.

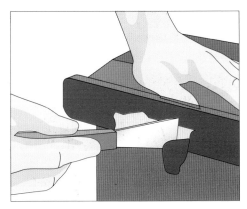

▲ Lift the softened paint with the scraper.

STRIPPING SHELLAC FINISHES

1 To remove shellac finishes, such as French-polished surfaces, apply methylated spirits to a small section of the surface with steel wool or a nylon scouring pad. (Strong liquid ammonia can also be used but the fumes are extremely unpleasant.) Wearing rubber gloves and a face mask, rub the pad back and forth, following the grain as closely as possible.

2 As you finish scrubbing the small area, use a cloth soaked with methylated spirits to rub off all excess shellac. Then move on to another area, making sure that you work on small sections at a time.

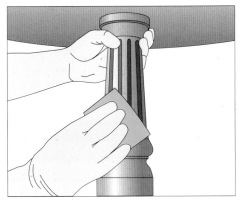

▲ Apply methylated spirits with a scouring pad.

3 Clean tight areas, such as grooves and curves, with a skarsten scraper. Then sand with medium- and fine-grit sandpaper.

4 If you will be using a solvent-based finish, set the object aside for a while so that the moisture in the air can raise the grain. If you are using a water-based finish, the same effect can be achieved by wiping the surface with a dampened cloth.

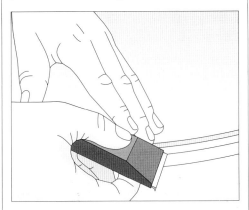

▲ Clean tight grooves with a skarsten scraper.

▲ Be sure to scrape out tight corners and edges.

STRIPPING VARNISH

1 Sand the surface roughly with a medium-grit sandpaper. This will help the paint stripper to penetrate the waterproof coating. Then liberally apply paint (or varnish) stripper with an old brush.

2 Leave the surface until the varnish begins to bubble and lift—this can take 1 to 4 hours. Scrape off the softened varnish with a paint scraper and use a triangular shavehook for corners and grooves. Any areas where the varnish does not come off will need a second application of stripper.

3 Sand down the surface with medium- and fine-grit sandpaper. Then wipe down with a tack cloth to remove any residue.

HINTS & TIPS: Stripping

• If you have a large piece of furniture, it may be worth using a commercial stripping company. Some businesses use non-caustic methods which, although invariably more expensive than caustic techniques, are safer for delicate objects. Chunky pine items or pieces that are not that valuable, can be treated with caustic chemicals. However, when the object is returned, wash it down with vinegar to neutralize any remaining caustic soda solution. Allow the piece to dry and sand it before applying the new finish.

• If you are unsure if the surface you wish to strip is coated in shellac or varnish, try rubbing a small corner with some fine wire wool soaked in methylated spirit. If the wool becomes clogged with a brown, sticky 'gravy', the surface is coated in shellac and can be stripped by continuing the procedure. However, if the surface has been varnished, only surface dirt will cling to the wool and so paint stripper will be required.

STRIPPING WALLPAPER

Until you actually start to strip wallpaper, you will not know if the task ahead is going to be easy or time-consuming. Some paper comes away without the aid of scrapers or soaking. In some cases though, you will need to soak wallpaper off by washing the wall with hot water and a sponge again and again until the old glue dissolves—you may also need to use a flat scraper or putty knife.

When all the paper is off, wash the wall with hot water again to remove old glue residue completely and then sand the entire surface with medium-grit sandpaper.

▲ Lift the unstuck edges with both hands.

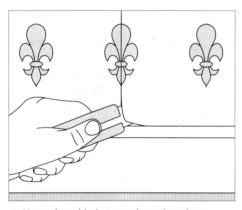

▲ Use a sharp blade to work up the edges.

FILLING

Gaps, holes, and dents are common defects. By filling these pits, it is possible to create a beautifully smooth finish, ready for decoration. There are many different fillers available.

When you buy a filler check whether it is sandable—those that tell you on the label to smooth before allowing to dry are probably not sandable and are more difficult to work with. Powder filler, mixed on a board with water and a putty knife, is beyond compare and is used by all the professionals. With sandable fillers, you can safely overfill the crack or hole, and then sand it down to a smooth finish when it is dry.

The little holes that appear in plasterboard where the screw attaches it to the wall are best filled with a flexible, sandable wood filler, which will move to expand and contract, and may prevent the hole from reappearing.

Before starting, knock out any areas that look as though they will eventually need filling and refill them. It is worth the extra few minutes.

• CELLULOSE FILLER: Popularly used for most small dents and holes around the home, this filler can be used on wood as well as plaster. Although it is not ideal for large cracks, the filler helps provide a smooth surface for rough-grained pieces of wood, and for the rough ends of manufactured "wood" surfaces such as chipboard.

• WOOD FILLER: There are many types of specialized wood fillers available. Water-based, ready-mixed varieties are the easiest to use and are suitable for filling small holes and cracks, and sealing around bad joints in wood. They come in a variety of wood colors, as well as plain, and sand down well to a very fine, hard finish. Some fillers are bought in powder form, which is mixed with water to form a smooth paste.

• CHINA FILLER: A special china filler can be bought at craft suppliers and sometimes at antique stores. Use it to build up small missing areas on china edges, and to fill any cracks and chips. It takes on the appearance of china and gives a fine finish when smoothed off and hardened.

HINTS & TIPS: Filling with pumice

Surfaces that are to be given a clear coating can be filled with powdered pumice. Moisten a clean cotton pad with methylated spirits and dip it into sifted pumice. Coat the entire surface of the object using a circular motion, applying a gentle, even pressure. When the grain is completely covered, wipe away the excess with a clean cloth.

HINTS & TIPS: Tinted wood filler

If you plan to leave the wood partly showing for any reason, such as when liming or colourwashing it, it may be a good idea to use a tinted wood filler for filling holes and cracks.

• PUTTY/FILLER KNIFE: This is a broad blade, used to force different fillers into difficult cavities. Although these knives are very similar to paint scrapers, their blades tend to be more flexible, helping to make the action of pushing filler into cracks, and leveling flat against the surface, much easier.

FILLING GAPS AND HOLES

1 Sand around the outside of the hole and remove any dust. Apply some filler with a filler or putty knife. Spread the blade over the hole, pressing the paste into the recess. Scrape away any excess paste and allow to dry. If the filler shrinks slightly as it dries, apply another layer as before. Then sand with a fine-grit sandpaper.

2 If areas of the wooden surface have been compressed, rather than actually gouged or pitted, try removing the dent by putting a thick, damp cloth over the area and then placing a hot steam iron over it. The steam should help to raise the compacted wood, without the need to use any filler.

PRIMING

Preparation of the surface includes ensuring that any decorative technique finish will be applied to a receptive base.

A range of primers and sealers is available. Check with the paint store for a primer that is specially designed for your surface. Plywood, for example, can be safely primed with two thinned coats of the paint that you intend using. Oil-based eggshell paint is recommended for this. There are also primers for shiny surfaces such as plastic, tiles, and melamine, which have been formulated to grip to the surface. Thin the primer with water or turpentine according to manufacturer's instructions and apply two coats for a smooth finish.

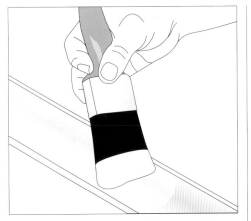

▲ Apply primer to bare wood before painting.

• ACRYLIC PRIMER: This quick-drying primer is generally used for sealing wood, although some brands are also suitable for metal, masonry, and other materials. It is usually white in color and very fast-drying. However, if acrylic primer is applied to bare wood, a second coat (or a layer of undercoat) may be required.

• OIL-BASED PRIMER: This is a slow-drying, durable primer that is useful for surfaces that do not easily accept or grip acrylic primers, such as some metal and plastic surfaces. Oil-based primers are rarely needed if you are dealing with wooden furniture. The fumes emitted by oil paints are particularly strong so be sure that there is plenty of ventilation while you are working.

• HIDE GLUE: This can be used as a preparation for gesso or as a base for gilding. The sealer can also be applied to paper to prevent the penetration of varnish or water.

• RUSTPROOFING PRIMER: Sometimes known as red oxide paint, it is helpful to apply rustproofing primer to any metalwork that you have brushed or sanded. This should get rid of any remaining rust and prevent further development. Although the primer should not be needed for new galvanized metal or tin, do apply the coating to any surfaces that are likely to rust or that are to be decorated using water-based paints. It is also a good idea to use it as a base for objects that are to be gilded. Normal primer can be used on items that will definitely not have contact with water.

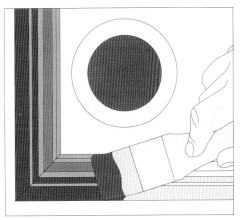

▲ Use rustproofing on metalwork.

• SANDING SEALER: This spirit-based sealer is ideal for applying to new, stripped, dark, or heavily knotted wood. (Knotting fluid, an oil-based solvent, can be used on individual knots, although it should not be used for surfaces that are to be coated in water-based paints.) Sanding sealer provides an excellent base for waxing.

▲ Use sanding sealer on wood for varnishing.

FINISHING SEALANTS

Many surfaces, particularly wood, are porous and need sealing before you can start applying final coats of paint or varnish. Similarly, when a decorative paint technique has been used, it is often necessary to use a finishing sealer in order to protect the surface and prevent damage or aging. This is important with objects that are kept in the garden and are subject to extremes of weather.

Most finishing sealers comprise either varnish or wax. They work by sealing the painted, stained, or natural surface so that the decorative finish is not damaged by general wear and tear, or by the chemicals that may come into contact with it.

VARNISHES

Unlike transparent stains that are simply absorbed into a wooden surface and require additional sealing, varnishes form a clear, protective layer. Most conventional varnishes are made with polyurethane resins that provide a heat-resistant, scratchproof, and waterproof finish. They can be used on painted surfaces, or on wood that has been carefully sanded and wiped clean with a tack cloth.

The range of varnishes is enormous. They are either water- or oil-based and come in a variety of finishes, including matte, satin, and gloss. Some tinted or stained varnishes are also available but these do not sink into the wood like ordinary stains. This means that additional coats of clear, protective varnish should be used as a sealer.

• OIL-BASED VARNISH: There are numerous types of oil-based varnish, all of which are generally slow-drying. Polyurethane types are the easiest to use and are available in matte (almost no shine), satin (semi-gloss), and gloss (high sheen) finishes. To get the protection of a gloss finish without the increasing shine, apply coats of matte or satin varnish over one coat of gloss.

Sometimes available in spray cans that avoid brush marks, oil-based varnishes can usually be reapplied within 8 to 24 hours. These varnishes are generally more durable and heat-resistant than water-based varnishes (see below), but they can yellow with time, possibly spoiling the decorative effect. Oil-based varnishes are, however, ideal for sealing water-soluble crackle varnish.

• WATER-BASED VARNISH: Increasingly popular, water-based acrylic varnishes are widely available in gloss, satin, or matte finishes. A flat varnish is also available, which provides even less sheen

---

HINTS & TIPS: Oil-based varnish

Several thin layers of varnish always provide more protection than a couple of thick coats. Whenever you apply a second coat of varnish, rub down the surface lightly with a very fine abrasive paper and dust off – this will ensure that the next coat adheres well.

than a matte coating. Acrylic varnishes are milky in appearance but dry to a clear finish and are nonyellowing. However, the matte and flat versions contain chalk, giving them a cloudy appearance when a number of coats are applied. This makes them unsuitable as a sealer for techniques that require many layers. These finishes are also softer and less durable than satin or gloss varnish.

Some brands of acrylic varnish contain polyurethane for extra toughness, but most offer an average level of resistance, which should be suitable for most home furniture. (Items that receive a lot of wear, such as children's toys or furniture, may need stronger types—try using a varnish designed for outdoor use.) Water-based varnish is usually dry to the touch in about 20 minutes and can be reapplied after two hours.

• SHELLAC: Shellac is the naturally occurring resin of the lac beetle and is mixed with methylated spirits to form a fast-drying varnish. This traditional product is widely used for furniture restoration and French polishing. It should be applied to small areas of the surface by brush and then rubbed in using a round ball of lint-free cloth.

Shellac comes in a variety of grades and colors and is sold under many different names. Use clear shellac sanding sealer, white French polish, or white button polish for sealing

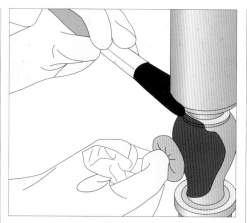
▲ Wear rubber gloves when applying shellac.

wood, paper, and paint. Use brown French polish or garnet polish for staining and aging, in addition to sealing. French enamel varnish is transparent shellac with added dye and can also be used.

• CELLULOSE LACQUER: Usually available in a spray can, cellulose lacquer gives a glossy protective finish for water-based

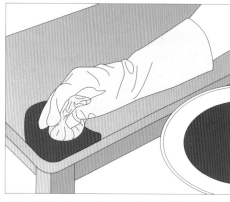
▲ Apply shellac to large surfaces with a cloth.

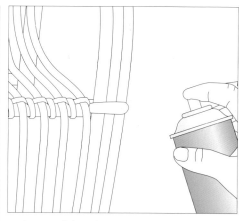
▲ Spray cellulose lacquer in a light, even coat.

decorated surfaces. However, it should not be used with oil-based mediums because the cellulose thinners, which are used to dilute the lacquer, act like a paint stripper on the oil.

HINTS & TIPS: Varnishing tools

Although it is possible to apply varnish with any soft household paintbrush, specialist varnish brushes hold more liquid and so are better for covering large surfaces. Flat hog's-hair brushes are the best, usually available from specialist craft and decorating shops.

APPLYING VARNISH

1 Prepare the surface of the object by sanding first with medium- and then fine-grit sandpaper. Wipe thoroughly with a tack cloth, ensuring that there is no dust remaining on any part of the surface, including any grooves.

❖ VARNISHES & WAXES ❖

TYPE	SOLVENT	SHEEN	TIP
ACRYLIC VARNISH (BRUSH)			
• FLAT	Water	Low	Nonyellowing and durable.
• MATTE	Water	None	Nonyellowing and durable.
• SATIN	Water	Medium	Nonyellowing and durable.
ACRYLIC VARNISH (SPRAY)	Water	Medium	Nonyellowing and very durable.
ACRYLIC VARNISHING WAX	Water	Medium	Nonyellowing and very durable.
BEESWAX POLISH	Mineral spirits	Medium	Can yellow with age, durable.
FURNITURE WAX	Mineral spirits	Medium	Nonyellowing and durable.
CELLULOSE LACQUER VARNISH (SPRAY)	Mineral spirits	High	Nonyellowing and very durable.
SHELLAC	Methylated spirits	High	Nonyellowing and very durable.

2 Dip a thoroughly clean brush in the varnish and, without removing the excess, work the brush over a sheet of brown paper. This will expel the air from the bristles and ease out loose hairs, preventing them from sticking to your intended surface.

3 Apply the varnish with gentle strokes, taking the brush around the lip of drawers or doors. Try to avoid overloading the surface with varnish as this will cause runs or sags.

4 Allow the varnish to dry completely hard (possibly taking 1 to 3 days) before lightly sanding, dusting, and applying additional coats.

WAXES

Wax finishes are usually applied over a varnish coating, helping to provide a soft sheen. The greater the number of coats you apply, the better the sheen that will be produced.

• TINTED PASTE WAX: A blend of several waxes, paste wax has a good resistance to water and fingermarks. It can be applied to painted furniture and creates a seal for crackled, aged, and peeled-paint techniques. The wax is available in different colors, but choose carefully because some will cause yellowing.

• CLEAR WAX: Clear furniture wax is also effective and can be used for creating an aged appearance on furniture. Use it over paint or wood where you do not want a color to adhere, such as areas of wear. Clear liquid wax is particularly good for this but tinted versions are also widely available.

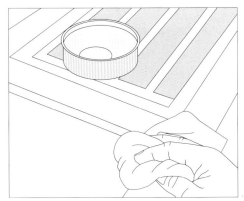
▲ Apply several coats of wax for a good sheen.

APPLYING A WAX FINISH

1 To create a protective sheen on a surface, lightly sand it down with fine-grit sandpaper and then wipe the surface with a tack cloth.

2 Apply the wax with steel wool or a nylon scouring pad, rubbing the surface with long, straight strokes. Make sure the wax is rubbed right into the grain and try not to leave any build-up of wax on the surface.

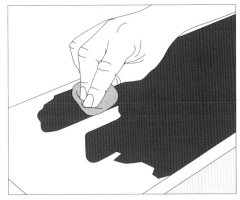
▲ Rub the wax into the grain with steel wool.

3 Within a couple of minutes of application, rub the surface with a lint-free cloth to even out the coating. The surface will feel sticky but continue to rub, changing to a clean section of cloth whenever it clogs.

4 Rub the surface for as long as possible to create a polished finish. Hold the object firmly while you polish, grasping it through a clean cloth to keep oils from your skin from transferring to the wood.

5 Repeat the process at least once more. The greater the number of coats, the more enhanced and refined the final finish will be.

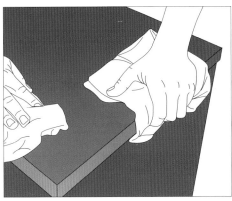
▲ Hold the item with a cloth while polishing.

TRACING & CUTTING

Basic drawing and cutting techniques are often essential to complete the projects in this book. Instructions for detailed work are given in "Advanced Paint Effects" (see pages 42–75), but simple procedures to help make basic tasks easier are listed below.

PLANNING TOOLS

• RULER: Essential for measuring and marking designs, rulers should be sturdy and long. Centering rulers of 18in (45cm), available from graphic art suppliers, are very good. If you need a straightedge for cutting out, invest in a metal-edged ruler—plastic and wooden edges may get sliced by the blade.

• T SQUARE: This is useful for keeping corners accurate, but any rectangular object can also be used for drawing edges. You may find a plastic T square more useful because you can see guidelines beneath.

• WATER-SOLUBLE PENCIL: This is ideal for marking wood because any unwanted lines or smudges can be wiped off later.

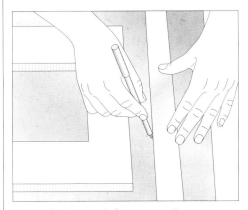
▲ Use drawing tools for accurate lines.

PLANNING A DESIGN

1 Always plan in advance. If you are making alterations to a piece of furniture, take measurements of all the dimensions and draw on a piece of scrap paper where fixings will be required. Make sure that if the item is to be functional, any alterations you make will be of sufficient strength and adaptability. For example, if you are adding shelves to an old cupboard, think about the size of the items to be stored and maximize the room available.

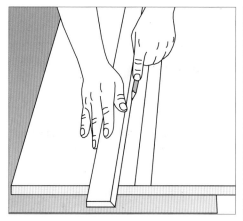

▲ Measure and mark all dimensions.

However, remember to allow enough space for access. Similarly, decide whether the original positions of hinges or screws really are the most useful, or whether alterations are needed.

2 For large items that need matching shapes, such as two pieces of wooden scroll trim, create a template out of paper and draw around it onto your wood. This will ensure symmetry in the shapes, and will also help to minimize wood waste.

TRACING

Always be patient when you are tracing items and spend time on the preparation. For example, make sure that your stencil and tracing material are securely fixed—with the slightest wobble the inaccuracies begin. If the material you wish to trace onto is opaque, use a light box to help you see the design more clearly. You may also stick the design on a window, position your medium on top, and then trace over it.

TRACING A DESIGN

1 Position a sheet of tracing paper securely over the design. Slowly follow the design with a pencil. For intricate patterns, rotate the design and paper, rather than your body.

2 Follow the outline on the reverse side of the tracing paper with a heavy (No. 2) pencil. Then put the tracing over your chosen surface, right side up, and follow the outline again. The heavy graphite on the reverse side should transfer to the surface. Then cut out the design.

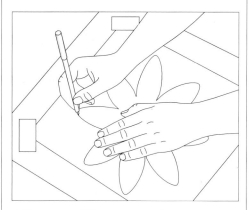

▲ Trace around the secured design.

CUTTING TOOLS

The secret to effective cutting is sharp equipment—blunt blades cause untidy edges and slips. The projects in this book involve cutting out a variety of items including wood and paper.

• SAWS: There are many different types of saws available, both for heavy-duty work and intricate cutting. It is best to use a fretsaw for tight curves

in wood or plastic and a hacksaw or heavy-duty tin snips for cutting metal. To cut out detailed shapes, cut away most of the surrounding excess material before trying to follow the intricate outline.

• SCISSORS: Use sharp scissors and reserve them solely for craft work, rather than also using them for odd tasks around the home that might cause them to become blunt. Ordinary scissors can be used for removing excess paper or card stock before using a craft or utility knife.

• CRAFT KNIVES: Generally, craft, or utility, knives offer more flexibility and accuracy than scissors when it comes to cutting out intricate designs. Craft knives are good for cutting straight lines, particularly on semi-thick materials such as cardboard, but precision artist's knives, which can be held like a pen, are better for handling difficult shapes.

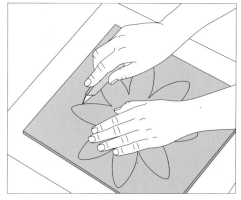

▲ Use a craft or utility knife for cutting out.

Knives that have replaceable blades are particularly useful and, once mastered, can provide crisp edges. Change the blade as soon as the cutting becomes heavy or difficult—going over a slice twice leads to rough and inaccurate edges.

• CUTTING MAT: A cutting mat is essential for protecting your work surfaces. Although thick pieces of cardboard make a temporary alternative, knives will soon penetrate the board, blunting the blade and making a clean first cut very difficult. Self-healing mats are the best option because they last for years and have guidelines.

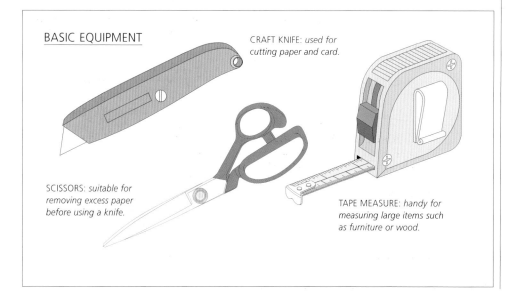

BASIC EQUIPMENT

CRAFT KNIFE: *used for cutting paper and card.*

SCISSORS: *suitable for removing excess paper before using a knife.*

TAPE MEASURE: *handy for measuring large items such as furniture or wood.*

❖ SURFACE PREPARATION ❖

SURFACE	CLEANING	SANDING	BASE COATS
CHIPBOARD			
• WOOD VENEER	Wipe with damp, but not wet, lint-free cloth.	Fine-grit sandpaper.	If necessary, apply acrylic wood primer, latex, or oil-based undercoat.
• MELAMINE-COATED	Wash with detergent solution, using a lint-free cloth, and allow to dry.	Wet and dry paper.	Speciality primers available.
HARDBOARD			
• PAINTED	Wash with detergent solution, using a lint-free cloth, and allow to dry.	Fine-grit sandpaper.	Use oil-based primer on oil-based paint and water-based primer on water-based paint.
METAL			
• BARE	Brush off any rust, wipe with mineral spirits and steel wool.	Wet and dry paper.	Metal primer or rustproofing primer, followed by acrylic primer for water-based paint.
• COATED	Wash with detergent solution and remove any coating with an appropriate stripper.	Wet and dry paper.	As above.
PLASTICS	Wash with detergent solution, or mineral spirits.	Wet and dry paper.	Specialty primers available.
PLYWOOD			
• VARNISHED	Brush well with a stiff brush, then wash with detergent solution and a lint-free cloth.	Fine-grit sandpaper.	Wood primer and oil-based undercoat where necessary.
• UNPAINTED	Wipe with damp, but not wet, lint-free cloth.	Fine-grit sandpaper.	Wood primer and undercoat.
WOOD			
• PAINTED	Wash with detergent solution, using a lint-free cloth, and allow to dry.	Remove loose flakes with a scraper and stripper then use coarse-, medium-, and fine-grit sandpaper.	Wood primer, and oil-based undercoat where necessary.
• UNPAINTED	Wipe with damp, but not wet, lint-free cloth.	Fine-grit sandpaper.	Wood primer and undercoat.
• SEALED	Wash with detergent solution, using a lint-free cloth, and allow to dry.	Remove loose flakes with a scraper and stripper, then use coarse-, medium-, and fine-grit sandpaper.	Wood primer and undercoat where necessary.
• VARNISHED	Brush well with stiff brush, then wash with detergent solution and a lint-free cloth.	As above.	As above.
• WAXED	Methylated spirits.	As above.	As above.

INTERIOR DECORATORS OF ALL LEVELS OF EXPERIENCE CAN ACHIEVE SUCCESS WITH BASIC PAINT EFFECTS. ALL YOU NEED IS SOME PAINT, TOOLS, AND PLENTY OF PATIENCE. THIS CHAPTER PROVIDES YOU WITH A BASIC INTRODUCTION TO PAINT AND ITS USES. IT ALSO TEACHES YOU THE SKILLS NEEDED FOR BASIC PAINT EFFECTS, WHICH YOU CAN THEN USE TIME AND TIME AGAIN. ONCE YOU HAVE MASTERED THESE, ALL PAINT-EFFECTS PROJECTS WILL BE WITHIN REACH.

Basic Paint Effects

Using Paint and Color

BEFORE YOU CAN start manipulating paint to achieve paint effects, you must decide on the type of paint that you want to use. The range of paints and painting materials is ever-expanding and it can be difficult to identify the most suitable products for your job. Although there is rarely a right or wrong answer, some products, methods, and tools are better suited to certain techniques than others. In addition, mixing different types of paint can cause problems—for example, oil-based and water-based products should be kept apart—so plan ahead and think about the finish you want to achieve. Although some paints are designed for specific purposes, most can be adapted or added to other mediums, creating an even greater array of potential results.

▲ There are many types of paint available.

CHOOSING PAINT

The selection of paints, varnishes, and other paint products that are available can be confusing. Listed below are some of the most common types of paint. On pages 26–29 is a paint chart with useful tips about how to use some of the available paint products.

PRIMERS

Usually oil-based, primers are applied to raw wood to help seal the surface and prepare it for additional paint coverage. Its oil content makes primer ideal for very porous surfaces, but it can be slow-drying.

A different type of primer, rust-proofing primer, is used as a base paint for metallic surfaces. It should be applied as soon as any rust has been removed from the item, helping to prevent further corrosion. (See pages 16–17 for more information.) Primer not only seals the base but also ensures that the top layers of paint dry and cure properly.

There are other ways of priming wood. Some manufactured wood products can be primed with two thinned coats of the paint you intend using. This is particularly successful if you are using oil-based eggshell. Thin the paint until it has the consistency of light cream.

Check the paint store for a primer specially designed for the surface you are treating. There are primers for shiny surfaces such as plastic, tiles, and melamine, which have been formulated to grip firmly to the surface. Thin the primer and apply two coats to achieve a smoother finish.

WATER-BASED PAINT

Also known as latex paint, these are relatively inexpensive paints that are available in either flat or satin finishes. They are most commonly used for painting walls, but can also be used on furniture—½ pint (0.25l) tester pots are ideal for painting small items. Latex paint can be thinned with water to make a wash; it can also be mixed with glaze or tinted with acrylic, universal stains, or powder pigments to make a range of unique colors. When you apply a water-based paint, you are effectively applying a skin of colored plastic and water. The water evaporates and you are left with an even coating of plastic. Keep windows closed when you are applying water-based paint, but then open them as soon as the work is finished.

OIL-BASED PAINTS

Oil-based paints come in flat, eggshell, and gloss finishes. Gloss paint tends to create a crisp, clean effect, which is not ideal for making an item look worn and old. For this reason, most people tend to use flat or eggshell oil-based paints, both as base coats and to make glazes for decorative finishes.

Oil-based paints give a much tougher finish than water-based paints and are particularly useful in light-colored glazes where crackle glaze, and the addition of varnish, would be too yellowing. The only drawback to oil-based paints is that they take a long time to dry and need at least 24 hours between coats. To tint oil-based paints, use artist's oil paints or universal stains, which are stronger and cheaper than artist's oils but not quite as subtle.

▲ Choose your paint color carefully.

TRADITIONAL PAINTS

A recent development in the production of paints, traditional paints are a variation on latex paint. Natural pigments, rather than the synthetic ones used in normal paint production, are used to make the mixture. The paints also contain chalk, a traditional ingredient used in paint-making, and dry to a flat finish that appears much lighter than the color in the paint can.

Most of the paints include modern binders and, though they have the feel and look of old-fashioned "milk paint," they have the advantage of a greater degree of durability. However, they are easily marked, so painted surfaces need to be protected with wax or varnish. But, remember that applying varnish and waxes over traditional paints will darken them and take away their chalky appearance.

Traditional paints are more expensive than standard latex paint but they are definitely worth the investment, if you can afford them. The colors have a wonderful softness and subtlety, which makes them ideal for isolated projects such as furniture or accessories. They can be thinned with water and tinted in the same way as ordinary latex paint.

HINTS & TIPS: Professional or trade paints

Most manufacturers also make a special range of paints for the professional painter or "to the trade." These tend to be more intensely colored and dry more quickly. There are just as many colors available, if not more. Thin them and apply two or three coats to achieve a professional finish. Because they dry so quickly and thin so well, the extra time it takes to apply an additional coat is rewarded in the quality of the finish. Unfortunately, trade paints are made with a different formula to domestic paints and so it is not a good idea to mix them. Trade eggshell, for example, should not be painted with satin finish eggshell.

GLAZE

Glaze is an essential medium that can be colored for use in creating paint effects. In simple terms, it makes the color slippery and movable. The glaze is applied with a paintbrush or roller and then, while it is still wet, it is mani-

▲ Artist's paints come in a range of colors.

pulated with brushes, cloths, plastic, or anything you like. See pages 34–5 for further information.

ARTIST'S ACRYLIC PAINT

This paint is very quick-drying and durable. Its concentrated color makes it ideal for many types of surface decoration, including stenciling, printing, and general detail painting. It can also be used to color acrylic glaze, although the paint should be watered down a little first to avoid lumps.

Acrylics are also ideal paint bases, and can be sanded to create an old, distressed look. Although they are less cost-effective for covering large surfaces, they can be used on smaller items or diluted to make general washes. Acrylics are usually available in tubes or jars, and some special types, suitable for work such as fabric painting, are also available. Acrylic paint can be quite hard on brush hairs, so make sure brushes are cleaned thoroughly straight after use, before they dry out.

ARTIST'S OIL PAINT

Usually used for fine art, oil colors can also be used to tint any oil-based paint or glaze. However, they are slow-drying and will slightly delay the drying time of anything with which they are mixed. Paintbrushes must be cleaned with mineral spirits before ordinary water and detergent are used.

The most subtle of paints, artist's oil colors can be used for almost any decorative finish, including stenciling, although many people prefer to use faster drying media, such as acrylics. If you want to keep the effect simple and clean, however, there is often nothing

better than simply using oils to paint some scroll work or decorative feature onto an old varnished piece of furniture. If you want to speed up drying time, you can add drying oil to your paint mixture.

SPRAY PAINT

Available in easy-to-use cans, spray paint is produced in a large range of colors and finishes. Acrylic water-based spray paint, specifically intended for use in interior decoration, is ideal for almost all surfaces, including wood, metal, plaster, plastic, and glass. It can

▲ Spray paints are very easy to use.

be used for small projects such as stenciling, as the main color for doors and shutters and is especially suitable for children's trunks and toys because it is nontoxic. You can also buy spray enamels for metals and glass, pearlized finishes, and polyurethane varnishes. Apply the paint in several thin coats rather than one heavy one, so as to avoid paint buildup and runs.

GOUACHE COLORS

Although relatively expensive, these colors are extremely strong and are ideal for tinting water-based glazes or for painting directly onto a surface.

DRYING OILS

Drying oils can be added to any type of paint in order to speed up the drying process. There is much controversy surrounding their effect on the final finish, but they are worth using if you are pushed for time. They are almost essential if you are using oil-based glaze colored with artist's oils. Drying oils are not used with water-based paints.

Paints and Their Uses

Product	Quality and finish	Thinners	Use for	Apply with	Number of coats
Primer	Preparation for raw wood. Prevents wood from swelling.	Water or turpentine (check the can).	Raw wood.	Brush or small roller.	1
Undercoat	Matte finish, thin surface preparation, and sealer.	Water or turpentine (check the can).	Walls, woodwork.	Brush.	1
Latex flat	No shine, general-purpose coverage.	Water.	Walls, new plaster.	Large brush or roller.	2
Latex satin	Satin sheen, general-purpose coverage.	Water.	Walls, murals, and base for glaze work. Not suitable for new plaster.	Large brush or roller.	2
Eggshell	Satin sheen, general-purpose coverage.	Mineral spirits or turpentine.	Walls, woodwork, and metal.	Large brush or roller.	2
Gloss	High shine, durable.	Water or turpentine (check the can).	Woodwork, doors.	Good-quality brush.	2
Wood stain	Color without varnish for raw wood.	Water or mineral spirits.	Raw or unvarnished wood.	Lint-free cloth or brush.	1 or 2
Varnish—polyurethane	Oil-based wood and paintwork protection. Choice of shine.	Mineral spirits or turpentine.	Wood and to protect paintwork.	Good-quality brush.	Up to 8
Varnish—acrylic	Fast-drying protection for wood and paintwork. Choice of sheen. Nonyellowing.	Water.	Wood and to protect paintwork.	Brush or roller.	Up to 8
Wax	Protection and shine for wood.	N/A	Bare or stained wood.	Lint-free cloth.	3
Oil-based glaze	Transparent.	Mineral spirits or turpentine.	Mixing with artist's oil colors to make colored glaze for paint finishes.	Brush or roller.	1 or 2

Washable?	Approximate area per quart (one coat)	Notes	Drying time between coats	Drying time final coat	Undercoat required?
N/A	130sq ft	Thin to a watery consistency. Rub down with sandpaper when dry.	2–4 hours	N/A	No.
N/A	130sq ft	Stir well. Rub down with sandpaper when dry.	Oil-based—8 hours. Water-based— 2 hours.	N/A	N/A
No.	105sq ft	Do not stir and avoid frost.	1–2 hours	8 hours	No, but dilute first coat for raw wood.
Yes, soapy water. Do not scrub.	105sq ft	Dark colors require 3 or more coats.	1–2 hours	8 hours	Latex flat.
Yes, household cleaners. Avoid ammonia.	160sq ft	Stir well before and during use.	8 hours	24 hours	Primer or commercial undercoat.
Yes, household cleaners. Avoid ammonia.	130sq ft	Slow to apply—use good-quality natural-bristle brush. Oil-based is more durable.	4–8 hours	24 hours	Primer.
No.	85sq ft	Apply generously with brush or cloth. Stains do not protect wood; always wax or varnish when dry.	1–3 hours	1–3 hours	No.
Yes, soapy water.	105sq ft	Use thinned and apply several coats for the greatest luster. May yellow as coats build up.	4 hours	24 hours	No.
Yes, but do not scrub.	105sq ft	Difficult to apply as evenly as polyurethane varnishes. Not as durable but fast-drying and crystal clear. Do not use on oil-based paints.	1 hour	8 hours	No.
Yes, with more wax or soapy water.	85sq ft	Apply just like shoe polish, buff with a soft cloth between coats. Pure beeswax best for new wood; rewax often.	3 hours	N/A	Wood stain (optional).
No.	Depends on consistency.	Good workability for ½ hour. Cheap way to extend color.	6 hours	N/A	Oil-based eggshell base.

Paints and Their Uses (continued)

Product	Quality and finish	Thinners	Use for	Apply with	Number of coats
Craft paint	Intense colors for detailing and small areas.	Various.	Small craft projects.	Soft brush.	1 or 2
Artist's oils, crayons, and pastels	Intense, pure colors in stick form.	Oil or turpentine.	Detailing and drawing on walls, furniture or paper.	N/A	N/A
Powdered pigments	Intense colors from natural earth and mineral pigments.	Water.	Making homemade paints for color washing.	Brush or roller.	1
Spray lacquer	Low or high sheen, durable, wide color range.	Cellulose thinners.	Stencils and basic coverage.	Spray from the can.	1 or 2
Glass paint	Transparent or matte.	Acetone.	Painting glass of all kinds. Transparent detail work.	Soft artist's brush.	1
Blackboard paint	Flat black, very opaque.	Methylated spirits.	Interior matte finishes, chalkboards.	Brush.	1 or 2
PVA glue	General-purpose sealer.	Water.	Walls or woodwork to seal or stick.	Brush.	1
Kitchen and bathroom paint	Moisture- and steam-resistant paints.	Water.	Kitchens and bathrooms.	Brush or roller.	At least 2
Melamine primer	Primer for shiny plastic surfaces.	Water.	Preparing shiny surfaces for painting.	Brush.	2
Tile primer	Primer for tiles.	Mineral spirits (best to throw the brush away after use).	Preparing tiles for paint.	Brush or small gloss roller.	2
Textured wall paint	Heavy plaster-like wall and ceiling paint with a textured finish.	Water.	Textured walls.	Range of tools to create different textures.	1

Washable?	Approximate area per quart (one coat)	Notes	Drying time between coats	Drying time final coat	Undercoat required?
Yes, do not scrub.	N/A	Better quality than poster paint. Widely available in small quantities.	½ hour	N/A	N/A
No.	N/A	Allow to dry for 3 weeks or more before varnishing.	N/A	N/A	N/A
Yes.	N/A	Can be mixed with oil- or water-based products.	N/A	N/A	N/A
Yes.	N/A	Extremely durable; wear a mask when spraying.	1 hour	10 hours	Spray undercoat.
Yes, do not scrub; check label.	N/A	Brushstrokes always show; vivid color selection. Use acetone to thin these paints.	1 hours	4 hours	No.
Yes, water only.	105sq ft	Fast-drying, easy to repair and patch up.	1 hour	4 hours	No.
Yes, soapy water.	130sq ft	Dilute 1:1 with water. Apply with brush.	1–2 hours	N/A	No.
Yes.	85sq ft	This is really just acrylic latex eggshell paint.	2 hours	8 hours	Save money by undercoating with latex.
N/A	50sq ft	For best results, sand lightly before priming.	2 hours	16 hours	N/A
N/A	50sq ft	Do not overdilute.	16 hours	24 hours	Ammonia based, work in ventilated area.
No.	105sq ft, depending on textures.	Good for hiding cracked or lumpy plaster.	5 hours	N/A	Not needed if applied quickly.

PAINTING TOOLS

A visit to an art-supply, a craft, or a hardware store will reveal the vast array of painting tools available. Finding the right tool can be expensive—many manufacturers will lead you to believe that a different tool is required for every task. In fact, many pieces of equipment are adaptable. As long as they are cleaned and well-maintained, brushes should last several years.

PAINT APPLICATORS

There is a range of paintbrushes available. Even standard brushes, which are suitable for basic paint application, vary in size and quality. While cheap brushes seem more appealing, they are more likely to shed and may ruin the finished effect.

• BASIC ARTIST'S BRUSHES: These come in a variety of shapes. "Flats." have a square end, helping to produce thin imprints, whereas "filberts," which are also flat, gently taper into a conical shape at the end. Round, fine-pointed brushes are ideal for painting intricate designs, although these must be stored carefully as they are prone to damage.

• HOG-FITCH BRUSHES: Good, all-purpose brushes, these natural-bristle brushes are usually used for oil painting and can be round, flat, or dome shaped. Extremely versatile, they may be used for painting narrow bands of color, applying glue, waxes, and gilt creams, touching up paint, and tamping down metal leaf.

• STIPPLING BRUSHES: Stippling is the term used for finely lifting on or off very fine speckles of paint. Stippling brushes have stiff, dense bristles in a squared-off shape, and come in a variety of sizes. They are useful for many paint techniques, and are particularly good for blending paints and getting rid of hard lines and edges. A good quality decorating brush can be used as a cheaper alternative.

• SWORD LINERS: These long-haired, soft brushes are tapered and angled, enabling you to produce many widths of line simply by varying the pressure applied to the brushstroke. They hold a lot of paint and are often used by sign writers.

• SOFT-HAIRED MOPS: Usually made from squirrel or camel hair, mop brushes are round and are primarily used to apply metallic powder to gold size during gilding. They can also be used to remove surplus gold or metal leaf. A cosmetic blusher brush will do the job of a mop.

• DRAGGING BRUSHES: Sometimes confused with floggers, dragging brushes are used for graining. They have long bristles that are dragged through wet glaze, creating a wood-grain effect.

• FLOGGERS: A flogger is used primarily for making the tiny flecks characteristic of oak wood grain. It is about 2" (5cm) wide and has long bristles and a light, flat handle. After applying a wood grain with a dragging stroke, tap the end of the bristles gently against the glaze, letting them bounce on the surface. The bristles will flop about and spring from the surface leaving tiny flecks. Work down the grain starting at the top.

• SEA SPONGES: For sponging effects, natural sponges are the most popular tool. This is because their absorbency and irregular natural structure create attractive patterns. Always clean natural sponges thoroughly after use.

Artist's brushes   *Fine artist's brushes*   *Hog-fitch brush*   *Natural-bristle varnish brushes*   *Stippling brushes*   *Sword liners*   *Soft-haired mop*

• PAPER TOWELS: These are invaluable for applying shellacs and polishes, for rubbing in and wiping off paint, mopping up spills, and buffing waxes.

• PALETTE KNIFE: Flexible-bladed palette knives can be used both for applying wood filler and mixing oil colors on a palette. Finely shaped varieties can also be used for applying paint, producing an interesting texture and style.

• PAINT BUCKET: Although it is possible to paint out of the can, using a paint bucket or paint tray allows you to use small amounts of paint at a time. This helps to keep the remaining paint in the can clean and free from air (air will cause a skin to form on the paint).

• PAINT ROLLER: Suitable for large furniture surfaces, as well as walls and doors, rollers are ideal for quick coats of paint. Most can be fitted with a variety of replaceable roller sleeves.

APPLYING PAINT

The quickest way to apply paint to walls is by roller. However, if you thin the paint until it has the consistency of light cream, you can apply it with a large 4–6" (10–15cm) latex brush, known as a flogger among professionals. The paint will then settle without the brushstrokes showing and the wall will not take on the dimpled orange-peel effect, which is all too familiar these days. It may take three coats of paint but two will be enough if you are using trade paints.

When using oil-based paints, apply slightly thinned paint in a "crow's foot" fashion, which means crisscross in every direction. Lay off the paint by gently stroking the brush in a single direction. You will find that all the brushstrokes level out to give a smooth surface. Never apply the paint too thickly because a skin will form on top while the paint underneath will stay soft and eventually peel. A rub between coats with fine-grit emery paper is recommended. If you buy a couple of sheets of medium-grit emery paper (about 180 grit) you can turn them into fine by simply rubbing two small pieces together.

CHOOSING AND MIXING COLORS

The variety of colors now available in different paints and mediums can make choosing a final shade difficult. In order to mix colors effectively, it is useful to understand the basic principles of how colors interact.

PRIMARY COLORS

The three primary colors—blue, red, and yellow—are the source of all other hues. By mixing one primary color with another, for example, blue with yellow, you create what is known as a secondary color (in this case, green). The range of subtle shades of green that can be mixed is vast. If blue is mixed with yellow in a ratio of 2:1 (or vice versa), you create an intermediate color. The same applies to the other primary colors.

Finally, a tertiary color is created by mixing all three primary colors together in various percentages. As an exercise in trying to find the right color combinations, it can be useful to examine a color wheel (see below). The area between each of the primary colors on the color wheel is a secondary color.

COMPLEMENTARY COLORS

These are colors that appear opposite each other in the color wheel; very simply, red is opposite to green, yellow to purple, and blue to orange. These colors react strongly with each other, often becoming more vibrant if they are used side-by-side.

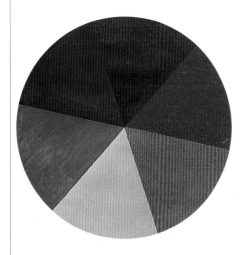

▲ The color wheel will help you mix colors.

CHOOSING COLORS

Ultramarine blue

Yellow ocher

Prussian blue

Raw sienna

Cerulean blue

Burnt sienna

Viridian green

Red ocher

Oxide of chromium

Venetian red

Raw umber

Cadmium red

Burnt umber

Alizarin crimson

▲ Useful acrylic pigment colors.

HINTS & TIPS: Shading & tinting color

• A "shade" is made by adding raw umber to a paint color, helping to darken it and reduce its vividness. This will tone down any pigment, even white, immediately giving it an aged appearance.

• A "tint" is created by adding white to a color. This reduces the strength of the hue and makes the color more opaque.

If complementary colors are mixed in equal quantities they become dark gray and muddy, but adding just a touch of one to the other will tone it down without making the color look dead.

COLOR MIXING

There are no rules about which colors should or should not be mixed together. Many unlikely combinations can produce very interesting shades—it is simply a question of experimenting and developing an eye for color. With practice, you may find that you come to know immediately how a certain color will be affected by adding another pigment to it.

NATURAL PIGMENTS

Natural earth pigments, which are warm and soft, tend to be quite easy to live with and are extremely adaptable. These colors have been used in paint-making for centuries; they are literally

▲ Mix colored pigment with medium gradually.

made of finely ground earth and are very inexpensive. With the addition of white they make very pretty pastel shades. Cooler shades of green and blue can also be chosen, from beautiful mineral colors.

MIXING PIGMENT WITH PAINT & PAINT MEDIUM

One economical way of creating a range of hues is to add powdered pigment to a paint medium. It can be added to latex or traditional paint, but do this gradually and mix it thoroughly to avoid thickening the paint too much. Remember that even if the paint looks adequately mixed in the can or bucket, it may look less so when painted onto a surface.

▲ Use small amounts of powder pigments.

However, this unevenness of color can sometimes add to the object's charm and produce a more authentic aged appearance.

Artist's acrylic colors and universal stains can be used in place of powdered pigment. Most types of pigment and medium are compatible with each other, so feel free to experiment with different variations. Do, however, make sure that you are using all water-based or oil-based products—never mix them. Also, when you are mixing pigment with paint, work in a room that is well-ventilated and take care not to inhale the pigment powder, as it can be toxic.

For darker or more intense shades, pigment can be mixed with PVA medium or glue and water, or with artist's acrylic medium. This will create a rather plastic paint without texture, but it is good for painting detailed designs.

When diluted, this paint is also ideal for color washing and glazing. If you are using acrylic glaze for a textured effect, you will only need to add a small amount of pigment and it is not necessary to add water.

▲ Artist's colors can be mixed in paint medium.

TROUBLESHOOTING

WRONG COLOR

It is best to color test one patch of wall before you paint the whole room but if you are still not happy with the color you have applied, you could glaze over it (as long as it is fairly pale) using a simple paint technique, such as color washing (see pages 36–7) or ragging (see page 37). Your base color will be toned down by doing this but it will still glow through the transparent glaze.

If the color looks too dark, try sponging one or two lighter colors on top. Your base color will show through but the whole effect will become lighter and mottled. If you are using two or more colors for sponging, use the lightest color last.

UNEVEN SHEEN

If the paint you have used either does not have as much shine as you would like, or is too shiny, there is a solution.

Buy some latex glaze with a gloss, eggshell, or matte finish, and apply a single coat of this on the dry paint surface. Latex glaze looks like milk when wet but dries clear.

THE PAINT IS WAXY

Careless preparation can often prevent oil-based paint from drying, or cause it to dry with a waxy feel. If you are painting a wooden surface, you should always prime the surface first. Primers provide not only a smooth surface on which to paint, but also a base on which the top color will cure (dry and set) fully. If you have overlooked priming the surface, wash the paint away with plenty of mineral spirits and steel wool, and start on a primed surface.

If the paint is drying very slowly with a waxy feel to it, then you have probably applied the coats too thickly. The surface of the paint is beginning to dry and cure and is sealing the moisture underneath.

If you can, leave the paint for a week and see if it dries. If the paint does not dry, scrape it off, wash the wood with mineral spirits and steel wool, and start again.

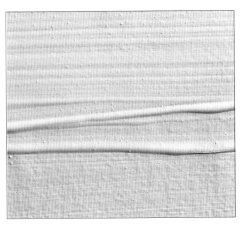

▲ Sagging.

▲ Cracking.

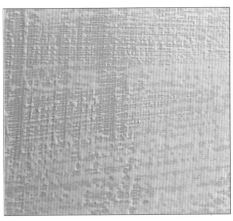

▲ Cissing.

SAGGING

This occurs when the paint has been applied too thickly or each coat has not been allowed to dry fully before the next was applied. To deal with sagging paint, you must first allow it to dry fully and then rub the offending areas down with wet and dry sandpaper (use it wet for best results) until it is perfectly smooth. Then paint the sanded parts again using the same number of coats as you have used on the whole area.

SPILLED PAINT

Every decorator's nightmare is to spill paint on the carpet. If the paint spill is small, allow it to dry without touching it at all. It can then be removed from the carpet pile with sandpaper. Water-based paint spills can be removed by washing the area with plenty of water and then blotting with clean cloths. Larger oil-based spills will have to be washed with mineral spirits and then with soapy water.

STAINS SHOWING THROUGH

Even old, dry stains, perhaps from a previous flood or damp patch, may work their way through the new paint. Seal the old stain well, using a stain-blocking solution, and then paint over it. (Apply the stain block direct from the can and allow to dry out fully before you start to paint.)

BRUSHSTROKES SHOW

This happens when the paint is so thick that it cannot settle evenly on the wall. A quick rubbing with medium-grit sandpaper and a coat of thinned paint will work wonders.

CRACKING

Cracking is caused when paint or varnish is applied over a base layer of paint or varnish of different elasticity before it has been given long enough to cure (which can take up to a month). For example, two separate brands of varnish may react with each other and form cracks. To deal with cracking you must allow the surface to dry and then sand it before repainting. But, you could consider leaving the cracking visible. It is a popular aging technique and many people seek this particular decorative effect (see pages 55–6).

NOT ENOUGH PAINT

If you notice the potential disaster of your paint running out, you can stretch your paint by diluting it a little with the appropriate thinner. You can also make sure that you use every drop of the paint that you have soaked your rollers and brushes with, rather than washing it away into the sink. Sometimes you can buy a small tester pot of latex color to help finish that last corner. If you are working with a color that you mixed yourself, and which cannot be repeated, then one wall or section of your room will have to be painted in a similar or harmonizing color.

CISSING

This term is used to describe the appearance of paint that is resisting the surface on which it is being applied. It usually occurs when water-based paint, such as latex, is being applied over oil-based paint. For large areas, you will be forced to buy new paint in oil-based form. For smaller areas, try washing the surface with detergent and a light scouring pad to remove any grease that may be sitting on the surface. If the paint still resists, you will have to resort to using oil-based paint.

CHALKING

Prevention is much better than remedy for chalking. Sometimes gloss or satin surfaces become dry and powdery, completely lose their shine and give off a chalky powder when rubbed. Using a high-quality paint will help to avoid this aging process because they are more likely to be light resistant. If you do encounter chalking, then wash the surface with a detergent solution and rub it with wet and dry paper until the chalk stops coming off. Then repaint using a better quality paint.

DRIPPING

Drips, or "nibs," in the dried paint surface are usually oversights that were left while the paint was drying. Rub the dried drip away with fine-grit sandpaper and repaint the area. On high-gloss finishes you may need to apply a final coat over the entire area to disguise where you removed a drip.

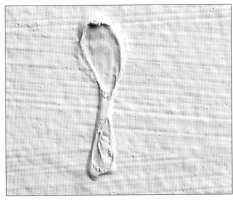

▲ Dripping.

Paint and Glaze Effects

SOME YEARS AGO the world of decorative effects underwent a dramatic change. For the first time, we began to see interesting mottled effects on the interior walls of public buildings, which were clearly carried out with paint as opposed to wallpaper. Like most trends in fashion and interiors, the paint effect is, of course, not new. Back in the 1930s and '40s when money was scarce, it was a cheap alternative to wallpaper. At that time, the effects were achieved using hazardous chemicals. Today, we can buy safe formulas of the required ingredients. The scruffy edges of some of the early work were not long tolerated—the paint effect has cleaned up its act and made a niche for itself in the world of interior decoration.

EQUIPMENT & PREPARATION

The good news for any keen amateur is that there is little to creating paint effects except for one special ingredient—glaze. Called oil glaze or acrylic glaze—and sometimes scumble glaze—it is a slippery feeling medium that makes it possible to move paint around on a slightly shiny surface before allowing it to dry.

So, in basic terms, add some glaze to a chosen color and make the paints slippery. Brush this on a wall that has been painted with latex satin and then move it around with a cloth, bag, brush, cork, or piece of newspaper and then let it dry.

PREPARING THE SURFACE

All paint effects, with the exception of color washing, must be worked on a surface that is smooth and at least a little bit shiny. The colored glaze will move around against this surface and can be worked until you are happy with the result. Matte surfaces soak up some of the paint and will leave blotchy marks showing where, for example, the fully loaded brush or cloth first touched the wall and a greater amount of the paint soaked in. You will not be able to slide the colored glaze around on a matte surface or lift any of it off in order to expose flashes of the base color as you would in rag rolling. Even color washing will look more professional if worked on a surface with a sheen.

The preparation coat must be good, at least two coats thick. Any misses in the shiny base coat will soak up glaze and appear as a blotch.

You must fill and smooth uneven surfaces prior to painting and remember that the glaze coat will sit firmly in any cracks or dips in the wall and will appear darker. A paint effect is not a way of dealing with lumpy walls unless you want to emphasize the irregularities.

GLAZE

Make sure that the glaze you buy is compatible with the paint that was used as a base coat. When the base is latex satin, which is water-based, you may use an acrylic or an oil-based glaze. When the base is oil-based eggshell, you will only achieve a good result by using oil-based glaze (sold as transparent oil glaze). A water-based or acrylic glaze will not adhere to an oil-based surface—it would be like trying to paint a plastic container with children's poster paints.

Color the glaze with either artist's paints from tubes or with ready-mixed paint from the paint store. Use a small can of eggshell or satin for oil-based glazes, or a small can of latex satin for water-based glazes. See "How to mix a glaze" (opposite) for information on the quantities that you should use. You can color a glaze only with compatible products: water-based into water-based or oil-based into oil-based.

▲ Once you have applied a glaze, you can manipulate the paint into various decorative finishes.

▲ Glaze is the key ingredient in most paint effects.

You will already be aware of the fact that wall paints tend to dry a little darker than they look in the can. Glaze, however, dries a little bit lighter. Watch out for the words "student quality" on tubes of artist's paints. They may be cheaper to buy but the colors will fade to an unattractive brown after just a year.

APPLICATORS

You can apply glaze to the surface with a small roller before you begin to manipulate it into the finished effect, but it is much easier to use a household brush. You must work in sections so that the glaze does not begin to dry before you have worked it, so you will only be applying paint to a small area at a time. Rollers also tend to soak up about a pint of moisture before you can use them and so cost more to use.

The following examples of paint effects outline the variety of items that can be used to create interesting effects. Anything from old cotton cloths to the best department stores' shopping bags can be used to create these effects. It is easy to experiment because a glaze can be wiped off a prepared wall as long as it has not been left for longer than several minutes. This means that you can sample some of the effects before deciding which one looks best on your walls.

WORKING FAST

Be aware of the fact that once you have chosen your desired paint effect and started working, you will need to move fast because glazes start to dry after several minutes and any overlaps will show up as a "watermark" or dark line. When you get to a corner, do not stop until you have brought your painting to a neat edge. That said, with the exception of marbling, paint effects are quick and easy to apply.

Two people working in tandem is a good way of speeding up the process—one person applies the glaze and the other works it into a paint effect. If you do this, it is not advisable to swap jobs because the way in which the first person dabs and manipulates the effect will always be slightly different from the next person and differences will show up.

ACHIEVING A PROFESSIONAL FINISH

Sometimes when you look at a surface that has been decorated with a paint effect, you can see the brushstrokes showing where the coat of glaze was first applied before it was manipulated. You are supposed to be able to see these brushstrokes underneath a color wash and you can leave them to show through beneath any effect if you want. However, if you gently stipple, or jab at, the freshly applied coat of wet glaze with the tip of your paintbrush, you can eliminate the brushstrokes and achieve a smoother finish.

Many paint effects require that you move your working hand around in large strokes or that you jab at wet glaze in a back and forth motion and so it can be tricky to continue the effect into hard-to-reach areas, such as behind radiators or around wall sockets. Where possible, remove obstacles. Or you can paint right over an outlet, for example, and wipe it clean immediately with a clean cloth. Glaze will not adhere well to plastic surfaces, such as switch plates, so it is not a good idea to leave the paint there because it will start to chip over time. Getting behind a radiator is always a challenge but you could try putting your tool on the end of a long stick.

COPING WITH YELLOWING

Glazes of all varieties age much faster than regular latex paint and will darken considerably in the space of about two years in areas where they do not get any light, such as behind a picture. If they are exposed to light, they will eventually lighten up again.

Many glazes will yellow slightly over time, particularly those with blue in the color mix. A paint effect on a radiator will tend to age faster than that same effect on the walls.

HOW TO MIX A GLAZE

Two quarts (2l) will be more than enough to cover a 13 by 13' (4 by 4m) room in any of the paint effects shown in this section. Put the glaze into a large paint bucket and then add the color of your choice, little by little, stirring as you go. Test the mixture on a piece of paper, adding glaze until the mixture brushes onto the paper looking glossy and slightly transparent. It should be the same consistency as table cream and can be thinned with water or mineral spirits, depending on whether it is water-based or oil-based. Normally, you will need 1 pint (0.5l) of colored paint or a whole 1 oz (35ml) tube of artist's colors for this. Artist's oil paint is usually more intense and you will need less if you use this.

Mix thoroughly until the colored glaze is smooth and even. Get rid of any lumps in the mixture at this stage.

▲ Mix the glaze in an old dish.

A kitchen balloon whisk is handy for removing lumps if you can spare one for mixing paint.

USING OIL-BASED GLAZES

When using an oil-based glaze for a technique that involves rags and cloths, be sure to spread them out flat and let them dry fully before throwing them into the dustbin. Oil-based glazes warm up when they are left in screwed up rags and can self-combust. This does happen from time to time, especially during warm weather. So be sure to remember to hang your dirty rags on the ladder to dry out overnight or take them away to a cold place where they can dry spread out, not left in little balls.

HINTS & TIPS
Oil- vs water-based glazes?

Advantages of water-based glazes:

- The brushes are easy to wash.
- They do not smell.
- They are cheaper.
- They dry very fast.
- They are less shiny.
- Wet rags are not combustible.

Advantages of oil-based glazes:

- They dry slowly and give you longer to work them.
- The luster of an oil-based glaze is beyond compare.
- They are more durable when fully dry.
- They smell fantastic (if you like the smell of linseed oil!).

WORKING IN SECTIONS

It is important to keep the edges of the work wet while you work in order to avoid drying marks where the overlaps occur. Work in 3 by 3' (1 by 1m) sections and remember which section is the oldest (albeit only minutes older). So, work the first section on the left-hand, top corner of a wall and then move onto the next section, just to the right of it. After this, move down and work a section just below the first and then back up to the top. Then move to both sides of the second row

that you just started; one to the right and one just below it. Continue in this way over the entire wall.

You will find that you are building up a broad diagonal design of squarish blocks with more blocks along the top. In this way, you will find that you do not leave a wet edge of paint for too long and therefore will avoid making unsightly watermarks.

SMALL ITEMS

All paint effects can be miniaturized for use on boxes or items of furniture. You will not have to work in sections as described above and will be able to cover whole sides with glaze at one time. Use a smaller cloth or brush than you would for a wall to achieve a tighter effect.

REPAIRS

If you need to repair a paint effect, then try to patch the smallest area possible because overlaps on the rest of the wall will show up as a dark patch or line. Better still, repaint the whole wall, working neatly in the corners.

COLOR WASHING

This technique gives a brushy or swirly finish, depending on how it is applied. Color washing is just what the name describes—the washing of a color over a prepared wall.

Using a large, 3 to 4" (8 to 10cm) latex brush, apply the glaze in random, backward and forward brushstrokes in every direction. Leave a few patches of the base coat showing through and always apply the glaze thinly. Do not overload the brush but just dip the tips

▲ Color washing gives a lovely mottled finish.

of the bristles into the glaze. If you are working on a matte surface, you can expect to see darker areas of glaze where the new brushload of glaze first touches the wall and then paler areas where it begins to run out of paint. On a satin or eggshell surface, you will be able to move the glaze by brushing over it until it is more even.

Work in long, bold strokes, starting the brushstroke from your shoulder—and be prepared to touch up the ceiling after you have finished the walls—so that your big strokes look even over the whole wall. It is much better to paint onto the ceiling than to have noticeably smaller brushstrokes all around the top of the room.

If you choose to use a cloth for color washing, all you have to do is dip it into the glaze mixture and wring it out well. Then wipe the color onto the wall in swirls, just as if you were washing the walls down with soapy

▲ Color washing with a brush.

▲ Color washing with a cloth.

water. The result on a matte finish will be random circles of glaze in a mottled effect. If you have painted the base coat with satin or eggshell, you will again be able to move the wipe marks and rub them in until they are softer and more even.

One of the added advantages of using a shiny base coat is that there is no need for you to dip and wring the cloth out—just dip it gently against the surface of the glaze in the paint bucket and get it to the wall that you are decorating as quickly as possible so that it does not drip all over the place. Thereafter, the excess blob from the first touch can be blended beautifully onto the wall.

Color washing is an ideal effect for kitchens and can be built up in layers from light to darker tones to produce beautiful Tuscan effects. The basic technique of color washing by cloth is also ideal for aging and shading around the corners and edges of any paint effect once it is fully dry. Just rub the glaze in completely so as not to leave too many marks from the cloth.

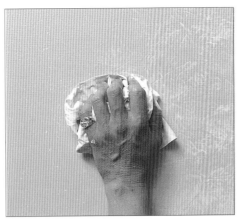

▲ Ragging or ragging off.

RAGGING OR RAGGING OFF

Probably the most common paint effect, ragging is more textured than color washing. The most common mistake is to assume that the colored glaze is applied using a cloth. As there are no rules in paint effects, it can indeed be dabbed on with a wadded up cloth. True ragging, and probably the one that you have seen most often, is actually the removal of colored glaze from a surface with a dry cloth. The subtle difference in technique makes

a world of difference. Apply glaze to the wall and then stipple out the brushstrokes by jabbing all over the wet surface of the glaze with the tips of the bristles. Take a wadded up ball of cotton cloth in the palm of your hand, about as big as a large orange, making sure that any threads are tucked into the palm side of the cloth. Now dab the rag at random over the wet surface. The glaze will lift away from the wall onto the rag and will reveal some of the base coat from beneath. Twist your hand around so that you do not create a repeated image of the imprint of the rag.

Ragging is often used with colors close to each other such as dark-yellow glaze over a pale-yellow base coat. It is good for those who prefer to experiment with textured surfaces.

RAG ROLLING

The natural progression from the ragging technique, rag rolling is slightly more even and shows evidence of repeats in the pattern. Once again, it is best to remove the original brushstrokes

▲ Rag rolling.

with stippling but this is not essential. Thinly apply the glaze in sections about 3 by 3' (1 by 1m). The glaze should cover the wall but should not be applied so thickly that it runs or dribbles. Jab out the brushstrokes with the tip of the brush and then wad a ball of cotton cloth into the size of a large orange. This time, make sure that any loose threads are buried firmly into the core of the ball. Now simply roll the ball of cloth very firmly over the section of wet glaze. The glaze

▲ Ragging can produce soft terra-cotta tones that are reminiscent of the Mediterranean.

▲ Rag rolling produces a soft texture on this wall.

deep shine. It is just perfect for the area below a chair rail if you are using another technique, such as ragging, above the rail. Try painting the wall in bright red and bagging over the top of this with a deep crimson.

Ordinary supermarket bags produce a neat, tight texture while coarser, heavier bags produce results that are more like ragging and a little wilder. Try a few before you start so that you can decide which you like best. You need a few bags of the same type to cover a whole room.

DRAGGING

The most uniform of paint effects, dragging is so popular that the overall pattern is even available as wallpaper. One quick try at dragging will make you realize that it is foolish to pay for this effect in a wallpaper as it is easy, and fun, to do yourself.

▲ Dragging.

You need the glaze to be fairly thin for dragging, certainly no thicker than table cream. It is more successful if you use a dark color over a pale base than the other way around.

You will need a dragging brush for this; it is a brush about 3" (8cm) wide and about $^1/_2$" (1cm) thick, with coarse bristles about 4" (10cm) long. Do not use bristled flogging brush because the 6" (15cm) long bristles will drive you mad before you get halfway through the job. You can use an ordinary household brush for dragging but you will find the process slower.

Happily, dragging does not have to be worked as quickly as other paint effects so you can safely answer the telephone

will again lift off onto the rag. Work in random directions for a soft finish or, alternatively, work up in straight lines if you want to see the repeats more clearly. Move on immediately to the next section and do not stop until you have reached a neat edge in the corner of the room. You will need a good supply of clean cloths for this technique as they tend to become soaked, at which point they stop lifting the glaze from the wall.

BAGGING

This is not the most elegant name for a paint effect but surely one of the most elegant to look at. Bagging is even simpler than ragging because there is no need to remove initial brushstrokes. It has the appearance of leather and is very effective in situations where a heavy finish is required.

Brush the glaze onto the wall, again working in sections about 3 by 3' (1 by 1m) and keeping the edges wet as you work. Turn a plastic grocery bag inside out (to stop the print from adding to the wall decor) and scrunch it up in your hand. Now dab the bag

all over the wet glaze and watch as the glaze magically begins to take on a thick texture. Move onto the next section immediately.

This technique is really simple and the results are truly stunning. Bagging is even better if you work on an oil-based glaze that is as thick as jam because it takes on an actual three-dimensional texture as well as the flat texture of the paint effect. You will need to use neat oil glaze and artist's oils from tubes to mix a really thick glaze. It is advisable to add about a teaspoon of drying oil to this kind of glaze mix or it will take at least a week to dry. It is worth the effort though, because oil-based bagging creates a

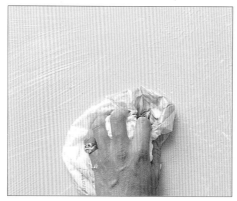

▲ Bagging.

between sections. This is because of the uniformity of the effect and the fact that you will work in 6" (15cm) wide sections around the room from ceiling to floor. Use a plumb line that falls from the ceiling to the floor in order to keep the lines as straight as possible.

Apply a 6"- (15cm-) wide strip of glaze all the way up the wall. As you become more competent, you will be able to apply wider sections.

Hold a dragging brush flat against the wall at the very top of the strip of wet glaze with the handle pointing toward the floor and, as the name suggests, drag it all the way down the wall. The brush will lift away the glaze where the bristles touch the wall and leave fine stripes of glaze behind. Try not to stop and lift the brush halfway down because it will leave an uneven mark. For a lighter and more delicate effect, redrag the same strip and lift even more glaze away.

Wipe the brush regularly to keep it from becoming clogged with old glaze. You will need to trot up and down a ladder a lot for this technique and should, where possible, work from the top of the room to the bottom. Move down the ladder with the brush pressed firmly against the wall and keep it moving as evenly as you can.

You may already be aware of the fact that the stripes in dragging are made by the bristles at the point where they meet with the ferule, into which

they are rooted, and not by the tips. This is why it is important to press relatively firmly and be sure that the paintbrush contacts the wall along its entire length. The length of the bristles and tips serve to feather and soften the stripes. If the strips of glaze do not drag evenly into fine stripes then the glaze is too thick.

STIPPLING

Timeless and classic, stippling in its purest form is one of the most difficult effects to perfect and it takes some practice and energy to master it fully. Yet it looks so very undaunting and so understated. If you ever find yourself looking at a large wall space that has been perfectly and evenly stippled, stop awhile to appreciate it.

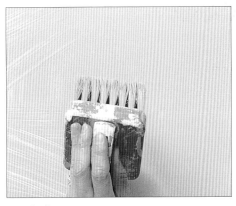

▲ Stippling.

You may be forgiven for not noticing that a stippled paint effect has been added to a wall because it needs close inspection before you can see the tiny pin-prick texture in the glaze. Working with oils is recommended because they dry slowly and allow you more working time, thus minimizing clouding and patching. Oils also take on a gentle texture that is not evident when working with water-based glazes.

For a classic stipple, you will need a glaze mixture that is not too runny; like table cream and no thinner. Apply this to the wall in sections of about 3 by 3' (1 by 1m) as evenly as you can.

Immediately take a stippling brush and tap the flat bristles onto the glaze in soft jabbing motions. A paintbrush that is approximately 3" (20cm) wide will prevent you from tiring too

quickly. Keep moving over the wet glaze and wipe the tips of the bristles whenever they stop lifting the wet color. After you have moved over the whole wet square, look for dark patches and jab the stippling brush directly into their centers. From the center of the dark patch, work gently out toward a lighter patch, using exactly the same jabbing motion. What you are doing here is evening out the paint by moving excesses from the dark patches into the lighter areas.

Work the next square and "share out" the paint that overlaps the previous square to keep a mark from showing.

Most stippling has a gentle, cloudy effect. This is easier to achieve and you will not need to concentrate on moving the paint around to ensure an even finish. You may also use a stippling tool that looks as though it is made of plastic turf for a more obvious stippled look.

Follow the same principles for this technique as for classic stippling but pay less attention to the even finish. If your overlaps begin to show as obvious squares then it may be worth changing the shape in which you apply the wet glaze to the wall. Try using oval shapes or very wide diagonal strips. Incidentally, quick stippling makes a good sky effect if worked in pale blue over white and you can add some quick and convincing clouds following the sponging technique on page 53.

FROTTAGE

The French speakers among you will realize that this is the French word for "rubbing." As with most of the basic paint effects, it describes the technique accurately because it is nothing more than a layer of glaze that has been rubbed with a sheet of paper.

That said, the frottage effect is bold and random—it will create a more radical finish than those of the aforementioned techniques, especially if worked in layers changing from light to dark. Frottage can be shaded dramatically into corners or highlighted to bring feature areas forward into a room. Because this technique is big, it is not suitable for very small items.

▲ Dragging produces a subtle effect.

A large tea tray is about as small as you can go and still create a good effect; any smaller and your finished item may look scruffy.

Frottage is also the basic technique for making the effect of old, cracked plaster, so it is worth mastering if you are interested in developing your skills to include trompe l'oeil—another French word, this time meaning "trick of the eye" but more accurately described as realistic painting (see pages 52–3).

Once again the base must be soft sheen or shiny. For basic frottage, apply the glaze in large, uneven sections, as big as you can comfortably reach from your ladder or standing position. Don't panic at the idea of big sections because frottage is very quick to manipulate. You must, however, be able to reach the whole glazed section safely with both hands so do not lean too far from the top of a ladder.

When the glaze has been applied to the wall, immediately press a large torn piece of newspaper flat onto it and pat the surface all over. Now, pull the paper off carefully so that it does not tear, to reveal a blotchy, wet, and somewhat rippled texture. Move over and reapply the paper in this way until the whole section has been frottaged. Continue across the entire wall using the same color and techniqe. You will find that the same piece of newspaper will end up going a long way.

That is all there is to frottage really. You will find that some of the newsprint ink comes off on the wall, leaving very effective smudges and shading. Sometimes though, the newsprint is so cheap that you may see an exact mirror image of the text

appearing on your wall. The broadsheets seem to work better than the cheap tabloids! If you prefer not to have these marks, then use large torn sheets of brown paper. Use a piece of paper with torn edges to prevent any straight lines from showing up.

Frottage is one of the effects that really benefits from being worked in layers of differing shades. Let the first layer dry fully and then start again with a deeper tone, perhaps leaving some areas and patches of the first layer unpainted. A third layer can be applied more heavily into corners to produce an aged and tarnished effect and then a final, much lighter coat over areas that naturally catch the sunlight such as the chimney breast can work to make the walls look very three-dimensional.

Just like a wallpaper with a really big pattern, frottage works best in larger spaces and can look too messy in tiny rooms such as foyers and bathrooms. When the tool used for a paint effect is as big as a sheet of newspaper you really need a large flat space for it to work fully.

You could try using a base coat of primrose yellow and then adding three layers of frottage, first matching the colors of pale dried bricks, then of terra-cotta flowerpots, and finally of dried earth. To take frottage further, see the mock plaster effect on page 49.

With the exception of sponging, the techniques outlined above are the basis for all basic paint effects. Sponging and stippling do not require a glaze medium and are described on page 41. Once you have mastered these basic paint effects you will be ready to move on to some of the more adventurous finishes such as softening techniques. These in turn lead to the very satisfying effects such as mock stone and marble.

COLOR TONING

TWO-TONE EFFECTS

Any of the above paint effects can be two-tone by using two different color glazes and applying the glaze to the wall or item in random patches. Remember that the two colors will mix together in places as you mani-

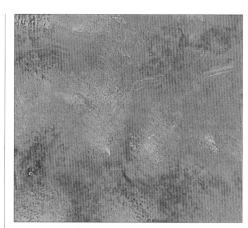

▲ First, rag a yellow glaze to the wall.

▲ Add cream glaze to produce a mottled effect.

pulate the glaze. This means, for example, that blue and yellow used together will result in some green patches here and there. If you would like the two colors to be unblended, apply the first, leaving lots of spaces for the second, and allow it to dry before adding the second color.

SHADING

Once the first coat of a paint effect is fully dry, you can shade into the corners of a room or item to give it a well-used and aged appearance by simply rubbing on some darker glaze.

All you need to do is mix a weak glaze in a darker color by using less color than usual and additional clear glaze. Then rub it into the first coat around the corners and the top of the room, perhaps also along the bottom of the room. Curve around the corners. Use the technique for color washing as outlined on page 36. Raw umber is the best color for aging most paints but try yellow ocher for very pale yellows. The finished result is stunning and shows a real attention to detail, which is often missed in our hurry to get the job done.

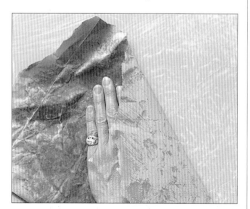

▲ Frottage.

BLENDING COLORS

As long as you are prepared to work fast, you can successfully use two or more colors to create a blended effect—such as sunset colors graduating from dark at the top to light at the bottom of the wall. For effects such as these, you need to work as before except in bands along the wall, working from the darkest color up to the lightest or the other way around.

Do not be tempted to work a single band of color all the way around the top of the room before moving onto the lighter shade. Instead, work one wall at a time so that the colors remain wet and easy to blend. An oil-based medium will be more successful because of its slow drying time. Overlapping the colors by 1' (30cm) or more will save you from having to mix lots of graduating shades since they will blend when they are in place. It is a good idea to have two people on the job for blending because speed is of the essence.

▲ Work quickly when blending colors.

SOFTENING COLORS

Softening is probably the most important technique for those who would like to develop a full range of decorative painting skills. It is worth practicing until you get the hang of it because the results are very satisfying. Softening removes brushstrokes and gently smudges and blends a finish. For example, a brushy color wash can be softened while wet to produce a very different finish in the form of gentle clouds of color. Softening is essential for marble finishes and helpful in most mock stone or wood looks.

Unfortunately, the essential tool, a badger-hair softener, does not come

▲ Soften the finish with a badger-hair softener.

cheap. They are available in art-supply and craft stores, as well as in some home-improvement centers. You can expect to pay at least five times as much as you would for a decent household brush of the same size. Badger-hair softeners, as with other expensive brushes, benefit from being washed carefully and left to soak for a day now and then in a good hair conditioner. A 3" (8cm) badger-hair softener will serve well for most techniques. In a pinch, you can use another natural-bristle brush, but the result will not be as smooth as that achieved with a badger-hair brush.

The bristles are long, soft, and floppy and, by flicking them gently across the wet surface of oil- or water-based paint, you will see the edges of the brushstrokes begin to go out of focus before blending softly into the background. Tickle the brush in one direction and then the opposite direction. Repeat this until no brushstrokes are visible. It is possible to eliminate your painting marks completely but this tends to take time and practice.

Of course, if you are working on an area that will not be subject to close inspection, such as the area of wall above a picture rail, you will not need to achieve an immaculate finish. For furniture and smaller items, however, it is really worth making the effort to achieve the best possible finish.

ADJUSTING THE SHEEN OF THE FINISH

Once your paint effect is complete, you may wish to make it more or less shiny. While today's glazes are durable enough

to survive without a coat of varnish, you may want to coat the wall with a product called latex glaze coat. This product can also be used on wallpaper and is available in matte, satin, or gloss finish. It can be applied by brush, or very slowly by roller (so as to avoid foaming and unsightly bubbles). It goes onto the wall looking like milk but will dry clear. As most paint effects are slightly shiny, this is a good way of making a matte finish. Latex glaze coat is unfortunately not suitable for use in kitchens and bathrooms where you would be advised to use varnish.

Varnish often contains a degree of yellow stain because it is designed to make wood look more beautiful. Use clear varnish if you want to keep the color exact. Acrylic varnishes are best for a clear finish but, of course, cannot be used on an oil glaze. If in doubt, test a small area first.

HINTS & TIPS:
Paint effects that do not require glaze

Some paint effects do not require that the paint be movable once you have applied it to the wall. The position in which you apply the paint is the position in which the paint will be left to dry.

• Sponging: First wet and squeeze out the sponge in warm water so that it is soft and pliable. Any paint can be used for sponging but water-based latex is particularly easy to work with. Dip the sponge into a shallow tray of your chosen color and then apply two or more gentle dabs of the paint onto some scrap paper to dab off any excess paint. Then gently begin to tap it against the wall. The hairs and protruding pieces of the sponge (not the whole sponge) should make contact with the wall. Repeat the tapping of the sponge and keep your hand moving around so that you do not sponge the same area twice.

• Stippling: Stippling takes on an entirely different effect if the paint is stippled onto the wall and not worked with a glaze. All you need are three shades of paint, one very light, one medium, and one dark. Gently dip the tips of a wide stippling brush into the medium color first. Apply the paint to the wall in patches or long, squiggly lines using a gentle jabbing of the brush so that it goes on in little dots with no brushstrokes. When the brush runs out of paint, dip it into another of the three shades and repeat against the first area of paint while it is still wet. The two colors will blend where they meet to make a third shade. Repeat with the third color.

Once you have mastered the basic techniques, you will be ready to move on to more challenging projects. This chapter shows you how to create eye-catching and exciting faux finish effects including metal, stone and wood, as well as letting you in on a number of painting tricks. It also shows you the exciting decorative paint finishes that you can achieve with the aid of a stencil or a stamp.

Advanced Paint Effects

Metal- and Stone-finish Effects

ADD A UNIQUE TOUCH to your decorative scheme by using metal or stone, from the weathered surface of verdigris to semi-precious stones such as lapis lazuli. However, the genuine article can be expensive to buy and cumbersome to handle. Thus, the aim of many paint effects is to re-create the finish of a particular type of metal or stone.

The following techniques will enable you to take the first steps toward achieving the finish you desire. Before you start, think about the style that would suit the object you intend to decorate. Tortoiseshell, malachite, verdigris, porphyry, and lapis lazuli work well on small items, while granite, marbling, faux stone, and mock plaster are effective in covering entire walls or a large area, such as a fireplace.

VERDIGRIS

Verdigris is one of the most popular paint finishes and is a very useful treatment for any items that are supposed to be made of metal but are in fact made of something else. When brass and copper are left out in the weather, they corrode and age, producing a greenish powder. This corrosion is very easily imitated in paint and can therefore be used to make any item look like it is a really old piece of brass or copper. There is a wonderful secret ingredient in the form of rottenstone—a gray powder pigment made from crushed rocks, which will give a more realistic appearance than plain paint. Although it is not essential, you should be able to find some in a good art-supply store and will be more pleased with the results of your verdigris if you use it.

All you need to bear in mind when working mock verdigris is the fact that it has a fairly dry and powdery-looking

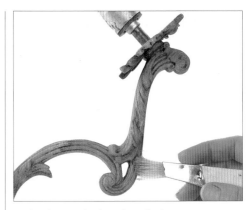

▲ Apply two shades of verdigris green.

finish. Work with the paint as dry as you can, forcing as much whiting into the mixture as it will take, and dab the colors on randomly. When painting a verdigris effect, you can cake your brush with powdery paint mixture.

Gilding the item in patches with copper leaf (see pages 69–70) will also allow you to leave a few little spaces here and there through which the copper leaf can shine. It will help to make the article look as if it is indeed genuine copper underneath. Or you could add in some gold highlighting after applying the green base color.

Using two shades of verdigris green or a mixture of pthalo green, white, and raw umber artist's acrylic paints, mix up a cake-type mixture of each color in separate jars by forcing as much whiting powder into the mix as you can. If you have no whiting powder, use acrylics only and apply the paint in many sparse layers.

Jab the two colors at random all over the surface, allowing them to overlap and blend with each other

▲ A verdigris finish is a very effective way of aging an object.

▲ Highlight the edges with gold.

here and there. If you want to go one step farther, then you could apply some rottenstone when the paint is still a tiny bit wet by jabbing on the powder using a dry brush. It will stick to any wet paint and make the item look very old and dirty.

To protect a verdigris finish use a matte varnish rather than oil-based paints because it is not supposed to have any shine.

TORTOISESHELL

A good starting point for stone effects is tortoiseshell because it does not require too much intricate detail and it is so rarely seen in its genuine form these days that no one will notice if your attempt is realistic or not!

Work on a base of pale yellow so that it shows through the paint that you are about to apply. You will need to make three shades of brown paint. Mix some glaze with a good squirt of artist's color in raw sienna, raw umber, and, if you can get it, transparent yellow ocher, which is great for tortoiseshell. If not, then use another burnt-type color. This

▲ Varnish tortoiseshell to a high shine.

technique requires a much more concentrated, color-intense mixture than is used in the basic wall effects.

Using a square-ended artist's fitch (a grand word for a cheap artist's brush, made of hog's hair with a long, pale wood handle) about ½" (1cm) wide, apply patches of the various colors in small oblong shapes, the same shape as the end of the paintbrush. Apply a random selection of the three colors and leave some spaces for the background color to shine through.

It is best to work diagonally across the surface of the item you are painting rather than from side to side. Imagine a checkerboard or crossword-puzzle grid, with all the black squares replaced with a variety of the three browns and then turn it diagonally.

Now take a badger-hair softener and gently brush the wet paint in the direction of the painted oblongs, back and forth a few times. Then prepare for the magic as you brush the opposite way using the same light motion. Suddenly the regular oblongs of color begin to merge into the background. Wipe the badger-hair softener from time to time and repeat this over and over until all of the brushstrokes disappear. Immediately wipe away everything you have just done, all the way back to the pale yellow background and do the whole thing again but this time make it a bit more irregular. You will soon see that a few variations in the size of the dashes of colored glaze make a significant difference.

Tortoiseshell looks great if it is varnished four or five times with thinned gloss varnish when it is completely dry. You will find that a thinned varnish is easier to apply evenly to the object.

MALACHITE

This is a very messy technique so prepare to be covered up to your elbows in green glaze. It is very simple, though, and unlike most of the mock-stone techniques, this one does not require any softening.

Work on a base of aqua or pale turquoise. Mix a glaze using about a

▲ A malachite finish is very striking.

tablespoon of glaze and a teaspoon of artist's color in pthalocyanine green, which is a deep bluish green. If you ask for fallo green, the supplier will know what you mean. You will also need to make a glaze mixture using a dash of raw umber. Now apply the green all over one side of the item on which you are working, using a stippling or jabbing motion so that you do not make brushstrokes. Incorporate a tiny dash or patch of the brown here and there.

Now take a small piece of cardboard, about 3 by 3" (8 by 8cm) torn from a larger sheet and draw it across the surface just as if it were a paintbrush you were dragging. Move slowly and in broadly recognizable circles. The irregular edges of the card will scrape away some of the paint leaving the familiar trace marks of malachite. You will find that giving the card a little wiggle here and there helps to make the malachite look more natural. Some pure dots of the brown about the size of the diameter of a pencil eraser will also help. If you overlap the circles, you will end up with something very like the real thing.

Once again you will need to varnish this finish and may want to build up a number of coats so that the slight ridges in the finish are eventually buried deep in the layers of varnish.

GRANITE

With such a large variety of granite paint on the market, it is easy to trick the eye into believing that a speckled granite paint effect is the real thing. One simple method is to mix a granite-colored paint using various shades of green and adding dark green, silver, and black glitter for the speckle, or mica, effect. Apply over a pale base coat for best results.

Another possibility is to stipple the base with a mixture of cream, light brown, and fawn paints (which will blend into a host of browny shades) and then spatter first with white and then very sparingly with burgundy or caramel. But of course there are no rules on the colors.

Another method is to begin by stippling on some of the colors you have chosen for your granite using the same technique as verdigris (see page 44) or stippling (see page 41), that is to say, use a very dry, cake-mix-like paint on a lightly loaded brush. Make sure

▲ A granite fireplace.

▲ Apply a mix of paint and glitter on a pale base.

that the paint is not caked onto the item, though, because while this will work for verdigris, it is not effective for mock granite. Add some rottenstone if you have it, but go easy at this stage.

When the base is completely dry, you can start on the speckles of granite, which you create by spattering the object with three shades of paint in tiny droplets. Using an old toothbrush, dip the bristles gently into a thinner mix of paint. Tap the brush gently on the edge of a pot to get rid of excess paint and then, holding the toothbrush about 1' (30cm) away from the surface, gently rub your fingers along the bristles. Watch out for traveling droplets of paint that can flick quite a long way.

MARBLING

Marbling, the paint effect that everyone wants to learn first, is a separate art form in itself. You will find that some expert help and practice will really make a difference in the results you achieve if you are trying a complicated marble. That said, some are quite simple to copy—all you need is a bit of patience and a badger-hair softener, which is so important for marbling that it is really not worth doing unless you have one.

Likewise, although marbling can be carried out in acrylics, the luster and depth of real marble is only achieved when working with oils—artist's oils, straight from the tube and thinned with a drop of oil-based glaze. As oil paints dry slowly, adding a tiny dash of drying oil will help to speed up the process.

The first rule of marbling is not to rush. Work gently and you will be

amazed at what you can turn out. Prepare the surface with two coats of oil-based eggshell paint in the base color, which is normally white or cream.

FANTASY MARBLE EFFECT

It is best to start with a fantasy marble effect so that you will see some fairly speedy results, which have the air of marble without actually imitating a stone.

Squirt a couple of inches of two paint colors (for example, yellow ocher and raw sienna) in two colors onto a palette or mixing tray. Take a paintbrush no more than 1" (2.5cm) wide, dip it lightly into one of the colors and then dab it into a small dish of glaze (with some drying oil mixed into it if you have decided to use them). Move the brush around on the palette until the paint mixture is really smooth and there is not much left on the paintbrush.

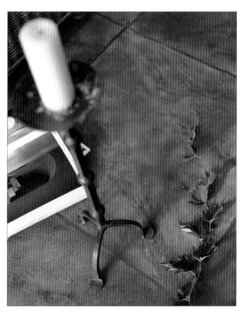
▲ Create a fantasy marble effect.

Now apply this first color onto the painted surface in soft, squiggly lines that are roughly diagonal and all going in the same direction. It is very important that the paint is thin and that you are not applying it so thick that it makes a textured surface. Leave quite a lot of the background unpainted. You may join the squiggles in Y shapes in places. Immediately repeat this with the next color, filling more of the background but leaving a little of it unpainted.

Now immediately stroke a badger-hair softener backward and forward in the same direction as you have painted. You will see the colors begin to move and smudge. Brush again in the other diagonal direction—the paint will begin to blur around the edges and the squiggles you applied will widen and spread out, with some blending into each other. Continue brushing in both directions until all the brushstrokes have disappeared completely. Now you should have the base of a marble finish, without any veins.

For a more realistic finish, dip a tiny brush into some mineral spirits and run it lightly in the same diagonal direction as before. Perhaps dot it lightly against the paint here and there or spatter a fine spray of spirits. You will see the paint open up, revealing the base color as soon as you touch it to the surface. Try dabbing a crumpled piece of cloth onto the surface here and there and then resoftening, but remember that this is marbling and not ragging.

If you are happy with the marble base at this stage, then let it dry fully before continuing. By doing this, you will be able to wipe off any mistakes in the veining without destroying the base.

Apply the veins in one of the colors already used but this time use thicker paint. Use the thinnest artist's brush you can find for this with bristles about ½" (1cm) long. Hold the brush as lightly as you can and gently pull it down the diagonal flow of the marble base. Look at a real piece of marble and copy the vein structure—this will make life easy as you build up a network of veins. Don't make right angles to join the veins, but join them to each other in the way a ramp joins the highway, making a V shape. You should be able to trace all the veins to the edge of the piece so that they never appear out of nowhere. You can soften these veins to make it look like soft marble.

When this is completely dry, apply a second vein structure. Use the thinnest brushstrokes and a very weak paint mix to apply the secondary veins. This will produce the almost invisible veins that close inspection of the real thing reveals. Varnish the completed marble several times using thinned gloss varnish.

▲ Realistic marble is convincing.

REALISTIC MARBLE EFFECT

Having come to grips with how softening oil paints can produce a marble effect, try imitating one of the popular white marbles, which is often used to make countertops and café tables.

Begin by making the surface slippery so that you can smudge the effect—wipe it all over with a drop of straight glaze, like greasing a cake pan before baking. As you did before, dip a paintbrush approximately 1" (2.5cm) wide into a squirt of Paynes grey oil paint on a palette and then into glaze and drying oil. Dab any excess paint off onto the palette until the brush is almost empty of paint.

This time, don't paint the color onto the surface, but jab it on very lightly

▲ Paint using roughly diagonal strokes.

with gentle stippling strokes. Again aim for broadly diagonal, but not clear, stripes. Leave most of the background unpainted. When stippling the paint onto the surface, tap over and over each part until you cannot see the imprint of the shape of the brush. Repeat this with a slightly darker application of Paynes grey with a touch of raw umber in it.

The next thing that you need to do is soften the overall effect with a badger-hair softener. Gently allow the colors to smudge into the unpainted background. Most of the background should remain white and you can wipe off any paint you want to remove at this stage and resoften. The secret of this marble finish is sparsity of paint. In fact, you only really need a hint of color on your brush. Apply the veins in a thicker Paynes grey as before.

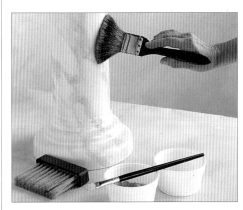

▲ Soften the effect with a badger-hair softener.

These two techniques—painting on the background of the marble and stippling on a tiny amount of color—form the basis for nearly every type of marble effect. Soon you will have enough confidence to copy those you see on buildings and floors.

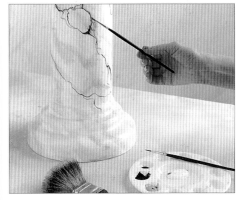

▲ Apply the veins using Paynes grey.

FAUX STONE BLOCKS

Having successfully turned out a mock marble you are well on the road to more serious trickery of the eye. The best starting place for murals and theme painting is a stone wall, which is so very easy to re-create. If anything, stone blocks are more laborious than they are difficult.

Use a very pale base coat of latex flat paint and divide the wall up into a rectangular pattern, using a level and a plumb line to keep things straight. Make the blocks as big as possible, as this will mean less work for you.

Make a dirty stone paint color by mixing gray glaze with small quantities of black or white colorizer or artist's acrylics paint. Mix the color slowly because these hues are very powerful and you need to take care to achieve the correct shade.

▲ Sponge the paint on the wall.

Sponge the paint on the wall so that it is thicker in some places than others. Work each block separately and try not to go over the edges. Some painters prefer to use a grid of thin masking tape, but the method here is faster and looks more like a dry stone wall.

Now darken the paint a little with a dash of raw umber and add a second layer of gentle sponging. Make sure that you apply thicker paint in the corners of the blocks and sponge a few patchy areas on each brick.

Add a tiny hint of a darker color to each block of stone. You should see the effect of stone right away as long as you remember to work each block individually and are not lazy about staying within the edges! Remember to keep the sponging gentle; don't press too hard.

▲ Use a dark crayon to add the shadows.

When this is dry you are ready to work some magic with oil crayons from the art store. Outline the top and right-hand sides of each rectangle by drawing along it by hand in white—don't use a ruler. Smudge each line by running your finger along the crayon line. Now outline the bottom and left-hand side of each block with a crayon darker than the color of the blocks. Use a dark brown for sandstone colors and very dark gray for gray stones. Again, smudge the lines by running your finger firmly along them to produce a feeling of light and shade. Now tidy up the corners and draw in an occasional crack with sharpened crayons. Soften the effect with a fine brush.

▲ Use a dark-colored glaze to produce a Gothic end result.

▲ Blend in any obvious drawing lines.

MOCK PLASTER

This is a step forward from frottage (see pages 39–40) and an intriguing way of creating cracks that can be used when painting mock stone walls. It takes longer to execute than straightforward frottage but the finished effect is very rewarding.

Use the same technique as that used for frottage for the first coat of paint—apply a light terra-cotta to create a deep red plaster or a muted pink for a lighter finish. When the first application is completely dry, apply a darker glaze to fill an area about 3 by 3' (1 by 1m) and press a piece of torn paper against the wet glaze. Pat it into place and then, before removing the paper, jab a paintbrush over the torn side of the paper in stippling motions from the wall and onto the paper and back again. Lift off the paper carefully and you will see that the stippling has made the image of a crack in the paintwork.

Instead of working along the wall in a uniform fashion, apply the next piece of paper so that you continue the crack line. Build up more layers of deeper tones for greater effect. Apply a flat varnish to mock plaster so that it looks really dry and powdery.

PORPHYRY AND RED LEATHER

Like granite, porphyry relies on the spattering of paint to bring it to life. Real porphyry is deep red and very rewarding to recreate in paint. Oil-based paints are recommended because of the resulting depth and luster. This means that you will have to allow plenty of drying time between the steps.

Using a glaze made of oil glaze and Alizarin crimson oil paint, dip a cloth into the glaze and wipe the prepared object (which has been painted with satin or eggshell paint) in swishy circular motions. This will look like a tight color wash. Cover the remaining the glaze to stop it from drying out while the background dries.

Next, add an extra squirt of Alizarin crimson to the glaze so that it becomes very intense in color and as thick as jam. Make another glaze in the same

▲ Spatter paint on to create a porphyry effect.

way but add some Paynes grey to give a very dark red. A few drops of drying oil will help here because oil paints can take weeks to dry. It is best to use two round brushes (domed sash brushes). First, dip one into the red glaze and stipple the paint onto the surface, making it fairly even. Then add some of the darker red glaze in patches here and there and stipple the two colors into each other so that they blend. The darker patches should not look like blobs. Keep the surface thick and color intensive.

If you prefer, you can adapt your effect at this stage to look like faux red leather. While the paint is wet, press a piece of plastic sandwich bag flat onto the surface (as you did with frottage) and peel it away to create a leather effect. Experimentation and keeping the paint thick are key in this effect.

For a perfect deep-red porphyry finish, allow the stippled surface to dry and then spatter it with white, Paynes grey, and dark red paint. If deep red does not fit with your color scheme, you can use a terra-cotta base color instead (see "Porphyry Picture Frame" project on pages 106–7).

Neither of these effects need to be softened and both benefit from a couple of coats of gloss or satin varnish.

LAPIS LAZULI

Lapis lazuli is one of the most important semiprecious gems in the world of painting and art because it is the purest form of ultramarine blue. The stone itself has tiny flecks of gold and sometimes even marble-like veins.

It is best to paint onto a background of gold so that any gaps or spaces in the paintwork will glint through, looking like the flecks of gold in genuine lapis lazuli. Spray the item all over with gold spray paint and let it dry completely. Mix some artist's oil paint in ultramarine blue with a touch of oil-based glaze or linseed oil and a drop of the all-important drying oil. Then stipple this mixture all over the surface using small, sharp jabbing motions at random. Occasionally, touch the tip of your brush into some darker blue paint, such as Prussian blue, and continue the stippling. This deeper color will liven

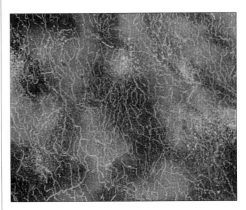

▲ Use a deep ultramarine blue for lapis lazuli.

up the overall effect and will also provide some realistic variation.

Once you have covered the whole area, check for any brushstrokes that are visible and stipple them out carefully. The surface should have the tiny indents of your paintbrush tips all over it. Now soften the effect thoroughly and carefully using a badger-hair softener, creating a soft, smudged surface so that no brushstrokes show through. Use the softener in all directions—remember that this is not a marble effect and so the brushstrokes should not all follow a definite diagonal direction.

Finally, while the surface is still wet, gently scratch through the surface in tiny squiggles, perhaps using the sharpened point of a feather or a kitchen skewer. The gold base will be revealed through these scratches. Lapis lazuli is so often seen in its highly polished form that the paint effect looks even better if given a few coats of high gloss varnish after it is completely dry.

Wood-finish Effects

THE TEXTURE AND FINISH of wood has long been admired by interior decorators. If you do not have much wood in your home and want to re-create its effect, then use a wood-graining technique to produce a faux mahogany or oak finish. If, on the other hand, your house is full of different types of woodwork, then use a paint technique such as wood staining or liming to add interest and variety. Wood stains come in a wide range of colors that enable you to experiment with different hues. Liming, or pickling, is a traditional technique best suited to open-grained wood such as oak, maple, and pine. In the past, floors and furniture were treated with lime wash to prevent damage by insects. Today, there is a paint effect that simulates this finish.

WOOD GRAINING

SIMPLE WOOD GRAINING

Wood graining, like marbling, can be as simple or difficult as you choose to make it. In its most basic form the imitation of a grain is no more than a form of dragging (see pages 38–9). Try dragging an earthy brown glaze over a terra-cotta base and let your dragging brush wiggle slightly here and there. Even this will look convincingly like wood and the addition of a few strokes with a softening brush or some fine, intense, deep-brown dashes will further enhance the effect.

Once you have achieved this finish, add knots in the wood by dotting a single blob of glaze, about ¼" (0.5cm) in diameter, onto the dragged surface and then redrag around this dot. Move the brush around it as you come down the grain and you will develop little "heart grains" as if there was once a branch attached at that point.

MAHOGANY FINISH

For those who are aiming to achieve even more intricate woodgrains, a base of smooth latex satin or eggshell is essential for the best results.

You will need to get hold of some pure crystals of pigment from an art supplier in Van Dyke brown or raw umber. Mix a heaping teaspoon of these in a shallow dish with some vinegar. The crystals will not all dissolve but most of them should. Now dip the tip of a flat household paintbrush or varnish brush into the

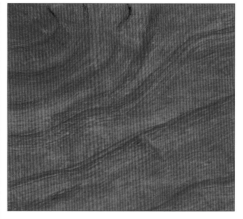

▲ Classic wood graining is easy to re-create.

mixture and brush it up and down all over the surface that you plan to paint. Do not use too much; all you need is just a thin layer of color. Drag this as before, but let your hand wiggle as you drag the brush through the vinegar mixture. The effect you achieve will be amazing.

Drag a badger-hair softener through the grain in places to soften the finish. You can experiment with all sorts of different brushes to find the best ones for opening up the grain and those that close it most effectively. Make knots by painting a dot and dragging around it. When the vinegar starts to dry out, you only need to redip the tips of your brush in the mixture to get it going again.

When you are happy with your graining, let it dry for a few minutes and then repeat the process using a mixture of oil-based glaze and a dot of raw umber oil color. This time though, do not coat the entire area but run some lines of the dark glaze down the lines of your existing piece as enhancements to the depth of color.

You may find that you need to wipe the whole board clean and start again several times before you finally achieve a perfect woodgrain finish.

OAK FINISH

To achieve an oak-grain finish, use a pale yellow base and a raw sienna pigment. Drag the grain in the same way as you would for mahogany and then, when the paint is still wet, flick the end of the long bristles of a flogger brush gently onto the surface. This produces the tiny light streaks that are characteristic of oak.

▲ An oak-floor finish is ideal for a study.

STAINING WOOD

Staining real wood does not mean you are limited to using just one color. You can experiment to produce intricate designs by using a few different colors of wood stain. The key is to prevent one color of the stain from spreading along the grain of the wood and blurring into the next. Just as a trench will keep cattle or animals from straying out of their designated area, a groove in the wood will prevent wet stain from straying beyond where it is meant to go. So, if you plan to stain untreated wood in many different colors, you must carve the outline of your design into the wood.

▲ Apply wood stain direct from the can.

First, draw the design lightly in pencil onto the wood. Complete the design before you start to cut the wood or apply the colors so that you can be sure that it fits in properly.

Now, score deeply into the wood along the outlines using a good-quality utility knife and plenty of blades. A ruler with a handle on it is a highly recommended investment because it will keep your hands away from the blade. Pay particular attention when scoring along lines that go across the grain because this is where the stain will spread most rapidly.

Using a soft artist's brush (No. 6 or No. 8) apply the stain, working from the middle of each section toward the edges. Hesitate for a moment or two before you paint right up to the edges because the stain will be soaking in and may do this part by itself.

▲ Apply at least three coats of varnish.

If the stain does go into the next section you might be able to scrape it away lightly with the blade of the knife. Rescore this line because it was obviously not deep enough to prevent soaking through.

When the design has been colored and has dried, wipe the surface with a clean, dry cloth to pick up any excess stain before varnishing the area with at least three coats of clear varnish.

LIMING

Liming, also called pickling, is a technique that was once only achieved using lime powder. Today, however, the grain of wood is highlighted and filled with a pale paste while the main body of the wood remains visible. A very popular effect in kitchens, liming lightens a wood and has the effect of softening the usual hard lines that are associated with plain, dark wood.

▲ Apply liming wax with steel wool.

Liming works particularly well on deep-grained hardwoods such as oak and will not be as successful on smoother woods such as pine because there is nowhere for the pale paste to sink into.

There are liming/pickling pastes on the market, but you may choose to make your own by mixing whiting powder into wax.

First, rub away any old sealant from the wood with sandpaper and remove any old paint that might remain. Now open up the grain of the wood by stroking fairly hard with a stiff wire brush along the grain of the wood. If you want to achieve a very limed look, brush harder to scratch some new grain into the wood.

The first thing that you need to do is to brush away any dust from the wood. Then rub the wax or liming paste into the grain with steel wool, always going in the direction of the grain first, then briefly across it, then along the grain again. You will be filling the grooves with the paste. There will be a lot of excess paste, so buff this off with a soft cloth. Some brands of paste are buffed while wet and others when they dry, so read the instructions before starting.

Do not varnish limed wood because varnish may lift the liming paste out of the grain, but a coat of clear wax applied a couple of days after the liming process will add a luster to the surface and help to protect it against moisture. Be sure that the liming is fully dry before you polish with wax.

▲ Gently buff the finished effect with a cloth.

Painting Tricks

THERE ARE A NUMBER OF painting tricks that every interior decorator should have up his or her sleeve to make life easier. Trompe l'oeil is one of the most difficult paint effects to get right, but the tips offered in this chapter will help you to re-create stunning lifelike images on your walls and furniture. Aging is a common paint trick that will enable you to make brand-new objects look like antiques. There are also two types of crackle finish that can transform any uninspiring pieces of furniture. Crackle is, in fact, an aging paint effect that simulates what happens when an incompatible paint type is painted over another. *Craquelure*, on the other hand, produces a glazed, crazing effect on your item.

TROMPE L'OEIL

Avid paint-effects fans often ask for books on the subject of trompe l'oeil. The French phrase for "trick of the eye" describes a painted object or mural that looks so very real that you are mistaken into believing it is.

Think about this and you will soon realize that art galleries are filled with amazing paintings that look like photographs of the real thing. We wonder at the painters' skill and marvel at how anyone finds the time for such attention to detail. And yet we expect to be taught a quick way of painting trompe l'oeil, just because it is going straight onto the wall. Trompe l'oeil is a genuine skill that should be admired and appreciated. It is the skill of the

▲ Project the image that you want to re-create onto the object and fill in the original lines.

fine artist using all of his or her know-how and equipment without a canvas.

If you have been successful with some of the paint effects outlined earlier, such as wood graining (see page 50) and mock stones (see page 48), then you are well on the way to a satisfying mural in basic trompe l'oeil.

PAINTING FROM PICTURES

Here are some tricks to get you started. The ultimate trick of trompe l'oeil, which is used by set painters in film and theater, is to project a slide photograph of your subject onto the wall or a piece of furniture you wish to paint. This will help you to get the outline shape perfect. Take the photograph up close, especially if you are working in a small room and won't be able to pull the projector back a long way. Keep the projector in exactly the same position and check your work from time to time. It does take time, but it is the most enjoyable way of learning how to paint and the results are stunning.

This technique is particularly helpful when you are attempting murals of natural scenes. When you next go for a walk in the country, remember to take a camera with you and take

▲ The finished project is eye-catching.

photographs of trees or plants that you come across. By projecting natural images such as these onto your walls, you will be able to reproduce them exactly and bring the countryside into your home.

PAINTING SKIES

Once you have tried basic sponging (see page 41) and are comfortable with the technique of delicately dabbing paint with a natural sea sponge, you will be surprised at how realistic a summer sky you can paint. Suitable as the background for murals, and frequently used for ceilings and children's rooms, a basic sky can be painted onto a matte surface and takes very little time to complete.

Start with a weak white paint and increase the intensity of the paint as you build up layers. First, tear a large sponge in half or quarters until it is the size of a tangerine. Dampen the sponge in water so that it is soft and dip it into the weak mixture of paint on a palette or tray. Tap the excess paint from the sponge by dabbing it a couple of times on scrap paper, so that it is not too soaked in paint. Dab the sponge gently onto the wall, making the shape of a goldfish bowl—a circle with a flat bottom. Then make another of these shapes, just overlapping the first but with the flat bottom at the same level. Repeat, but this time make more of an oval shape with the same flat, level bottom.

Every time you reload the sponge or overlap onto existing sponged paint, you will add new depths of color. In some parts of the wall, increase the amount of paint on your sponge, and in others, let the sponge almost run out

▲ You can use a sponge to paint trees.

of paint. You will by now be seeing the puffiness of white clouds appear.

Take a look out of the window on a slightly cloudy day and you will see that clouds often have a flat bottom. Although not all do, it is an easy way of tricking the brain into thinking it sees clouds. You will also notice that clouds are not entirely white and so a gentle addition of some very pale gray just along the bottom of the clouds and around the same side of each puff will make them look even more realistic. Add a few highlights in pale yellow to create the effect of summer sunshine.

PAINTING SCENES

For scenic trompe l'oeil, paint the whole wall as a sky (see above) and then put the details over the top so that any spaces you leave look intentional.

▲ Use a wide paintbrush for the background.

Block out the base of each piece of the mural in a pale color first. You could, for example, use various shades of green to draw the background of a landscape or a pale yellow for stone columns and statues. Apply obvious shading over the blocking mentioned above using a dilute wash of the next deepest shade. Highlight really light areas, such as where the sun catches a statue, with a dilute wash of white.

Remember to keep the light source relative to the room you are working in; make the highlights fall on the side of pieces where the sun really does come through the windows. Do not worry if the effect looks terrible at this stage of the process—it will soon be transformed.

The level of detail that you wish to draw is up to you. Trees are a good place to start—use a very fine

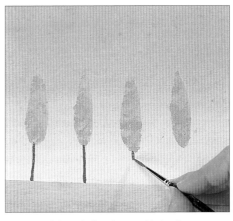
▲ Use a thin paintbrush to add detail.

paintbrush to draw thin trunks and a sponge to add the foliage.

To vary your painting, trace, copy, enlarge a design on a photocopier, or add textures—such as sand—to your paint. Use sharpened crayons instead of small brushes and fine-point markers for outlines. Gold pens are easier to work with than gold paint. Shade with pencils and use chalk first because it washes off. Remember that Impressionism is just as widely admired as realistic painting.

SHADING TRICKS

Build up shading with layers of a dilute wash and blend shadows into the main body of the subject with a softener brush. You can buy these long-handled, fan-shaped brushes in art-supply stores.

One way of deciding where shadows and highlights will fall on a painting is to imagine that it is snowing furiously through the window and that the wind is blowing so hard that the snow is coming in sideways. The places where the snow will hit your subject are the places to highlight with whites and the places the snow would have a hard time getting to are for shadows.

▲ This country scene is ideal for a nursery.

AGING

GLAZE AGING

Any paint effect can be given an aging treatment to make it look as though it has been in place for many years. The most obvious way to age an item is to make it look as though it has had several years of dust and grime—using a technique that only takes a few minutes. And then you could also add in mock cracks and wormholes or perhaps wear away some of the paint.

First, you must add the years of dirt to your item. Make a glaze in acrylic or oils in a color that is darker than the wall surface, such as yellow ocher for very pale walls or the famous raw umber for deep-colored walls. This glaze should be quite weak but not thin. Aim for a consistency as thick as table cream using about one teaspoon of artist's color per pint (0.5l).

Rub the glaze into the corners of the wall or item, making sure that it goes into cracks and corners and then, as the cloth begins to run out of paint, work toward the middle slightly. Do not rub glaze all over, however, because you will change the color completely instead of just aging it. Try to imagine where dirt would normally settle and apply more of the colored glaze to these areas. It is best to build up the appearance of dirt and the passage of time by applying more layers of paint rather than increasing the amount of dark color

▲ Rub down any edges with steel wool.

that you add to the glaze. Another popular method for aging painted work is to rub some of it away with fine-grit sandpaper or steel wool and then perhaps to add some aging glaze as outlined above. This removal of new paint can be heartbreaking, especially on mural work, but it is dramatically effective. Use only fine-grit paper because scratches from coarser papers look very artificial.

If you want to add woodholes, drill them using a small drill bit or just paint them on as little dots. To create cracks, run a tiny brush loaded with a dark-brown paint along the item, always in the direction of a corner or edge from where a crack might naturally have come. A touch of shading with white or a pale color where the sun might catch the edges of the crack can be very effective.

▲ Rub the aging glaze into the object.

TINTED WAX

A large variety of brown or antiquing furniture waxes are available, which can be used on their own or in combination with the varnishes and glazes already described. Walnut shades are particularly good for aging paint surfaces because of their antique color, as well as the feel and subtle sheen that they impart. Bear in mind that antiquing waxes may have a yellowing effect on the painted surface beneath.

▲ Dark tinted wax.

If the wax is to be applied to a varnish finish, make sure the base is a flat varnish, so that the wax can adhere properly. Or rub a satin-finished surface with fine steel wool to help remove the shine before applying the wax. Apply the wax with a cloth or paper towels and leave it for about half an hour before buffing to a good sheen.

CRACKING

There are two types of cracked finish, both of which are popular decorative treatments—crackle and *craquelure*. They are fundamentally different from each other so the first thing you need to decide is which of the two effects is most suitable for the object or item that you are decorating. If the label of the product you are buying does not show a picture of the effect then ask for further details because the two names are often confused. *Craquelure* tends to be more popular than crackle but neither effect is suitable for covering very large areas, such as walls or doors, because both require quick work and are difficult to control.

CRACKLE

This is where the top layer of paint is cracked and split just like an old, painted gate that has been subjected to extremes of cold, hot, wet, and dry weather. Before the paint actually begins to peel off, it cracks along the lines where the painter applied the paint. Crackle is suitable for large areas, such as columns or pillars, as long as you work it in vertical or horizontal sections and do not try to cover more than 9 by 9" (60 by 60cm) or a 12" (30cm) vertical strip at a time.

Apply a base coat of water-based latex paint and allow it to dry completely. This is the color that will peep through the cracks and splits in the paint. Using a brush, paint a good coat of crackle glaze in one direction only—the direction in which you want it to crack. You may use a roller instead of a brush but it will make the end result more scruffy. The crackle glaze will eventually dry clear.

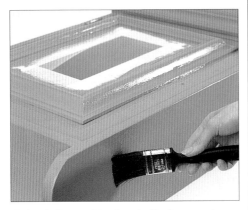

▲ Apply the crackle glaze to the base coat.

When the coat of crackle glaze has dried, apply the top color—again use a latex paint and brush, and paint in whatever direction you want to see most cracks appear. Load your brush

▲ Apply the top coat of latex paint.

▲ A crackle finish makes an object look old.

fully and apply confident, single strokes of paint. Do not rebrush over any of the initial brushstrokes. In minutes you will see the cracks begin to appear as the top coat dries and shrinks. Protect the finished effect with two coats of varnish.

CRAQUELURE

Remember what happened to that non-ovenproof plate that you once put under the broiler? The glazed surface cracked into a pattern of tiny squares and irregular shapes, all joined together to form a close network of almost straight lines. As time has gone by the cracks have stained and now the surface of the plate is a darker pattern than it was originally. This is the effect produced by *craquelure*.

The technique is perfect for any article that can be treated in small sections—such as one side of a box at a time. Water-based *craquelure* paints are more reliable and easier to control than oil-based *craquelure*.

First, paint your object until you have achieved a perfectly smooth finish in the main color—water-based eggshell is superb for this. *Craquelure* is supplied in two parts, step 1 and step 2. When the base paint is dry, apply a layer of step 1 *craquelure* all over the item and also to a small test piece that you can touch to test if it is dry. Use

two coats if you are looking for smaller crackles. Let this dry fully before painting a coat of step 2 onto the item and then allow it to dry for 15 minutes or so before studying the item very closely for tiny cracks in the surface of the top coat. Touch the test piece of paintwork and, if it is beginning to feel dry, you should start to see the cracks. These are caused by the fact that the top coat has a different elasticity than the bottom coats and it splits as it stretches.

Finally, when the item is fully dry and you can see the network of cracks on the surface, wipe it all over with a cloth dipped in a tiny dot or two of artist's acrylic in an aging color such as raw umber and then wipe the surface clean. The dark paint will now be sitting in the cracks and they will be easily visible.

Protect the finished object with two coats of varnish.

HINTS & TIPS: Helping *craquelure* to dry

If you find that your *craquelure* is taking a long time to dry, you can help it along by heating it gently with a hair dryer—be sure to use it on a low setting though. It is best to leave your decorated piece to dry on its own, perhaps under a warm lamp or near a radiator. Avoid using *craquelure* technique on a rainy or humid day because the cracks will need a considerable amount of encouragement to appear!

▲ *Craquelure* gives a crazed effect.

Special Paints and Techniques

SOME SURFACES AND FINISHES require special paints and techniques. Be sure to check beforehand if you need a special type of paint in order to complete your project successfully before you start. There are specially formulated paints available for most surfaces, such as glass, ceramics, and fabrics, that will enable you to be more versatile in your painting. Freehand painting and variations of this—such as barge painting and Scandinavian painting—are specialized techniques that are easy to master and that produce exquisite and unique paint finishes. It is best to begin with a small project that will enable you to see good, fast results. The success of this will fuel your confidence to attempt something larger.

GLASS AND CERAMIC PAINTING

There is a wide range of glass and ceramic paints available for the enthusiastic amateur. Most are acetone-based and durable enough to withstand gentle washing with soapy water (but do not use in the dishwasher or oven). Acetone is the primary ingredient of nail-polish remover—you may be more careful if you imagine that you are painting with nail polish! You can thin the paints (with acetone) until they are as light and gentle as watercolors, which can be blended together or dribbled onto the glass. Remember that they will dry quite fast and can only be changed by completely removing the paint with acetone once it is dry.

For a stained-glass effect, try to find imitation lead when buying the paint. It comes in tubes with a long, thin nozzle and can be squeezed directly onto the glass from the tube to outline areas of different colors with lines of imitation lead.

Use soft brushes for glass and ceramic painting so as to avoid any scratchy-looking brushstrokes; remember to clean the brushes immediately after use with acetone or nail-polish remover.

Decorative ceramics can also be painted using glass paint but will not be suitable for everyday dining. If you want to achieve a permanent design, check out stores where you can sit and paint your own design onto a plate and then leave it to be fired in a special kiln.

HINTS & TIPS: Spray painting glass

Glass paint looks particularly effective when applied with a spray can. It produces a light, misting effect, rather like frosted glass. See the "Fish Stencil Shower Glass" project on pages 193–5.

FABRIC PAINTING

When painting fabrics, always use paint specially designed for the purpose so that your handiwork will last. You will then be able to wash them, as long as you keep them apart from the rest of your laundry. Most fabric paints have a liquid consistency and soak into the weave of the fabric like colored inks. Some are thicker, though, and these will make the fabric feel slightly hard when the paint has dried.

It is best to stretch the fabric that you want to paint over a frame and pin it into position while you work. Secure it as tightly as a drum to achieve the best

▲ Glass painting can instantly transform uninspiring pieces of kitchenware.

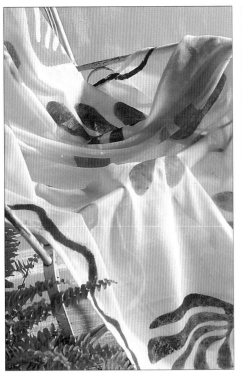

▲ Bright colors look great on white fabric.

results. If you are painting a design with the liquid paint, then the paint will soak along the weave of the fabric and may travel beyond the areas you want to fill. Outline the shapes with a product like gutta-percha to keep this from happening. Gutta is a type of liquid rubber that impregnates the fabric and provides a blocking point beyond which the liquid paint will not

▲ Special fabric paints are widely available.

be able to soak. Apply it through a nozzle—it is rather like cake icing, only much finer. It washes off, leaving the painting perfectly smooth; it is available in a range of colors.

All fabric paints must be sealed when dry, either with a hot iron or by steaming them over boiling water for a few minutes. The product you select will give the recommended method.

For interesting mottled effects, try painting a wash of various colors onto a square of silk and then immediately, while it is still wet, sprinkle rock salt onto the silk and allow it to dry. The salt absorbs the color and pulls the paint into amazing starburst shapes.

Fabric can be stamped, masked, and then painted or freehand painted—thicker paints and fabric pens are recommended for stamping.

FREEHAND PAINTING

There are some decorative paint techniques that do not require any equipment except a small artist's brush and a palette loaded with colors. Freehand painting a small embellishment can often be faster than making a stencil or stamp.

See trompe l'oeil (pages 52–3) for a brief outline of some of the tricks you can bring into play, such as slide photography and carbon paper. Of course, for small-scale projects, you can always use tracing paper.

A good way of building up your confidence is to start by stenciling a design onto a wall and then using a small artist's paintbrush to shade in and embellish the stenciled background. You can then use the stencil as a guideline, just as if you are painting by number.

Of course, freehand work does not necessarily have to be carried out with paints and brushes—you can use crayons, colored pencils, or spray paint. If you know exactly what finish you wish to achieve, ask for some advice at the art-supply or craft store because they will be able to tell you

which paints or products are best for your project. Otherwise, experimentation is the key to success.

You only need a limited palette of colors to get started—red, blue, yellow, white, and raw umber mix to make most of the basic colors, though you may like to add a deep green to the selection. Black is rarely used, except on its own. Add raw umber to colors to make them darker. Artist's paint from a tube goes a long way and is very economical. You will only need a little dot of color on a palette for most of the hand-painted ideas in this book. Avoid "student" or "school" paints because they will fade.

When selecting brushes, the middle-of-the-range soft ones, which come to a point when moistened, are a good starting point. Shorter bristles are easier to control but do not hold as much paint as longer bristles. Imitation sable is almost as good as the real thing and half the price. If you intend to paint any long strokes, such as a branch or flower stem, then a No. 4 "rigger" will be invaluable to you. It has long, soft bristles and flows paint onto the surface, allowing you to paint a long stroke without having to reload your brush. These brushes, as their name suggests, are used by painters of boats to add the rigging and ropes. Instead of buying a palette, you could always cover an old dinner plate with foil or plastic wrap, which cuts cleanup time.

Keep brushes wet and wash them as soon as you have finished; dry paint is very difficult to get off the brushes without spoiling their shapes. Do not allow brushes to stand on their tips in water for long periods of time because they will bend into a curve.

▲ Use tracing paper to transfer the outline.

▲ Freehand paint the detailed color.

▲ Barge painting is ideal for kitchen containers.

BARGE PAINTING

Barge painting decoration is the term used to describe the decorative finish traditionally associated with English canal boats. However, the decorative effect can be achieved on a range of furniture. Traditionally, the themes for canal-boat decoration are limited to scenes with castles and groups of roses and daisies. Yet there is plenty of scope for variation, both in terms of the design and method of painting. Although the rose-shaped strokes here might not suit the item you want to decorate, the actual method of painting can be used to create other designs or variations. Remember that traditional background colors for barge painting are dark, providing a suitable base for bold, striking colors.

TYPES OF PAINT STROKES

1. ROSE-PETAL STROKES
Paint the rose petals in this order: first, the two central petals; then, working from left to right, the three large outer petals; followed by the three smaller ones. Apply the stamens last of all, when the roses are completely dry.

Hold the brush upright and press it down so that half of it is flat on the surface. Then pull the brush toward you, lifting and curving it so that you finish the stroke with only the point touching.

2. USEFUL DECORATIVE STROKES
Hold your brush upright so that just the tip touches the surface. Then, moving from left to right and curving the line, dip the brush down and back up to finish on the tip again.

3. DAISY AND BORDER STROKES
Press the first quarter of the paintbrush onto the surface that you are painting and move it back, lifting it at the same time. As you gently pull the brushstroke across, you should finish on the tip.

4. THIN STROKES FOR STAMENS
Press the first quarter of the brush onto the surface and move it back, lifting it at the same time, so that you finish on the tip.

5. SMALL ROSE-PETAL STROKES
These are made by using the same technique as the one described in step 1, but by using less brush and curving upward.

6. LEAVES
Starting and finishing on the point of the paintbrush, pull it toward you, flattening it while curving it outward and inward. Start at the same point and make the second paint stroke in exactly the same way, but this time curve out in the opposite direction. Then finally, fill in the center of the leaf.

7. LONG AND CURVED STROKES
These are made in just the same way as the decorative strokes described earlier in step 2, only this time your brush must be well charged with paint and you should lift the paintbrush gradually as you move toward the point.

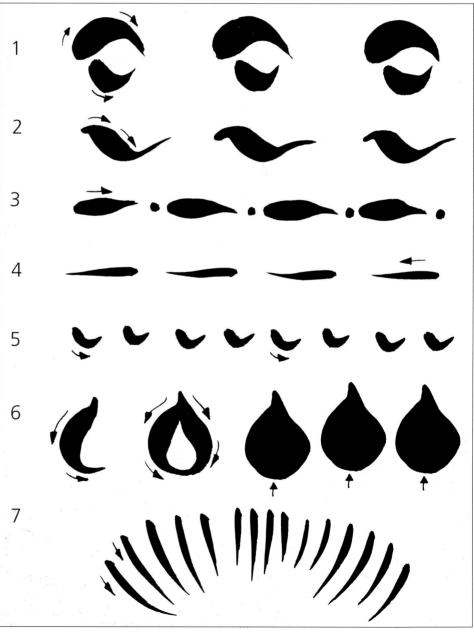

▲ Barge-painting paint strokes.

COLORS & SHAPES

ROSES

• YELLOW ROSE: Start the rose with an orange circle and paint the shadows with crimson paint. Using a clean brush, paint the top petals and the stamens in yellow.

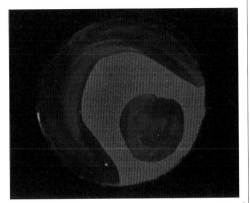

▲ Paint an orange circle with crimson shadows.

▲ Add yellow top petals.

• WHITE ROSE: Start the rose with a pink circle, made by mixing bright red and white together. Make the shadows with bright red and the top petals with white. The stamens are painted yellow.

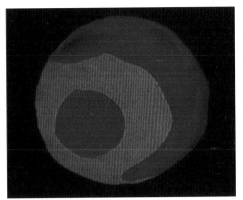

▲ Start with a pink circle and add red shadows.

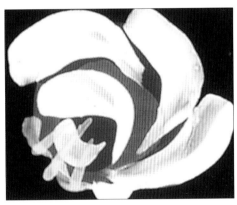

▲ Add white top petals and yellow stamens.

• RED ROSE: Start the rose with a crimson circle and add a little black to this to make the color for the shadows. Paint the top petals with bright red and the stamens in yellow.

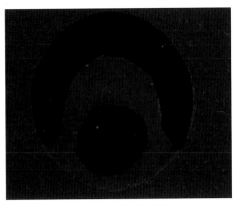

▲ Create a crimson circle with black shadows.

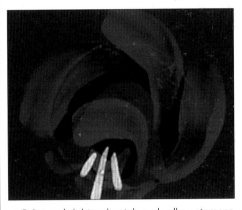

▲ Paint on bright-red petals and yellow stamens.

DAISIES

Daisies are begun by painting a circle of white petals. The yellow center has a small, bright-red brushstroke flicked around one side. These flowers are ideal motifs for connecting decorative features, and work well with roses.

▲ Add a yellow and red center.

LEAVES

The leaves are painted in lime green with a small smudge of tan paint at the base. The veins are painted yellow. All the filling lines and trimmings are usually painted in yellow, but you can use another color around them.

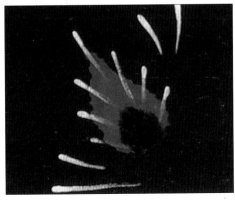

▲ Add yellow veins to the lime green leaf.

SCANDINAVIAN PAINTING

Just as with barge painting, there is a definite style about Scandinavian hand painting. Tiny swathes of painted flowers on a background of muted green or bright red and blue are the most common design in Scandinavian painting. All you need to do to emulate this style is to keep the painting simple. Instead of painting a flower petal by pulling the brush, just lay it flat and lift the brush off immediately. The shape made by a small artist's brush (a circle with the tip of the brushmark toward the center) is used repeatedly to make flowers such as daisies. A little yellow dot in the center will complete the image. Use the barge-painting technique to paint leaves.

Stenciling

STENCILING IS A SIMPLE decorative paint technique that can give a totally different look to your room or piece of furniture. It is an inexpensive way to create great paint effects. All you need is a little paint, a few pieces of equipment, and plenty of imagination. There is no end to its uses, whether for unifying the design scheme in an entire room, or adding that extra finishing touch to the most ordinary of objects in your home. You can use it on anything, ranging from the tiniest of boxes to a pillow or lampshade—even a window. If you are a first-time stenciler, start small and have a clear plan in mind. Time spent developing your stencil design and analyzing its shape, scale, repeat, and color scheme will dramatically increase your chances of success.

DESIGNING YOUR STENCIL

Craft stores are full of precut designs that are ready to use and the array can provide ideas for entire themes in any room of the home. You may, however, want to take the more original approach of designing your own image. Anything can become the basis for a stencil—from intricate Chinese dragons to simple pictures of children's toys. For many people, ideas for repeating patterns spring from existing home decoration, such as wallpaper or upholstery, or from various soft accessories and curtains found around the home. The simplest technique may be to trace elements of the pattern and rework them into your own design.

Try focusing on the more dominant elements in a design and remove them from surrounding shapes to see how they work alone. Remember, also, that single motifs are likely to need less reworking than a stencil that is to repeat continuously. For border patterns, leaves or scrolls are very useful as connecting links.

Flatten out the design, then trace it accurately line for line, using a fine-point marker or soft pencil. Take out any small or complicated shapes that

▲ Carefully trace elements of the design.

might prove impossible to reproduce— the idea is to create a design that is derived, rather than directly copied, from the existing decor. If necessary, take another sheet of tracing paper and make a new tracing that uses the main design elements.

Remember that stencils use "negative space"—that is to say, it is the area you cut out that creates the pattern. So negative space should always be completely surrounded by positive space (the uncut remainder of the stencil). There should be a constant

▲ Choose a design for your stencil.

HINTS & TIPS: Reversing the design

If you come across a design element that is perfect in size and shape for the stencil but is pointing in the wrong direction, trace it and reverse the paper, creating a mirror image. Remember that although stencil cards can be reversed, the first side will be coated in paint and may ruin the surface. It is advisable to cut out two stencil cards, marking one as the correct position, the other the reverse, and then use each in turn.

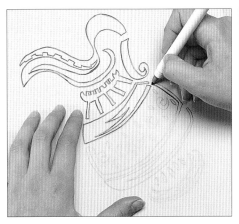
▲ Draw around the areas to be cut.

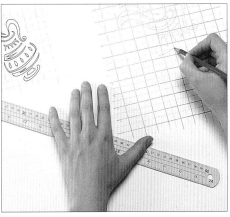
▲ Use a grid to enlarge or reduce designs.

border that is not cut or broken by the intrusion of another shape.

In some cases, it will be necessary to create your own borders or "filaments." For example, a bunch of grapes gains its original form through shape and color. To convey the shape of grapes, it will be necessary to create filaments that define the outline of the bunch and, within that, a few odd grapes. The same principle applies to more complicated flower or leaf shapes. For your stencil to work properly, you will need a space of around ⅛" (5mm) between each cut. Smaller filaments are liable to break and may allow paint to seep behind the stencil, causing the picture to bleed. For this reason, try not to leave too many floating, or unsupported, filaments. Isolated bridges (gaps) tend to make weak joints, which will move or break as paint is applied through the stencil.

SCALING UP AND DOWN
Some designs need to be enlarged or downsized from the original tracing. You can do this in a number of ways.

• PHOTOCOPYING: After measuring the desired size, photocopy the design to the nearest possible setting, keeping any intermediate-sized copies— they may prove useful later. It is also a good idea to make a few copies at the original size, ensuring that there will be sufficient versions to adapt for the final stencil.

• GRIDS: These can also be used for scaling designs up or down. If the original design is 8" (20cm) high and the required size is 16" (40cm), draw a grid over the pattern using squares measuring approximately ½ by ½" (1 by 1cm). On a separate sheet of paper draw another grid, each of whose squares is exactly double, that is approximately 1 by 1" (2 by 2cm). Draw the grid in ink so that, as the design is transferred in pencil by freehand, mistakes can be erased without affecting the grid markings. Then, either by eye or using a ruler, assess the position of each line within the squares on the smaller grid. Sketch the overall shape onto the larger grid, enlarging the lines to the correct size.

• PANTOGRAPHS: These can also be used for enlarging or downsizing images. Although using one of these gadgets effectively takes practice, the result can be a very accurate, refined enlargement of the original design. As you follow the outline of the smaller image, a pencil, resting in the pivoted levers, draws the same outline but to a specified scale. Once mastered, the device can be used for basic outline positioning before the remaining image is drawn freehand. Interestingly, many people

▲ Pantographs can be used for enlargements.

find that using a pantograph has actually helped them to improve their hand–eye coordination.

MAKING THE FINAL COPY
Before making your final copy, use cutouts of the various stencil elements to plan your design. Then make a fresh tracing so that the lines are completely clean and refined. Use fluid motions on the tracing paper with a soft pencil or small watercolor brush dipped in ink— remember that making a tracing will not damage the original underneath so be as relaxed and loose as possible.

The original, disjointed pencil marks should eventually be replaced with elegant lines, as you become more familiar with the tracing technique and the shape of the design itself. With confidence, your lines will become more constant and the design should start to flow a little more freely. This final version was known during the Italian Renaissance as a cartoon.

▲ Put the design together to check for gaps.

To check the symmetry of the design—and to identify any mistakes, unwanted marks, or poor proportions—try turning the picture over and viewing it from the back.

▲ Make a final tracing of the refined design.

MAKING YOUR STENCIL

STENCIL CARD

The next thing you need to do is decide what sort of stencil to use. The type of card (or transparent sheet) that is used is important because it will influence how fast and easy the pattern is to create. There are three main types to choose from.

• OILED MANILA CARD AND COATED CARD STOCK: The traditional choice for stenciling, oiled manila card is tough, durable, and easy to cut. However, it may be almost impossible to find. Coated card stock is harder to cut but may be more readily available. Symmetrical patterns also require careful tracing onto card, using a reverse tracing technique. Card stock is opaque and cannot be laid over the design on a light box, as transparent materials can.

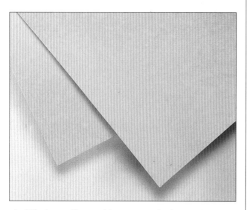

▲ Oiled manila card is opaque but easy to cut.

• ACETATE AND STENCIL FILM: The most durable stenciling materials, acetate sheets and stencil film are frequently used for stenciling projects. Their transparency enables you to see exactly what you are doing and assists with positioning the stencil in the correct

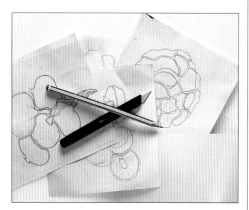

▲ Acetate makes strong, long-lasting stencils.

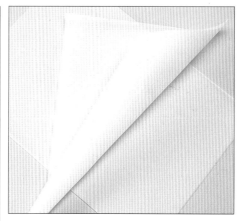

▲ Plan trace is both durable and easy to cut.

place on the wall of object that you are decorating. However, these are very smooth materials, so blades may slip on the surface. Always take care when cutting out a pattern and apply even pressure to the knife at all times.

• PLAN TRACE: A tracing paper that combines the best properties of both acetate and card, plan trace can be easily cut, is translucent, and is extremely tough. It may also be used in photocopiers, which makes copying, enlarging, or reducing of designs much simpler, while its fine density ensures that cut outlines are neat, clean, and crisp. Plan trace can be tricky to find but large art-supply stores and graphic suppliers may stock it.

TRANSFERRING THE DESIGN

If possible, photocopy the final design onto a sheet of plan trace. This will ensure that there is a back-up copy of the design, just in case anything should go wrong during the cutting stage. For transparent stencil cards, such as plan trace or acetate, the design can be immediately cut out, but for manila card or card stock, there are four different methods for transferring the design, each described here.

• CREATING A GRID: The least reliable of methods, the design can be transferred to card by drawing a grid on the card and copying the pattern. Use the same technique as that for scaling up and down, but this does require freehand skills and leads to fuzzy lines, which can be a hindrance for accurate cutting. Going over the pencil lines with a fine-point marker may help.

▲ Follow the outline with a series of pinpricks.

• PUSH PIN: Although it is quite labor-intensive, this method can be fun and was popular with stencilers during the Renaissance. Position the design on top of the card and push through the lines with a series of pinpricks. Judge the distance between the holes carefully—too far apart and they will leave only the barest of impressions; too close and the stencil card could end up becoming excessively perforated.

Ordinary needles and pins tend to produce holes that are too fine for this exercise. However, push pins, with their stout heads and long sharp points, generally make neatly rounded holes and are ideal for transferring designs through to the stencil card beneath. Ensure that the design and card are adequately anchored together, so that the original picture does not slip and alter the accuracy of the pin-pricks.

• CHARCOAL: A more faithful transfer can be achieved by rubbing charcoal through the pinpricks onto the card beneath. (Use a cotton ball to force the powdery charcoal through gently.)

▲ Rub charcoal through the pinpricks.

▲ Carbon paper can be used for transferring.

This method is ideal for repeating designs because the pinpricks only need to be made once—any number of transfers can be made simply by reapplying the charcoal.

• PENCIL OR CARBON PAPER: One of the simplest techniques involves liberally shading the back of the pattern with a very soft pencil. Then the design is positioned, right side up on the card, and the lines are retraced using a harder pencil or ballpoint pen. The pressure of the point should transfer the graphite from the other side. However, the transfer may be difficult to see, particularly on dark manila cards. In these cases, position carbon paper between the design and the card, and trace around the lines. The carbon will be transferred from its backing onto the card surface. Remember that typewriter carbon paper, as opposed to plain carbon paper, is actually more sensitive and therefore most suitable for this kind of work.

CUTTING THE STENCIL
Accurate cutting is vital when making a good stencil so spend plenty of time on creating the right shape. Always use sharp blades in your craft knife and be sure that they fit the handle properly. Use a cutting mat, which will protect the surface and minimize blunting of the blade. Scissors can be useful for large, flowing designs but, with practice, knives produce a much cleaner cut.

Start with the more intricate shapes as these tend to pull at the card. Avoid beginning with long or flat areas since these may distort or even tear as smaller, adjacent sections are cut.

While not recommended, it is easier to cut toward the body; keep the knife as close to an upright position as possible, in order to reduce the likelihood of slipping and causing injury. Steady the stencil by placing your free hand on the part of the stencil that has just been cut. Some longer lines are best cut by keeping the knife in a constant position and moving the stencil card. This tends to be less tiring and also increases the flow of curved lines. The shapes do not need to be cut exactly as they are drawn—it may help to make a series of short cuts, rather than one long one.

Having cut the design into the stencil, cut the stencil itself down to a more usable size. If the design is to fit a specific area, it is a good idea to cut the stencil to fit exactly. For a repeating border around a room, the top edge of the stencil must be exactly square, in order to keep the design from wobbling or running out as you follow the bottom edge of the molding. Marking the middle line of the stencil will make it easier to position. To do this, draw a square around the motif. By joining each corner diagonally, you will find the exact center of the design. Using a steel square, you can then mark off the vertical and horizontal midlines.

If the design is for a repeating border, trace one half of each of the neighboring motifs either side of the stencil. This will help with lining up the stencil for paint application.

HINTS & TIPS: Accidental cuts

Broken or cut filaments can be mended using masking tape. Make a rough or oversized splint with the tape and then cut the masking tape down to fit.

▲ Mend broken filaments with masking tape.

PREPARING THE SURFACE

CERAMICS
Use special ceramic paints to work directly on glazed ceramic tiles and unglazed ceramics such as terra-cotta. Make sure all surfaces are clean so that the stencils can be fixed easily. Apply the paint with a brush, sponge, spray, or mini-roller. Ceramic paints are durable and washable, and the manufacturer's instructions are given on the container.

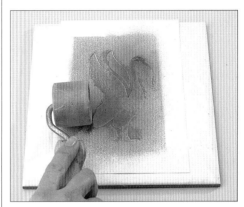

▲ Use a mini-roller to stencil onto ceramics.

PAINTED SURFACES
Stencils can be applied to surfaces painted with latex flat or satin, oil glazes, and acrylic glazes and varnishes, as well as to matte wallpaper. If you wish to decorate a gloss surface, stencil first with an acrylic primer, allow this to dry, and then stencil the colors on top. Surfaces to be stenciled need to be smooth so that the stencil lies flat.

FABRIC
Use special fabric paint for stenciling on fabric and follow the manufacturer's instructions carefully. Place cardboard or blotting paper behind the fabric while working and keep the material taut.

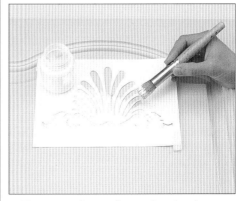

▲ You can apply stencils to painted surfaces.

▲ It is possible to stencil on fabric, but you will need special fabric paint (see pages 56–7).

If you are painting a dark fabric, best results are achieved by stenciling first with white or another light color. Heat seal the design following the manufacturer's instructions.

RAW WOOD

Sand the wood surface down to a smooth finish. Then fix the stencil in place and paint with a thin base coat of white so that the stencil colors will stand out well when applied. Leave the stencil in place and allow to dry, then apply your stencil colors in the normal way. When completely dry, you can apply a coat of light wax or varnish to protect your stencil.

GLASS

Before applying the stencil, make sure the glass is clean, then spray on a light coat of adhesive, and place the stencil in position. Spray on water-based or ceramic paint, remove the stencil, and allow to dry. If you wish to stencil

drinking glasses, use special nontoxic and water-resistant glass paint. An etched-glass look with stencils on windows, doors, and mirrors can be achieved with a variety of materials.

▲ Stencils can be applied to glass.

STAINED WOOD

If you are staining wood or manu-factured wood surfaces prior to stenciling, you have a choice of many different wood shades as well as a wide range of colors. If the base coat is dark,

stencil a thin coat of white paint on top. Apply your stencil and protect with a coat of clear varnish when the paint is completely dry.

POSITIONING THE STENCIL

ACCURATE MEASUREMENTS

There is nothing worse than a stencil that is supposed to be in the middle of a surface and is quite obviously not. Similarly disconcerting is a crooked motif or border that starts dropping halfway across a surface. To avoid this, find the middle of the design and mark a straight ruler, midline. Then match the middle of the stencil with the surface marking. For smaller flat surfaces, a steel square can be used to ensure that the line is a true right angle.

One of the cardinal rules of stenciling is always to start in the middle and work outward. This ensures that the

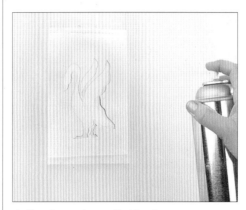

▲ Use a spirit level to get your stencil straight.

design is correctly balanced within the perimeters of the surface—even if the repeating stencil has been designed to fit exactly from corner to corner. By starting from the middle, any small fractions or gaps are kept to the less visible edges.

▲ Add color to white base coat on raw wood.

▲ Use a clear varnish on stained wood stencils.

▲ Use marker lines to position the stencil.

MARKING VERTICAL LINES

If you need to work out the vertical position for a stencil on a wall, hang a plumb line above the area that you plan to stencil and use a ruler to draw a vertical line with a piece of chalk or a soft pencil. You will need to use this method when creating an allover wallpaper design.

MARKING BASE AND HORIZONTAL LINES

Select the area that you are planning to stencil and take a measurement from the ceiling, doorframe, window, or edging, bearing in mind the depth of your stencil. Using a level, mark out a horizontal line. You can then extend this by using a chalkline or long straightedge and a soft pencil.

FIXING THE STENCIL IN PLACE

Small squares of masking tape can be used at each corner of the stencil to hold it in place, but check that the tape will not mark or remove any of the existing surface paint. Avoid drawing pins as they may leave permanent holes, and adhesive tack because it can raise the stencil away from the surface, allowing paint to seep or dribble. The best way to fix the stencil is with a nonpermanent adhesive spray, such as that used for mounting photographs. Avoid overspraying because an excessive layer can work as a paint remover, lifting the paint surface below.

If the stencil needs to be reapplied several times, wipe off the adhesive and apply a new coat—avoid adding continuous layers. In addition, take care when removing the stencil since delicate filaments may tend to stick to the surface and tear on lifting.

▲ Use spray adhesive to fix the stencil in place.

▲ You can use latex or artist's acrylic paint.

APPLYING THE PAINT

TYPES OF PAINT

Special stenciling paints are available but it can be cheaper and more creative to experiment with other types. Almost any paint can be used for stenciling, although some may have more advantages than others, depending on what you are painting.

• LATEX PAINT: Available in a variety of different colors, latex paint is water-based and extremely easy to use. It comes in two different finishes, flat and satin, which can create their own interesting effects when used in conjunction with each other. For example, stenciling a design in a slightly darker shade of satin over a flat base of the same color can simulate rich damasks or brocades. Alternatively, by isolating and stenciling one element in satin, you can lend a feeling of movement to the overall design, as the light is reflected by the paint's slight sheen.

• ARTIST'S ACRYLIC PAINT: Perhaps the most flexible and manageable of paints for stenciling, these are suitably durable yet water-based. They can be used straight or diluted, although very dilute mixtures are more likely to run under the stencil.

• SPRAY PAINT: Ideal for people who find hand-applied methods hard to master, spray paint is available from art, craft, and model stores in an increasing range of colors. Although these are appropriate for most porous surfaces, spray lacquer should be used for stenciling on surfaces such as glass, ceramics, or metal. Always apply spray paints in thin, even layers—almost a dusting—to avoid runs and dribbles. To achieve this, hold the can as far from the stencil as possible, using additional paper masking around the main stencil. Spray colors can be mixed by using successive, lightly sprayed coats because the paint hits the surface in tiny pinprick spots, which are easily offset by using different hues. Use spray paint only in well-ventilated conditions and always wear a mask.

Spray paint tends to be very fine and can travel into the smallest of areas. For this reason, always provide plenty of

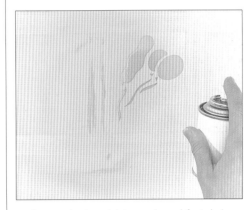
▲ Spray paint is quick to apply and fast drying.

masking around the outside of the stencil, to protect the surrounding areas. This can make using registration or centering marks difficult, so avoid using sprays for tight, repeating patterns. As with brushed or sponged stencils, any

▲ Mask off all edges if you use spray paint.

buildup of paint near the edge can lead to drips or dribbles, so keep the spray as fine as possible. Hold the can at a sufficient distance from the surface and apply several even coats, rather than one thick layer. See pages 28–9 for more information.

• ALKYD PAINTS: This provides many of the qualities of oil paint, with as fast a drying time as acrylic. The texture is buttery, so they do need to be thinned with mineral spirits or turpentine for stenciling.

• OIL PAINT: The choice of purists, oil paint is the trickiest type of paint to use for stenciling and it dries extremely slowly. However, for people who are practiced in oil-paint application and mixing, this paint can create beautiful transparent effects when mixed with a little varnish or oil painting medium. Extreme care must be taken when you remove the stencil after applying paint. Oil pigments remain unstable for at least 4 hours, which means that accidental smudging, by lifting the card too soon, is a hazard.

USING A SPONGE

Paint can be applied in a variety of ways for stenciling. For sponging, it is a good idea to use a "reservoir"— an extra piece of sponge that acts like an ink pad, helping to prevent irregular ink flow. Simply place the reservoir sponge in the bowl of paint and squeeze it firmly until it has taken up most of the mixture.

Then gently dab the reservoir sponge with the applicator sponge, until this too has taken up the paint. Dab the applicator sponge on a clean sheet of newspaper or an uncut part of the stencil, to check that the paint is not oozing or dribbling. A clean, crisp imprint means the sponge is ready for use. Then, starting in the middle of the largest cut, apply the paint with the sponge, working back so that by the time the sponge reaches the edges, a minimum of paint is being applied. The paint can be built up in layers, but this simple technique is ideal for a first practice run. It not only helps to provide a sense of what a sponged

finish will look like—it also reveals the final shape and image of the cutout stenciled design.

Smudgy edges are caused by a buildup of paint. Avoid this by starting in the middle of the design and gradually working outward, gently pushing the paint toward the outside edges. If the design begins to look a little insipid around the sides, try applying additional, light layers. Always allow each layer to dry, however, and aim for numerous light coverings, rather than one thick coat, which is likely to cause a buildup of paint and smudging.

▲ Dab paint gently using an applicator sponge.

Before deciding on a final method of paint application, it's a good idea to experiment with different techniques. Each method creates a slightly different effect, and it can be useful to try out the whole range of techniques before deciding on the final finish you want to create. Remember that all stenciling methods produce a slight clouding, but this is characteristic of a carefully worked piece and contributes to the three-dimensional charm of the decorating technique.

USING A BRUSH

If you are applying paint by brush, remove excess paint from the bristles onto newspaper before working through the stencil. Keep the brush at right angles to the surface, otherwise stray hairs may sneak behind the stencil and mark the surface. Gently stipple the paint through the stencil, working from the center outward to help avoid paint buildup and smudges. Keep a small dish or saucer of water and lots of dishwashing liquid at hand. If small smudges or dribbles occur, a timely

▲ Stipple paint lightly through the stencil.

wipe with a cotton swab should remove any problems or stray marks. However, most mistakes can still be rectified with a fine artist's brush when the paint is dry.

Other variations of brush application include feint oil painting and shadow stenciling. Feint oil application involves using artist's oil crayons rather than conventional paint. The oil crayon is rubbed onto a the surface and then a stiff brush is swirled into the color. Use this brush to press the color lightly through the cutout stencil in short

▲ Use artist's oil crayons for feint stenciling.

circular motions. The final effect should be a feint finish, softer than usual paint, together with gentle brushmarks.

Shadowed stenciling involves applying paint or artist's oil crayon colors in the same way. However, after the first application, the stencil is removed and repositioned about 1/16" (2mm) over the right- or left-hand edge. A lighter shade of the same color, or perhaps a subtle shade of gray, is then applied between the edge of the first coat and the border of the stencil. This creates a three-dimensional effect, providing the original stencil shape with a soft, decorative shadow.

▲ Reposition stencil to make shadows.

▲ Stick the cutout in position.

▲ Carefully lift the cutout with a knife.

HIDDEN STENCILING

The most subtle of stenciling techniques, this method is ideal for creating extremely soft finishes and projects that are designed to blend into a room, rather than stand out. It is achieved by coating the base surface in a very lightly colored glaze. Once this glaze is completely dry, the stencil is positioned over the surface and the same glaze is applied through the cutout, using a stippling motion. The stenciled effect is created by the double layer of glaze.

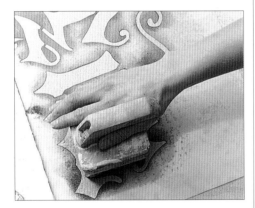

▲ Hidden stenciling is a subtle stencil method.

REVERSE STENCILING

A very simple version of stenciling, this technique does not require as much planning as other techniques and it is far less time-consuming overall. This is because the design does not need any filaments—the images are, effectively, cutout silhouettes.

Reverse stenciling is ideal for small projects in which the cutout will be used only once. Although the stencil can be removed and reused, it must be totally cleaned between applications. This means that acetate or stencil film, rather than oiled manila card or card stock, are most suitable for the job.

The idea is to cut out the stencil shape as a block—what is known as negative space in other stenciling methods actually becomes positive space in reverse stenciling. The chosen color of the stenciled design should then be applied to the object's surface. It is not necessary to coat the whole item, only the areas in which the stencil is to appear.

Once the base paint has dried, position the stencil over the top and stick it temporarily into place. Then use a brush to gently apply the top coat around the cutout, taking care not to lift the edges. Once these areas have been carefully covered, you can coat the rest of the surface more liberally. If it helps, go over the stencil itself, but make sure that the brush or roller action does not lift or move the cutout stencil beneath.

While the paint is still wet, carefully remove each cutout. (It may help if you locate and lift the corner using the tip of a craft knife.) Take care not to smudge the wet surface paint or damage the cutouts. Then allow the surface to dry completely. Remember to wash the stencils thoroughly if you plan to reuse them.

▲ Stipple around the edges of the cutout.

HINTS & TIPS: Storing stencils

If a stencil is to be reused, make sure that it is stored flat. Fix soggy stencils to a glass or ceramic surface with temporary adhesive spray, as this will hold them flat while they dry. Excess paint should be carefully wiped off before storage.

HINTS & TIPS: Stenciling around corners

• Stenciling borders around corners is particularly difficult, especially when it comes to matching up the design. To avoid mistakes, try the following method. When you have calculated where the stencil is to go and how many times it is to repeat, make a mental note of any halves or fractions of the design that will be needed to fit into corners. Be sure that every section of an area that takes a full repeat has been tackled before attempting to bend the stencil for fitting into corners. This is because bending stencils reduces their strength and life span, and can distort the design.

• Bending the design around a corner is best done in two stages, with time allowed for the first half to dry before applying the stencil to the adjacent surface. You will be surprised how a corner can cover up inconsistencies, as long as the top and bottom correspond with the stencil levels on the neighboring surface.

▲ A corner can hide any inconsistencies.

Gilding

POPULAR THROUGHOUT the world for thousands of years, gilding was even used to decorate the jewelry of the Incas and the ornaments of ancient Egyptians. Although the term is commonly associated with the application of gold, gilding can involve all kinds of metal leaves and powders, including silver, bronze, aluminum, and platinum. Gilding often provides the perfect final touch to a room, whether it is used on a picture frame, vase, or storage box. Creating the impression of an object made of solid, precious metal, the technique involves applying a very thin layer of gold to any base—even something as flimsy as papier-mâché. There are a variety of different methods for creating this effect, including gold leaf, gilding cream, and metallic powder.

MATERIALS & EQUIPMENT

The equipment and tools you need to create a gold effect will depend on the type of gilding you choose to use. Even so, you should not need to invest too much money in order to produce a stylish, extravagant effect. Before deciding on which technique to use, it may be a good idea to think about how much equipment you want to invest in, how much time you wish to spend on the project, and how intricate you want the final effect to be.

SANDPAPER

The variety of sandpaper needed will depend upon the surface of the item that is to be gilded. However, it is useful to have a range of coarse-, medium-, and fine-grit sandpaper at hand, and to work through the appropriate different levels, always finishing with a fine-grit paper. You can also use wet and dry paper on a slightly wet surface for a smooth finish.

▲ Sandpaper and bole for preparation.

CUTTING MATERIALS

Only relevant for gold-leaf applications, cutting materials can include scissors or a sharp craft knife. For the best results, however, it is worth investing in a gilder's knife, a long metal bar with a sharp edge. This knife can be used both to lift sheets of gold leaf, and to cut the medium in one sharp pull, rather than in a sawing action, which may cause the leaf to tear and damage.

PAINT

Depending on what you are decorating and the desired finish, you may find it useful to apply a coat of bole to the surface prior to gilding. Bole is a special type of background paint that works both as a filler for slightly rough surfaces and as a paint base. It comes ready-mixed and, once applied, is ideal for sanding down to a very smooth finish. Alternatively, a satin-finish paint, not matte or gloss finish, can be used as a base coat. However, make sure that the paint has the same base (either oil or water) as the gilder's size (see below).

ADHESIVES

Ordinary household varnish can be used to make gilding powder adhere to a surface. However, gold leaf requires a special type of adhesive known as gilder's size. The medium is used both to stick gold leaf into place, and to seal gilded and normal surfaces. It is available as a water- or oil-based product and, depending on the brand, can require drying times ranging from

▲ Gilder's size for gold-leaf application.

20 minutes to 24 hours. Gold leaf must be applied before the size is fully dry but when it is still tacky (much like gold powder on a varnished surface). If applied too early then the leaf will be marked by the wet size underneath, causing the gold to appear lifeless and dull. If it is applied too late, the leaf may not adhere to the surface properly, causing a poor and untidy finish.

BRUSHES & APPLICATORS

Brushes are needed for both tidying gold leaf and for applying gold powder. They should be as soft as possible—pony-hair or squirrel-hair brushes are ideal. If possible, keep gilding brushes aside purely for that job. Wash gilding brushes rarely; it is far better to tap them clean if possible. Use cotton swabs for gently pressing gold leaf into position, particularly in difficult or intricate areas. Velvet can also be used for pressing gold leaf over large areas, as well as for polishing gilded surfaces to a shiny finish.

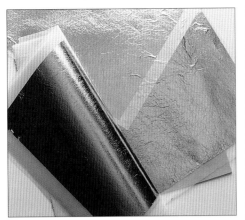
▲ Gold transfer leaf.

▲ Gilding cream.

▲ Gold powder.

THE GOLD EFFECT

Gold leaf, gilding cream, and gilding powder all have their different advantages. For example, while leaf is more time-consuming and complex to apply, it provides a long-term finish that is less likely to lose its luster than the other forms. Gilding cream is a popular choice for small projects or highlights—it is conventionally used for patching up gold work—whereas gilding powder is considerably more messy than the other methods, but it can be carried out with basic metallic powders and household varnish.

• GOLD TRANSFER LEAF: This is available in art-supply and craft stores. Transfer leaf is a very thin layer of gold or brass, supplied in small squares and lightly attached to tissue backing with a layer of wax film (see above). Professional gilders use specially designed cushions for applying leaf transfers, but it is possible to create a good finish simply with a soft brush or even a silk scarf—see the "Gilded Chair" project on pages 102–3.

Try not to touch the metallic surface until it is in place on the object, as it will stick to your fingers. Many people find the easiest way to lift the sheets is to use the bristles of a soft brush that has been swept across their cheeks. The light coating of grease from the face should provide just enough adhesive.

• GILDING CREAM: Commonly used by gilders for repair work, gilding cream is particularly handy for patching areas where the size dries and cracks (see above middle). The cream can also be used for small highlighting work.

• GOLD POWDER: This can be used as a quick alternative to leaf transfers (see above right), though it tends to be messier and will definitely require a protective varnish coat. The powder is applied to a surface that has been coated with varnish—the varnish should be allowed to partly dry, so that it feels tacky. Gold powder can also be used to patch up cracks in gold-leaf gilding. However, it is important to be sure that the powder is an exact match of the shade of the gold leaf.

APPLYING GOLD LEAF

Take some time to sand down the item to a really smooth finish. Leaf transfer is so thin that any rough patches will show through and mark the gilded surface. Once sanded, remove any dust residue with a tack cloth. Wipe ridges and crevices clean with a cotton swab.

If the item is large, or is to be totally covered in gold leaf, it may be worth applying one or two coats of bole, or a paint in the color of your choice. If the size for the leaf transfer is oil-based,

▲ Apply a coat of gilder's size to the item.

make sure that the paint you use is also oil-based. Once dry, sand the surface with fine-grit sandpaper and fine wet and dry paper.

Then use a soft brush to apply a thin layer of gilding size to the surface. Try to avoid leaving brushmarks in the coat. Although the size will be milky on initial application, it should dry to a clear, slightly oily-looking color.

Very carefully cut a single sheet of gold transfer leaf to the required size. Remember to leave some excess on each edge, so that each piece overlaps on the surface and can be trimmed later. However, bear in mind that transfer leaf will adhere to gilding size on contact, so avoid leaving so much excess that unwanted pieces stick to the surrounding wet size.

Press the leaf facedown on the tacky size, keeping the backing paper in place, and rub it with a cotton ball, soft brush or piece of cloth to ensure that it is firmly in position. Then gently peel away the backing paper, taking care not to lift the leaf from the object's surface. Repeat this process until the whole item is covered with gold leaf transfer.

▲ Brush away excess gold leaf with a soft brush.

▲ Apply tiny flakes of gold leaf for this effect.

Gently press the leaf flat with a soft brush. Although wrinkles may appear, these should disappear as the surface is brushed clean. Then, gradually brush away any overlaps and excess pieces of gold that remain. Any large pieces, known as skewings, that you have left can be kept for patching up corners and crevices.

Continue working around the surface, gradually brushing away wrinkles, loose flakes, and lumps. As you work around the object, small faults such as cracks or gaps may become apparent. These can be repaired—using the same technique described above—with the skewings. Alternatively, while the size is still tacky, touch up any cracks or gaps by gently brushing gold powder over the top of them.

Allow the item to dry completely— you will need to follow the guidelines on the can of size—and then polish it very gently using either a piece of velvet or a cotton swab. However, the gold surface will still be vulnerable to breaks or tears, so try to avoid using rough movements.

HINTS & TIPS: Working environment

Always be sure that the work environment is as dust-free as possible. Remember that wet size will be vulnerable to dust and particles for several hours, so if you are worried about dust rising and settling on the piece, try dampening the floors with a water spray, or putting down wet towels.

If you prefer the aged effect of the curtain pole shown left, use tiny flakes of gold leaf instead of whole sheets. It is always worth looking at the finish on gilded articles in stores and antique shops. Although the aim is to create as refined a finish as possible, using sheets of leaf will inevitably create some joints and overlaps. Note, however, that these are barely visible when the piece is looked at in its entirety.

Although the object is now gilded, it will not be able to withstand scratching or rough handling. The surface is also liable to tarnish with time. It is therefore important to protect the surface with a few coats of varnish.

AGING THE PIECE

In order to give the gilded finish an appropriately old and time-worn appearance, try adding some stain to the protective varnish. This can be applied all over the item, or simply to areas that would age and wear naturally, such as exposed corners.

First, apply one coat of clear, oil-based varnish to the surface and let it dry. Then mix a small amount of artist's oil color—either burnt sienna or raw umber—into a small can of varnish. Apply two coats of this mixture to the item, allowing each application to dry thoroughly. Then add more artist's color to the mixture to darken it even further. Apply this to creases or molded areas of the surface, and to any areas where dirt is likely to have settled over time, such as edges, grooves, or handles. Finally, wipe away some of the varnish with a soft cloth. The idea is to leave darkened varnish only where age may have led to tarnishing or grime.

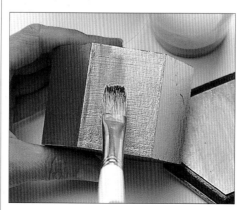

▲ Apply two coats of the stained varnish.

GILDING WITH CREAM

For a faster gilded effect, or for items that cannot be sanded, such as papier-mâché, gilding cream can be used instead. (The cream is also ideal for creating gold highlights on painted surfaces.) Cheap and easy to obtain, the finish will not polish to as high a sheen as leaf transfer, but it still creates an effective metallic surface.

The item can then be varnished with spray varnish or aged with a stain/varnish mixture as before. In the case of the star below, the darkened varnish sits comfortably in various crevices, creating natural low-lights and shaded areas.

▲ Use cream to gild unevenly shaped objects.

Begin by painting any raw surface with bole or your paint color. Once this has dried, use your fingers to rub gilding cream all over the surface gently. Be sure to cover all crevices and intricate areas—if necessary, use a cotton swab to insert cream into difficult gaps.

Allow the cream to dry for the recommended time (usually about

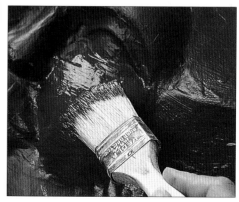

▲ Apply a coat of bole to raw surfaces.

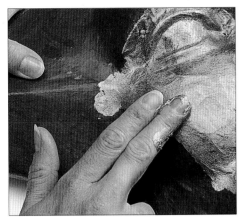

▲ Rub gilding cream over the shape.

two hours) and then buff the surface gently with a soft cloth. This will help to give it a slight shine and luster.

GILDING WITH POWDER

Another quick and satisfying way of applying a gold finish, gilding powder is less messy than gilding cream. It is also suitable for items that will have to stand up to quite a lot of wear and tear, such as lamps, handles, and doorknobs. However, the powdering creates a lot of dust, so be sure to wear a mask and try to work outside wherever possible. As with other gilding methods, apply a base coat of color or a couple of coats of bole to seal the surface. When the

▲ Apply a coat of varnish and leave until tacky.

paint is dry, apply a thin layer of gilder's size or varnish and allow to dry until it is just tacky.

Dip a clean, dry brush into the gold powder and gently brush it over the tacky size or varnish. Apply the gold powder fairly thickly as it will soak into the size. Brush away the excess until you can handle the item without too much powder coming off.

▲ Apply a coat of clear protective varnish.

If you prefer, use different colors of metallic powder for a varied effect. To do this, simply apply different colors directly to the surface and mix them together as they stick to the size.

Once dry, apply a coat of clear protective varnish to the object. If the item is to receive a lot of handling, use several coats, allowing sufficient drying time between each application.

OBJECTS FOR GILDING

Gilding can be applied to almost any surface, providing the base has been adequately prepared. It tends to be most effective when it is used in small areas, such as for highlighting trims and borders or on small room accessories such as lamps or frames. Gilding techniques can even be used on natural items such as shells or stones.

Whenever you use gilding as a decorative effect, try to resist the inclination to overuse the color. Gold, as well as silver, bronze, and other metallic colors, tends to look its best when it is used sparingly.

HINTS & TIPS: Color variations

Gilding does not have to be gold. Leaf powders and creams are also available in silver, aluminum, and copper, while creams come in a host of shades.

▲ Use a gloss varnish to produce this elegant finish.

Stamping

Printing designs on items of furniture or walls is not a new idea, but it has enjoyed a revival in recent years. It is an excellent technique for creating repeated patterns on flat, painted surfaces, and it tends to be less intricate than some other decorative methods such as stenciling. Stamped designs can be simple or complex, and much of their effect comes from a fairly casual, random application. This means that you rarely have to worry about achieving symmetrical effects or measuring accurate spacing for each stamp motif. Although rubber or wood are generally used for stamping techniques, it can be interesting to experiment with other mediums such as metal, sponge, or even halved vegetables (see opposite).

STAMPING MATERIALS

A range of different materials can be used to make printing stamps. The type of material you choose will influence the texture and definition of the print, as well as the durability of the stamp itself. For example, stamps that are to be reused frequently should be long wearing and easy to clean and maintain. Small, one-shot projects, however, could be decorated using homemade stamps that will be disposed of after one use.

▲ Use a sponge stamp for a textured finish.

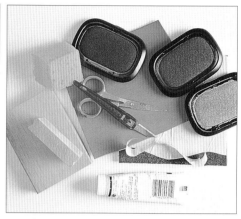
▲ A full range of stamping materials.

▲ Professional rubber stamps can be reused.

• RUBBER STAMPS: The most common type of stamp, rubber print blocks are able to withstand constant use over a length of time. Although mass-produced rubber stamps can be sophisticated, they can also be expensive if you use them on large objects that need more than one stamp. It is often more economical to make your own rubber stamp that can be adapted to your own needs.

• FIRM SPONGE, CORK, AND LEATHER: These are less durable than professional rubber stamps but they should last for a sufficient length of time. Materials such as these tend to create a textured finish, giving a more craft-like appearance.

• STAMP PADS: Stamp pads are available from most craft and stationery stores and are ideal for quick, simple stamping. Originally designed for fabric decoration, they are fast drying and can also leave a good, long-wearing finish on wooden surfaces.

• PAINT: Virtually any kind of paint can be used for stamping, although the type of surface on which the stamp is to be applied will influence the choice.

HINTS & TIPS: Making a mirror image

For a mirror image of the design, make another stamp by simply printing the first one directly on another piece of rubber. Cut around this image and stick down.

MAKING A RUBBER STAMP

To make your own rubber stamp, work out a rough design on paper. Then transfer or copy the design onto a piece of rubber, on the side that will form the top of the stamp.

Make sure that the design is simple and clean. The decorative effect should come from repeated motifs, rather than from complex shapes.

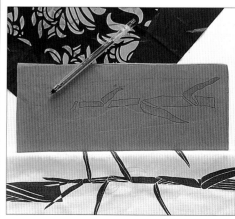
▲ Transfer your design onto a piece of rubber.

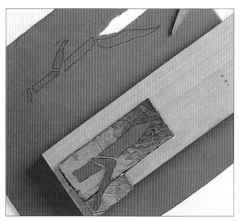

▲ Position the rubber cutouts on the foam.

▲ Cut away the excess backing foam.

▲ Stamping provides a rustic finished effect.

CUTTING THE STAMP

Use PVA adhesive to apply a piece of foam to a wooden block. Do not worry about keeping the foam neat—it can even be in several pieces—because it will be positioned behind the actual stamping surface.

Then, carefully cut out the rubber design using sharp scissors or a craft knife and cutting mat. Using the same adhesive, stick the cutout pieces of the rubber on the foam. Press firmly and add extra glue to any areas or edges where the rubber does not adhere properly.

TESTING THE STAMP

Apply an even coat of artist's acrylic paint to the rubber stamp with a chunk of smooth sponge. Then turn the stamp over and press onto scrap paper. This test image is how the final pattern will appear, so make any necessary changes to the shape at this stage.

Once satisfied with the design, cut away the excess backing foam with a craft knife. This will help raise the stamp above the block and prevent paint smudges as the stamp is applied and gently rocked on the final surface.

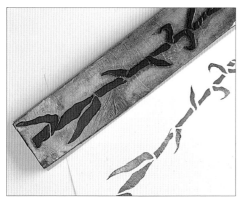

▲ Test your stamp on a piece of scrap paper.

APPLYING THE STAMP

Dab artist's acrylic paints with either a sponge or brush onto the stamp. (Other paints can be used but they should be both opaque and thick—about the consistency of heavy cream.) Test the stamp on some scrap paper to remove any excess paint, then apply the stamp to the surface of the object.

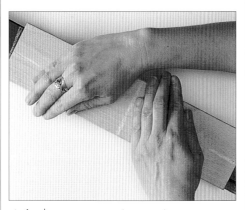

▲ Apply even pressure to your stamp.

Gently rock the stamp to ensure even pressure (it may help to practice this technique on scrap paper first). Then, holding the surface steady with your other hand, carefully lift the stamp in one swift, single movement.

Depending on the type of stamp material, it may be possible to reapply the stamp a few times before more paint is needed. Sponges, for example, absorb considerable amounts of paint and will not need new paint after every application. If this is the case, remember to press lightly for the first print and then gradually apply harder pressure for the following few applications. This should help keep the depth of color even throughout your design.

MAKING A VEGETABLE STAMP

Many firm vegetables, such as potatoes or carrots, can be used for cheap, basic stamps. However, they only work for one-shot projects, creating a semitextured finish. Cut the potato in half and wipe off the moisture. Cut around the template (such as the ivy leaf shown below) with a craft knife on the cut surface of a potato half. Then cut away the background until the design is high enough to make a sharp print. (See the "Ivy-stamped Chair" project on pages 150–1). Remember that vegetables exude moisture, so you will need to blot the potato with paper towels occasionally to prevent the paint from diluting or smudging.

▲ Use a craft knife to carve out your design.

THE INSPIRATION FOR YOUR PAINT PROJECT COULD COME FROM ANYWHERE, FROM THE PATTERN ON AN OLD TABLECLOTH TO THE TEXTURE OF AN AGING WOODEN GATE. IDEAS TEND TO SPRING FROM THE MOST UNEXPECTED OF PLACES, AND THE MORE UNUSUAL THEY ARE, THE MORE INDIVIDUAL THE PROJECT IS LIKELY TO BE. ALWAYS BE ON THE LOOK OUT FOR INSPIRATION, AND FOLLOW YOUR INSTINCTS. ALLOW YOUR IMAGINATION TO RUN WILD AND YOU WILL FIND THE CREATIVE CONFIDENCE TO TURN ALL YOUR INSPIRATIONAL IDEAS INTO PRACTICE AROUND THE HOME.

Finding Inspiration

Architectural Features

ARCHITECTURE DIFFERS a great deal from country to country and century to century. As such, there is a vast amount that might inspire you if you look closely at the architecture around you. The best way to find out about different styles of architecture is to get out of the house and visit as many different buildings and locations as you can. And as you are admiring the columns and arches, watch out for details that you might otherwise miss—the brickwork, the iron railings, the timber beams, and the small features on a door.

If you are a keen traveler, you will be able to find paint inspiration in architectural styles from all around the globe. When you have seen the classical architecture of Athens or Rome, you may be tempted to re-create the magical world

by using faux marble in your home. Once you have paid a visit to a splendid Gothic cathedral, you may be inspired to mirror its arches on your walls and ceiling using a trompe l'oeil paint technique. After observing the color-washed

charm of painted timber-framed houses, you may wish to add similar tones to your palette to use inside your home.
Once you have marveled at the subtle hues of past centuries in crumbling Mediterranean frescoes, you may wish to paint
your home in a combination of distressed ocher, sepia, burnt sienna, rust, and deep red, redolent of the long hot summers.
Another great way to get ideas is to delve into architects' source books. These are ideal, particularly if your design calls
for historical influences or structured styles. They are copyright free, packed with images, and available from the local

library or bookshops. And remember not to overlook the numerous small architectural details that may hold just the
inspiration that you are looking for. You may, for example, want to recreate the multi-layered verdigris that has built

up on a door handle, the distressed finish of an antique weather vane, the marble finish of the capitals of pillars and
columns, or the timber-framed effect of a Tudor-style house.

Stone, Wood, and Metal

THE COLOR AND TEXTURE of the surfaces of stone, wood, and metal have long served as inspiration for paint effects. The essence of the technique is to re-create the look of the surface using paint. From faux marble to wood graining, malachite to verdigris, liming to tortoiseshell, there is a great deal that can inspire you. Look closely at objects that you may take for granted such as a cobbled garden wall, a woven-wood basket, or a rusty metal wheelbarrow and think about how you can mimic their patterns and texture in your own house.

Among the most tactile of surfaces are smooth stone, textured wood, and gleaming metal. Inspiration can be found in all sorts of modest everyday objects such as freshly polished copper in your kitchen, a wooden gate in your garden, the

brickwork of your walls, or the rusty surface of wrought-iron railings in front of your house. Nature too provides a great deal in the way of inspiration—the smooth pebbles on a beach, the woodgrain in a branch fallen from a tree, or the glowing surface of gold. The best way to re-create metal, stone, or wood is to examine the desired surface closely and take careful note its structure, texture, and color. If you want to try your hand at marbling, for example, inspect the vein structure of the stone carefully—the veins should not crisscross or branch out like they do in a tree, but they should run at diagonals to one another. If you want to make your imitation marble look even more realistic, then you can divide your surface into sections to make it look as if it is made out of marble blocks. Another popular paint effect is

verdigris, inspired by the natural weathering of copper, brass, and bronze objects—over a long period of time, a layer of copper sulfate will slowly build up on their surfaces. Look closely at an example of real verdigris and think about how

you can best imitate it. Observe the areas in which the copper sulfate has started to form and how it spreads. It should appear to be running vertically down metal objects, so bear this factor in mind as you apply your paint.

The Past

ROM DISTRESSING to crackle glaze, from verdigris to liming, the purpose of many paint effects is to make objects look older than they really are. Inspiration can come from all sorts of different places. Look again at relics of the past that surround us every day—objects that are starting to decay and show signs of their age, such as metalwork, stones, natural features, or even museum artifacts. Think about the ways in which each of these different objects age and the sort of look that you want to re-create in your home.

Looking closely at everyday objects that are showing signs of age is a great source of inspiration for the interior decorator. This world that once belonged to the past is all around us and the more observant you are, the more you will notice it.

Examine how the rust has formed around the metalwork in your backyard and think about how it has affected the different features. Aging tends to show first on exposed corners and edges, or on parts of the object that have been

used most often, such as the handle of an old water pump. Stones and bricks take on an altogether different appearance when they start to age. Observe the flaking, distressed look of neglected brickwork and how its colors have subtly changed after years of exposure to rain and sunshine. Go for a walk in the countryside and have another look at natural features that are starting to show signs of age. You may find inspiration in the shape and texture of the twisted, knarled trunks of old trees or in the patterns formed by ivy that has run riot over trees and stones.

 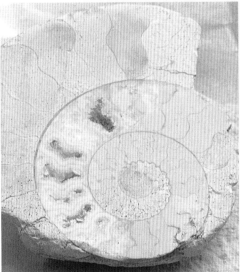 

Perhaps you could visit a museum and examine the artifacts on exhibit. Looking at ancient objects and fossils will help you to see how time takes its toll on different sorts of surfaces and structures. It is not hard to re-create such finishes.

Once you have mastered the paint techniques outlined in this book, you will be able to transform an inexpensive modern table or a brand-new cupboard into an antique-looking piece of furniture.

Flowers and Leaves

LOWERS AND LEAVES have served as inspiration for artists for many centuries, from William Morris to Klimt and Monet to O'Keefe. The unique variety of shapes, colors, sizes, and textures offers a wealth of potential for the interior decorator. If you are floundering, then get away from your paint and tools for a while and look to nature for ideas and inspiration—a quick trip around a garden or park should be enough. Or pay a visit to your local art gallery and take a look at how great artists have interpreted nature in their work.

The ever changing colors of leaves and flowers throughout the year are a rich source of inspiration for interior designers. Choose from the warm, muted tones of autumnal foliage, the delicate, tender aspect of spring's first growth,

the cool, stark colors of winter trees, or the vibrant, vivid hues of midsummer blooms. Each of these color schemes will have a very different effect on your house. Wintry blues will have a cooling effect, while summery oranges and yellows will warm even the darkest corner. The varied shapes of flowers and leaves are ideal for making stencils. Draw along the stem to create an outline of the basic shape and direction of a plant. Then break off the leaves and draw around them individually, leaving a bridge where the leaves are separate or where they naturally overlap each other. If you need to change the size of the plant, try drawing around it first and then increasing or reducing the size of your finished drawing on a photocopier. Then transfer your design onto card stock, acetate, or stencil film and you will be ready to

start. The leaf, which is often wrongly considered to be the poor relation of the flower, may also inspire you—the vein structure of a leaf may throw out some interesting ideas for paint patterns and its leathery texture can be re-created by

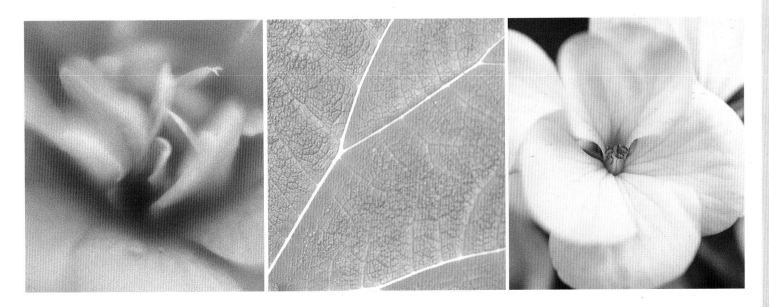

manipulating paint with a plastic bag. Look also at flowers and leaves from far-flung parts of the globe, which are becoming widely available, and bring a touch of the exotic into your house.

Textiles

THERE IS A WAY that you can find inspiration for your paint effects without even leaving the house. It is easy for us to get accustomed to the patterns and designs that surround us every day, so much so that we cease to notice them and overlook their inspirational potential. Take a close look at the fabrics that you have around you in the house—the curtains, the carpets, the towels, the pillow covers, and the throws. Each will have its own color, pattern, and texture that can serve as inspiration when you paint your house.

Start in the bedroom—look at the design on your curtains. Would it be possible to trace or adapt the pattern to use as a stencil? Perhaps the design could be reproduced on your walls in a matching border. If you don't have any leftover

material, you could always photocopy it on a color printer and use that instead. Next, move to the kitchen and look closely at the design on your dish towels—would you be able to reproduce this freehand on your cabinets? Perhaps you could mimic the tablecloth's checked pattern on your plates or curtains. The texture of many different types of fabrics can also be inspiring for the interior designer. You can use a trompe l'oeil technique to make it look as though your surface is covered in fabric—frottage, the multi-layering paint technique, will make a screen look as though it is covered in antique damask. Fabric colors can also be incredibly lush and rich. All you have to do is to choose which one you like best and then decide how you want to make it work in the color scheme of your home. Remember to observe how different

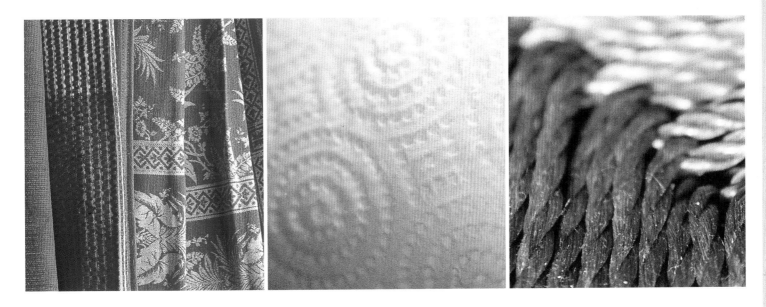

colors change in different lights. Some shades alter dramatically in artificial or evening light, compared with how they look in the daytime. Lilac can be a prime example of this—it looks much more pink at dusk than it does in the

morning sunshine. Once you have discovered a color that you like at all times of day, take a sample along to your paint or hardware store and they will be able to match it to the nearest paint color.

Art, Design, and Form

IF YOU ARE REALLY STRUGGLING for paint inspiration, why not visit your local art gallery or design exhibition. Looking at other people's work is an excellent way to get ideas of your own. Look at the shapes and forms that artists and designers have used and think about how you can incorporate such elements into your home. But art and design are not restricted to galleries—start to be aware of the forms, shapes, and colors that surround you every day. You may find inspiration in something as simple as a bowl of fruit or the cogs of a wheel.

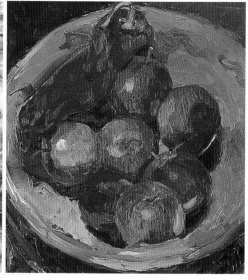

Looking at paintings and designs is particularly useful if you are planning to attempt some freehand. It is always helpful to examine how the work was put together before you start your own design. Look at the direction of the

brushstrokes, the paint type and thickness, and how the piece is constructed—what is the focal point and how does the picture develop from there? Look at the different techniques used by artists to form trees, flowers, or people.

It may be simpler than you think. And take note of the artist's subject matter. Maybe you could pick out a particular feature and incorporate it into a design for your home—Cubist blocks would make a stylish border and Art Nouveau motifs could be adapted into an inspirational stencil. Look also at the mood created by different colors—if you were to choose tones from the somber palette of Rembrandt or Caravaggio, you would give your home a very different feel than if you were to use the vivid hues of Matisse or Kandinsky. Take note also of the wonderful color combinations

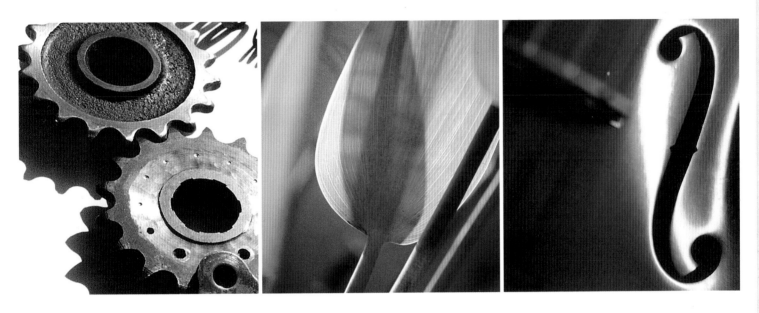

that surround you in the course of everyday life. Perhaps you will find inspiration in a checkered floor pattern or the gilded finish of a brass instrument. Watch the way that light falls on objects, for example, the mirror-like effect of the

sun glistening on the surface of water or spilling through a dark tunnel of foliage. Look closely at shapes that you might otherwise not notice, such as the sinuous curves of a violin or the delicate structure of an orchid.

Whether it is used for family get-togethers, sociable suppers, or elaborate dinner parties, the dining room is the place to indulge your sense of theater. Add striking accessories to create a particular mood or pluck up your courage and rejuvenate the furniture. This chapter is full of inspiring ideas for transformations, both great and small, to help you to create the perfect environment for good food and company, making each meal an occasion to linger over.

Dining Room Projects

Geometric Starburst Floor

THE STARBURST and geometric edges of this floor design are produced using a template; the result is truly stunning. This stenciled floor, which is about 21 by 21' (2 by 2m), took only two days to complete, with extra time for varnishing. You may find it comfortable to lie on a cushion or use a kneeling pad while working on the floor. Stand up frequently so that you can check your work. It also pays to walk away from your work for 10 minutes in order to shake off "artist's blindness." Coming back to a design with fresh eyes means you are more likely to notice any errors that might have crept in. This floor was not originally varnished, polished, or treated, so the stain soaked into the grain. If your floor is varnished to start off with, the design will not have the same depth of color and so it might be best to sand it before you begin.

❖ YOU WILL NEED ❖

Paper template

Steel ruler

Craft knife

Wood stain in colors of your choice

Plastic cup or glass jar

Deep tray

Household paintbrushes

Artist's paintbrushes

Varnish

1 Pin the paper design in the middle of the floor. Starting at the edge of the design, cut out each section individually using the steel ruler as an edge to aid firm and deep cuts that go through the paper and into the wood. These cuts form a border within which to paint and they also act as a barrier, preventing the stain from seeping into the wood outside the design. If you do not start from the outside of the design, you will find it hard to keep the template together as you cut it.

2 Pour a small quantity of each of the wood–stain colors that you have chosen into a plastic cup or glass jar and confine them to a deep tray while you work. You can also use this tray to put wet paintbrushes in, which will prevent them from rolling onto the unfinished work and spoiling it. Do not let your brushes dry when you take a break or the stain may harden on them.

3 Using a soft brush, very carefully fill in each section with the appropriate colors. You will find that the stain soaks into the wood quite quickly and travels right up to the cuts. Try not to leave a section before you have finished it completely.

HINTS & TIPS

When the work is finished it must be protected with a hard-wearing varnish to stand the test of time. Varnish your way out of the room before going to bed so that it has a chance to dry undisturbed. For the next few days, only walk barefoot on the floor while the varnish cures.

For more floor projects see:
Old Oak Woodgrain Floor pp113–15;
Sponge-stamped Floor pp128–9.

▲ Cut out the template with a craft knife.

▲ Use a tray for your stain and paintbrushes.

▲ Carefully fill in your design with a soft brush.

Painted Decanter and Glasses

STAINED GLASS is a wonderful way of brightening up any uninspiring pieces of glassware that you might have around the house. Even if you have not had any previous experience with glass painting, you will be able to achieve stunning effects extremely quickly and simply. This decanter and glasses were stained with special glass paints so that they could still be used for practical purposes—the paints are non-toxic and water-resistant so the colors will not fade after you have washed them several times. The decanter and glasses would make a great centerpiece on the table at a dinner party. However, if you are planning to stain glass for display-use only, you could use spray enamel, gold pens, and glitter glue instead.

❖ YOU WILL NEED ❖

Warm, soapy water and cloth

Methylated spirits

Wet and dry paper

Dry cloth

Gold outliner

Design for your stencil (see page 246)

Card stock, acetate, or stencil film

Craft knife and cutting mat

Squirrel-hair art brush

Translucent glass paint in rose and blue violet

1 First, you will need to prepare the glass and decanter by washing them thoroughly in warm soapy water and drying them well. Wipe them with a damp cloth and methylated spirits in order to remove any excess dirt and allow to dry. Rub over all the surfaces with wet and dry paper and wipe down with a dry cloth.

2 Squeezing the tube of gold outliner directly onto the glass, make large wiggly shapes around the sides. Use the templates on p246 to cut two stencils out of card stock or stencil film. Hold the star shape in place with your fingers and squeeze an outline around this. Use the fleur-de-lis stencil to decorate the top of the glasses. Allow them to dry for at least 10 minutes. You do not have to limit yourself solely to using stencil patterns.

3 Use a squirrel-hair art brush to fill in the color. Dip the brush into the glass paint and fill in the centers of the shapes that you outlined, alternating the colors each time.

4 Decorate the decanter in the same way as the glasses. The stopper is usually more tricky because it is smaller. Using the gold outliner, squeeze a swirling line on the stopper from bottom to top and then, with the brush and glass paint, create the same pattern as on the decanter. Treat your glasses with respect by hand washing them in warm, soapy water. Avoid using the dishwasher as this will shorten the life of your decoration.

For more glass painting projects see:
Brilliant Painted Glass pp155–6;
Fish Stencil Shower Glass pp193–5.

▲ Outline the design on the glass.

▲ Fill in the shapes with glass paint.

Checkered Walls

THE COMBINATION OF fresh yellow and green on the walls complements the crisp chair covers and creates a neat and airy effect in this bright dining room. Once you have managed to master the basic technique of color washing, more intricate designs such as checkered or striped patterns are relatively easy to achieve. In this project, the transparency of the glaze work allows the base color to glow through the pattern, providing an attractive depth and intensity of color where the stripes cross over each other. Painting these effects does not take long, but before you start to apply the paint, it is important to spend some time preparing, measuring, and masking the wall to ensure that you achieve a professional-looking finished result.

❖ YOU WILL NEED ❖

Yellow latex satin paint

Pencil

Long straightedge

Level or plumb line

Tape measure

Masking tape

1 quart (1l) acrylic crackle glaze

Artist's acrylic paint, or latex paint, for staining glass

Household paintbrush

Long piece of wood

Latex glaze coat

1 Carefully plan how the color scheme will work before you begin, to ensure that the pattern will fit in with the shape of the room. Paint the walls of the room in the yellow base color, using a paint that has a slight sheen, such as latex satin. For the best results, choose a base color that is paler than the desired color of the stripes or checks. If you do paint over a dark base color, more than one coat of glaze may be required to ensure that the pattern shows up.

2 When the base coat is fully dry, lightly mark the vertical stripes in pencil with the aid of a long straightedge and a level or plumb line. Then, position lengths of masking tape along the outside edges of the stripes, so that the areas you are going to paint are not obstructed. The stripes shown in this project are 10" (25cm) wide.

▲ Mix a glaze with the colors of your choice.

3 Mix a glaze, using acrylic crackle glaze with about a tablespoon of artist's acrylic paint or latex paint in the color of your choice. (Here two different shades of green—sap green and oxide of chromium—were added to produce a more unusual hue.) Add the paint color a tiny bit at a time, because, while it is easy to add more, it is impossible to remove once it has been added. Take care not to add too much color to the glaze because the aim is to maintain its transparent qualities.

4 Apply the glaze in a thin coat to the masked-off stripes, using a household paintbrush in a random, crisscross motion. Work as quickly as you can so that you only overlap wet areas of glaze—wet glaze meeting dry glaze will cause undesirable lines and marks to show in the final coat.

▲ Choose a base lighter than the stripes.

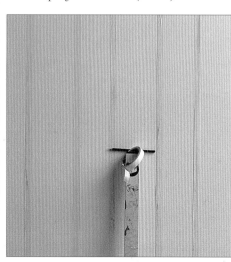
▲ Mask off the stripes.

5 While the glaze is still wet, carefully remove the masking tape along the edges of the stripes. Peel the tape slowly back on itself, making sure that it does not pull the base paint away from the wall.

6 When the vertical lines have completely dried, mark and mask off the horizontal stripes. To save measuring each stripe on the wall, which can be quite difficult to do accurately, mark a long piece of wood with lines spaced the appropriate distance apart from one another. Then work along the wall with the marked piece of wood and use the marks as guidelines for marking the position of the horizontal stripes.

7 In most homes the ceiling and the wall do not meet perfectly. Check this with a level before you begin to mark the horizontals. If the ceiling is not quite straight, make small adjustments of about $1/2$" (1cm) at a time on each horizontal stripe. These gradual alterations should create a more pleasing finished effect than one large adjustment, which will create a top or bottom stripe that is obviously out of kilter with the others.

▲ Apply the glaze to the vertical stripes.

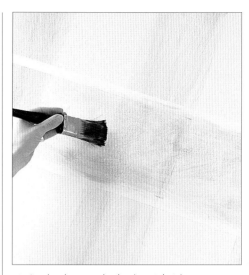

▲ Apply glaze to the horizontal stripes.

▲ Mark the position of the horizontals.

▲ Make adjustments to the horizontal lines if necessary.

▲ Remove the masking tape carefully.

HINTS & TIPS

• Horizontal stripes can be adjusted only if the ceiling is no more than 2" (5cm) out of line. If the ceiling is distorted any more than this, horizontal stripes (no matter how much they are adapted) will actually emphasize the problem. A ceiling that is severely uneven dictates that the walls should have only vertical stripes, rather than the checkered effect used here.

• Low-tack or cheap masking tape is ideal because it is less sticky than the more expensive brands.

• Plan ahead. If you need more glaze while you are working, avoid leaving a stripe half-coated while you mix the glaze, because it will begin to dry before more wash can be added.

For more wall projects see:
Color-washed Wall pp124–5; Children's Balloon Stencils pp184–5; Marbled Bathroom pp200–1; Repeating Border and Dragged Stripes pp208–11.

8 Mask off the horizontals, checking that there is always a 90-degree angle where the lines meet. Apply glaze to the horizontal areas, using the brush in a crisscross motion. When you have finished, carefully remove the masking tape.

9 To give the design extra longevity and durability, give the walls a single coat of latex glaze, in either a satin or matte finish, once the stripes are dry. Although this appears cloudy and milk-like when it is wet, the glaze dries clear to provide an additional protective coat over the walls' decorative finish.

▲ Apply a coat of protective latex glaze.

Color-washed Oak Sideboard

WITH PAINT EFFECTS, you can coordinate the furniture for one room and ensure that it all matches. The colors in the sideboard match the painting on the tartan-band table (see pages 100–1), which in turn complements the porphyry picture frame (see pages 106–7). The sideboard was already very decorative and so additional decoration was kept very low key. A cream-colored wash provided just the right note and worked well with the grain of the oak. A little faded color was added to echo the colors of the tartan on the table and chairs.

❖ YOU WILL NEED ❖

Fine-grit sandpaper

Tack cloth

Creamy off-white latex paint

Old tablespoon

Glass jar

Two 2" (5cm) household paintbrushes

Clean cloth

Gouache paint in various colors

Ruler

Artist's paintbrush
(sable or synthetic mixture)

Artist's liner brush (synthetic)

Sanding sealer

Clear matte polyurethane varnish

This old oak sideboard was revamped in subtle colors so that the grain of the wood shows clearly.

1 First, have the sideboard professionally stripped of its coat of varnish. This will ensure that the color wash penetrates the wood and displays its beautiful grain.

2 Remove the doors. It is often easier to deal with large furniture in pieces. Rub down with sandpaper and dust with a tack cloth.

3 To make the wash, spoon some of the cream-colored latex into a glass jar with an old tablespoon and add enough water to make a milky consistency. If you intend to treat other pieces of furniture in the same way, note the proportions used.

4 Apply a generous helping of the wash, brushing it out in the direction of the grain.

5 Leave for 15 minutes to allow the paint to sink in and dry a little. With a soft, clean cloth, rub the wash back to expose a little more of the grain. When the paint is dry, lightly sand and dust it with a tack cloth.

6 Mix up the desired gouache colors, diluting them with water to achieve the right tone. Then, using an artist's paintbrush, paint the carved flowers and leaves.

7 Using a ruler, mark a 1" (2.5cm) wide band around the edge of the top of the sideboard and divide it into 1¹/₂" (4cm) sections. With an artist's liner brush, paint them alternately in faded green and blue. Run a line of reddish tan color through the center of the band, then paint short lines across the middle of each blue section.

8 When the colors are dry, give the sideboard a coat of sanding sealer and allow it to dry before finally applying a coat of clear matte polyurethane varnish.

For more freehand projects see:
Tartan-band Dining Table pp100–1; Freehand-painted Tables pp110–12; Kitchen Accessories pp138–41; Hand-painted Chest pp206–7.

▲ Pick out the flower decoration.

Tartan-band Dining Table

THIS OLD DINING ROOM table had obviously been put to very good use over the last 50 years. But it looked somewhat out of date and there were also stains and small areas of missing and buckled veneer to be dealt with before the painting could begin. It was stripped professionally and then defects were repaired with wood glue and wood filler. The light, cream-colored wash and subtle tartan motif transformed this dark, heavy piece of furniture into a bright, more delicate-looking item, which fits well into a modern decorative scheme.

❖ YOU WILL NEED ❖

Small, flexible palette knife

Wood glue

Wood filler

Fine-grit sandpaper

Steel wool or coarse sandpaper

Tack cloth

Cream-colored wash (see page 98)

Clean cloths

Two 2" (5cm) household paintbrushes

Small pieces of stiff cardboard

Ruler

Pencil

Scissors

Artist's paintbrush
(sable or synthetic mixture)

Artist's liner brush (synthetic)

Gouache paint in various colors

Sanding sealer

Clear matte polyurethane varnish

This old dining table was badly in need of repair and renovation.

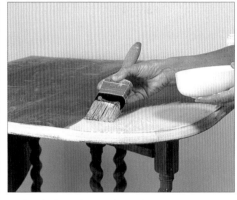

▲ Apply the color wash.

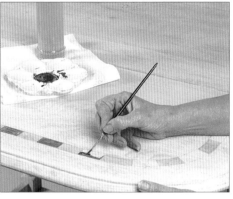

▲ Paint the decorative band.

1 Using the thin end of a palette knife, insert wood glue underneath any loose veneer and press the wood back into place. Allow it to dry completely, under the weight of a pile of heavy books.

2 Once the veneer repairs are fully dry, use the same flexible palette knife and neutral-colored wood filler to fill in any indentations that remain. Once the wood filler is dry, give the table a complete rub down with fine-grit sandpaper.

3 Here and there, especially on any areas of complicated molding or carving, where there are still traces of varnish, use steel wool or coarse sandpaper to strip back to bare wood. Then give the table a final rub over with the tack cloth to collect up all the dust and debris.

4 Paint the dining table with creamy off-white color wash in the same way as you did for the sideboard (see page 98).

5 A simple way to mark out a regularly spaced border is to use a stiff cardboard template. Cut a V-shaped notch with its point $2\frac{1}{4}$" (5.5cm) from the end of the piece of card and then position it with its unnotched end flush with the table edge. Move it around the table, making light pencil marks at the apex of the notch. These can then be joined to make a line following the edge of the table. Cut another piece of card and mark a line $3\frac{1}{4}$" (8cm) from the edge to give a 1" (2.5cm) wide band.

6 Divide the band into $1\frac{1}{2}$" (4cm) sections. With an artist's paintbrush, paint them alternately faded green and blue. Run a line of reddish tan color through the center of the band, then paint short lines across the middle of each blue section.

7 When dry, coat with sanding sealer and allow this to dry before applying clear matte varnish.

For more freehand projects see:
Color-washed Oak Sideboard pp98–9; Freehand-painted Tables pp110–12; Kitchen Accessories pp138–41.

Decorative Chairs

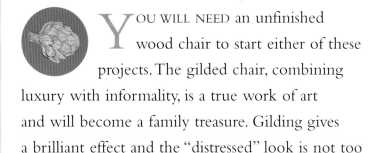

YOU WILL NEED an unfinished wood chair to start either of these projects. The gilded chair, combining luxury with informality, is a true work of art and will become a family treasure. Gilding gives a brilliant effect and the "distressed" look is not too difficult to achieve if you follow the instructions carefully. The stamped chair is deceptively easy, too; the artichoke shape makes a fine, compact decorative design and it also gives a hint of luxury. Stamps come in a great variety of shapes and sizes, so you can choose any motif that takes your fancy.

Gilded Chair

❖ YOU WILL NEED ❖

Medium-grit sandpaper

Tack cloth

Red brown water-based paint

Household paintbrushes

Gold leaf size medium (with an open-time of at least an hour) and brush

Cotton gloves

Silk scarf

Gold-leaf sheets

Shellac

Oil-based varnish

1 Sand the chair and remove the dust with the tack cloth. Apply two or three layers of the base coat, allowing each to dry.

2 Apply the size medium to the chair and allow it to set. The size is ready when your fingers will glide along it. Put on the gloves and have the scarf and gold leaf at hand. Never touch the sheets of gold leaf with your bare hands, as the oils from your fingers will discolor them.

3 Position a sheet of gold leaf above the surface and gently lower it onto the chair seat and lightly pat it down with your fingertips. The gold sheet will bond as soon as it comes into contact with the size.

4 Roll the scarf into a small, tight ball and rub it over the gold leaf to flatten the surface. Do not worry about gaps between the sheets (this creates an interesting effect) but touch up any really bare areas.

5 Coat with shellac and then apply three or four coats of oil-based varnish, letting each coat dry.

For more gilding projects see:
Gilded Mirror Frame pp119–21.

Stamped Artichoke Chair

❖ YOU WILL NEED ❖

Fine-grit sandpaper

Tack cloth

Household paintbrushes

Gouache paint in light olive and dark red oxide

Stamp with artichoke motif

Card stock, acetate, or stencil film

Craft knife and cutting mat

Piece of chalk

Stencil brush

Paper towels

Black waterproof ink pad and stamp

Satin varnish

1 Sand the chair with the fine-grit paper to achieve a smooth finish. Wipe it clean thoroughly with the tack cloth to remove all dust particles.

2 Using a household paintbrush, apply two coats of red oxide gouache paint all over the chair. Allow each coat to dry thoroughly.

3 Stamp the card stock or acetate with the artichoke stamp. Then cut around the outline with a craft knife to create a stencil.

4 Mark the position of each artichoke stamp on the chair with a piece of chalk.

5 Place the stencil on the marked positions. Dip the stencil brush into light olive gouache paint and dab it on a paper towel to remove any excess. Then apply paint through the stencil, working in a circular motion to build color and create artichoke shapes.

6 Using a waterproof ink pad, stamp over the outlines to fill in the detail on the artichokes.

7 When the chair is dry, apply two or three coats of satin varnish, allowing each to dry.

For more stamping projects see:
Sponge-stamped Floor pp128–9.

Antiqued Table

THIS TABLE WAS SPLIT and damaged when it was rescued from a junk yard—even some corners were missing. However, it was given a new lease on life with a distressed finish in a vibrant turquoise. Even the damaged surface and missing corners took on a certain charm once the table was painted. This antiquing technique simply uses a few cans of latex paint and works best on bare or primed wood. Surfaces that have been varnished or sealed should be rubbed down well with sandpaper to provide a good "key" before primer is applied.

❖ YOU WILL NEED ❖

Wood filler

Medium-grit sandpaper

Tack cloth

White acrylic primer

Household paintbrushes

Latex paint in brown and turquoise

Clean cloths

Methylated spirits (optional)

Acrylic matte varnish

1 Begin by filling in any large splits or holes in the table with wood filler, then sand well with the medium-grit paper and wipe the surface with a tack cloth. Apply a coat of primer to the table so that the latex paint will adhere well. When this is completely dry, apply a base coat of brown latex paint. Allow the base coat to dry thoroughly.

2 Apply a coat of turquoise latex paint over the dark brown base coat. Cover the surface completely, making sure that the paint reaches into every corner, the inside edge, and the underside of the table. Do not let this coat of paint dry out completely before the next step.

3 While the paint is still slightly wet, wipe off small patches from the edges and corners of the table with a cloth; these are the areas that would be the first to wear naturally. Use a damp cloth or one dipped in methylated spirits on any areas that are drying too quickly. If the paint comes off too easily and smoothly, reapply it and start again.

4 Once the table is completely dry, seal it with two coats of acrylic matte varnish. This dries quickly and can easily be recoated the same day—usually after an hour, depending on the room's temperature.

HINTS & TIPS

• If you find it difficult to judge the drying time for sanding the latex paint, an alternative method is to apply wax to the edges of the table after the brown base coat is dry. Then paint over this with the turquoise paint; later, chip it off to reveal patches of the brown underneath.

• To distress the finish further, you can apply a coat of crackle glaze between the base and top coats.

For more antiquing projects see:
Antiqued Iron Bed Frame pp178–9; Distressed Chest pp198–9; Aged Rustic Chair pp212–13.

▲ Apply the top coat very thoroughly.

▲ Carefully wipe paint from the edges.

▲ Finish the table with two coats of varnish.

Porphyry Picture Frame

THIS FRAME IS not very old but needless to say it was bought secondhand and was extremely cheap. It was an enticing item because it offers a range of interesting possibilities in terms of decoration as it is so wide and has an inset and some carving to add to its attraction. With its classical finish of spatter-painted black, cream, and gold, the frame now mimics porphyry—a type of granite used since antiquity. As a final touch a tartan ribbon was added to fit the decor of the room where the frame would eventually hang.

❖ YOU WILL NEED ❖

Damp cloth

White oil-based eggshell paint

Two 1½" (4cm) household paintbrushes

Fine-grit sandpaper

Tack cloth

Artist's oils in light red, yellow ocher, and black

Mineral spirits

Small natural sponge

Stencil brush

Piece of newspaper

Gold bronzing powder

Artist's acrylic varnish

Fine artist's paintbrush

Clear satin polyurethane varnish

Tartan ribbon (same width as frame inset)

Tube of nonstaining glue

1 Clean the frame thoroughly with a damp cloth. Apply a coat of white eggshell and leave for 24 hours to dry. Rub down with sandpaper and wipe with the tack cloth. Apply a second coat, allow to dry, and rub down and tack the frame as before.

2 Mix a little white eggshell with some red oil paint and a little yellow ocher and black to make a terra-cotta color. Add a tiny amount of mineral spirits and sponge all over the main part of the frame. Let dry for an hour or two, until no longer shiny.

3 Mix a little yellow ocher and the white eggshell to make a cream color and thin to a milky consistency with mineral spirits. Dip the end of the stencil brush in the mix and spatter some onto the newspaper by drawing your thumb across the tips of the bristles. This will remove any drips that may spoil the frame.

4 Spatter the cream paint over the frame. Let dry for a few minutes, then spatter over a little diluted black oil paint.

5 Mix a little gold bronzing powder with some acrylic varnish and spatter this lightly over the frame. Then, using the fine artist's brush and the same gold mixture, carefully pick out the indented lines around the frame, and paint the raised inner edge.

6 Allow the frame to dry overnight, then apply a coat of clear satin polyurethane varnish to protect it from wear and tear.

7 Cut the tartan ribbon into lengths to fit the frame inset. Cut the corners by following the original shape of the frame. Glue the ribbon onto the frame, smoothing it down carefully so that it lies flat.

HINTS & TIPS

If you have one, a glue gun is an easy way of sticking the ribbon to the frame.

For more picture frame projects see:
Limed Picture Frame pp230–1; Painted Frames pp232–3; Golden Pear Picture Frame pp234–5; Poppies Picture Frame pp236–7.

▲ Spatter the frame with cream paint.

▲ Use a glue gun to attach the tartan inset.

Used for socializing, rest, and play, the living room is one of the most flexible rooms in the house and can be treated as something of a blank canvas for your creative energies. You can start with some modest accessories, or go wild and decorate the whole room in paint effects. Whichever you choose to do, the result will be a room that is comfortable, stylish, and unmistakably stamped with your personality.

Living Room Projects

Freehand-painted Tables

A REPEATED DESIGN on nesting tables makes an unusually attractive item out of a very practical piece of furniture. Many people balk at the idea of hand painting a set of tables, on the grounds that although painting one successfully might be possible, painting the others to match would be too much to attempt. Once you have made your design for the largest table, however, nothing could be easier than copying it onto the other two. The painting does not require great artistic skill— patience and concentration are more important.

❖ YOU WILL NEED ❖

Wood filler

Palette knife

Fine-grit sandpaper

Tack cloth

Two 1½" (4cm) household paintbrushes

Primer

Pale yellow eggshell paint

Artist's oils in yellow ocher and raw umber

Glass jar

Mineral spirits

Old tablespoon

Natural sponge

Clear satin polyurethane varnish

Drawing paper and pencil

Masking tape

Tracing paper

Ruler

Soft pencil

Ballpoint pen

Acrylic craft paints

Artist's paintbrush

Sheet of glass (optional)

White or ivory candle

These battered old tables were covered in varnish and had to be stripped before work could begin.

1 The tables should be stripped of any varnish before you start— these have been stripped professionally. If there are any cracks or chips, apply wood filler using a palette knife with a thin, flexible blade.

2 When dry, rub down the tables with sandpaper, then dust them with the tack cloth.

3 As the stripped tables are extremely porous, apply a coat of primer. Allow this to dry, then apply a coat of yellow eggshell paint. Let dry for 24 hours, then lightly rub the tables down and tack them once again. Apply two more coats of eggshell—sand and tack after each application.

4 Prepare a slightly darker yellow paint to sponge the tables by putting some yellow ocher oil paint into a glass jar and adding a small amount of raw umber. Mix this to a creamy consistency with a little mineral spirits. Stir in some of the eggshell until the jar is about one-quarter full.

5 Smear a little of this mixture onto a dry tabletop to see if the colour is dark enough. Carefully add a little more yellow ocher and raw umber until it reaches the right shade. When you are satisfied with the shade, top off the jar with an equal amount of mineral spirits. The jar should now be half-full of paint glaze.

6 Clean the experimental paint smear from the table with a cloth soaked in mineral spirits. Turn one of the tables upside down, apply glaze to the legs, and then sponge it off with the natural sponge. Turn the table right side up and complete the top in the same way.

▲ Rub the tables down with sandpaper.

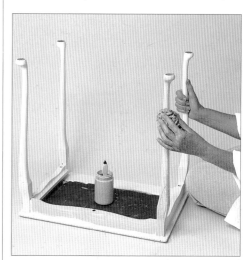

▲ Turn the table over to apply glaze to the legs.

7 Sponge the other tables in the same way and allow them to dry for 24 hours. Apply a coat of varnish to each table.

8 The next stage is to map out the design on your tables. In this case a border of very stylized ribbon and a bow, taken from some Victorian tiles, were used. Measure the top of the largest table and draw its proportions on a large sheet of paper. Draw a border 2½" (6.5cm) in from the first line.

9 Copy the design freehand along the border line, twisting the ribbon symmetrically as it turns each of the four corners. Mark the position of the bow halfway across the border at the front of the table and draw it in line with the ribbon.

10 When you have completed the border design for the largest table, tape a piece of tracing paper over the top of your piece of paper and make a tracing. Working on this tracing, measure along the longest sides of the border and make a mark halfway along each side. Using a ruler, join these marks with a pencil line that stretches across the center of the drawing. Repeat with the shorter sides so that the two pencil lines cross at right angles in the middle.

11 Take a soft pencil and repeat this on the tabletop to give two lines crossing at right angles. Using the same soft pencil, scribble all along the border on the back of the tracing paper. Then, placing the paper scribbled-side down, tape the tracing to the top of the table so that the crossed lines on the drawing match up with those on the tabletop, thus ensuring that the border is straight.

12 Go over the drawing on the tracing paper with a ballpoint pen—the graphite on the back of the drawing will transfer the design to the table. Remove the paper and, still using the original as your guide, paint the ribbon and bow with acrylic paints using an artist's brush.

▲ Apply a coat of varnish over the sponged glaze.

13 To prepare the design for the two smaller tables, reduce the size of the outer border (the distance between the table edge and the painted border), by ½" (12mm) on each table. Proceed in the same way for the middle size table: prepare your design on a sheet of drawing paper using your original tracing for the corners and the bow, filling in the slightly shorter sides freehand. Then trace the design, scribble on the back, transfer it to the table, and paint it in the same way as the large table.

14 For the smaller table, the ribbon will need to be slightly thinner to keep the design in scale, so once you have established the outside edge of the table and the position of the border on a sheet of drawing paper, you will need to copy the design freehand.

15 Once you have made the modified drawing for the smallest table, finish it in same way as for the other two, and then varnish all three tables.

16 Some tables have insets that take a sheet of glass on the top, in which case you can have a new piece cut for each as an added protection. For tables that don't have this feature, an extra coat of varnish is advisable. Finally, run a white or ivory candle along the runners and sides of the tables so they will move smoothly, reducing the risk of chipped paint.

HINTS & TIPS

• Use a natural sea sponge for sponging; its absorbency and irregular structure will create the most attractive effect.

• When tracing the design onto the table, don't lean too hard on the ballpoint pen or you could mark the tabletop. The graphite will transfer the design without the need to apply pressure.

For more sponging projects see:
Sponge-stamped Floor pp128–9; Hand-printed Blanket Chest pp164–5; Sponged Pot pp214–15.

Old Oak Woodgrain Floor

YOU MAY BE WONDERING why you would want to paint wood to look like wood. Perhaps your floorboards are beyond rescue—they have been filled too much and are too damaged to renovate to create a good natural finish, leaving paint as the only option. Or perhaps they have been painted already and re-painting them is easier than stripping them down completely. Or maybe you just want to create the look of a beautiful old oak floor. Wood graining can be a very specialized art practiced by master craftsmen to the highest exactitude, but don't worry; this project uses an easy, yet effective, technique to simulate a simple oak grain. You should plan to carry out steps 1 and 2, preparing the floor, the day before you apply the woodgrain effect.

❖ YOU WILL NEED ❖

Wood filler

Palette knife

Shellac

Sandpaper

Sand-colored acrylic eggshell for base coat

Household paintbrushes

Crackle glaze and colorizer

Bucket

Burnt umber artist's acrylic paint

Metal combing tool

Narrow paintbrush

Soft brush

Piece of real oak for reference (optional)

Polyurethane sealer

1 The day before you plan to apply the woodgrain effect, fill in any holes and knots in the floorboards using the wood filler and allow to dry. If the wood is bare, seal any knots with shellac and sand to a smooth surface.

2 Prepare the floor by applying a base coat of the sand-colored acrylic eggshell paint. You may have to apply two coats if you are painting over an absorbent primer. If the surface is already painted, sand it down to provide a "key" for the new paint to adhere to. Remember to paint in the direction of the grain and then allow to dry thoroughly.

3 Prepare a colored crackle glaze to apply to the woodgrain. Pour some crackle into a bucket and slowly add acrylic colorizer. Here a premixed colorizer, the color of medium oak, has been used.

▲ Add colorizer to crackle to make a glaze.

4 Paint on the crackle glaze in the direction of the grain. Paint the length of two or three floorboards at a time.

5 Add a dab of burnt umber acrylic paint straight from the tube onto the tip of your brush.

▲ Fill any holes or knots in the boards.

▲ Apply one or two base coats.

▲ Apply the glaze in the direction of the grain.

▲ Blend the burnt umber into the glaze.

6 Paint the burnt umber on the tip of your brush into the still-wet crackle glaze, blending it in. Pull a metal combing tool through the glaze in one direction to create a grain effect.

▲ Drag the comb across the glaze.

7 Drag the combing tool over the glaze again, but this time hold it at an angle to produce a mottled effect. Work quickly before the crackle dries. Soften the comb lines with a brush if necessary. Allow to dry.

8 Paint on the figuring (the marks in the end of a piece of wood) by diluting burnt umber acrylic paint and applying it with a narrow brush.

▲ Drag the comb at an angle to the first lines.

▲ Apply the figuring with a narrow brush.

9 Look at a piece of real oak as reference for the flow and structure of natural figuring. Stand back periodically to have a look at the overall effect. Soften the figuring, working gently with a soft brush in an outward direction.

10 Add sharper, straighter marks across the grain to complete the figuring. When completely dry, varnish the floor with two coats of polyurethane sealer.

▲ Use a large brush to soften the figuring.

▲ Complete the figuring with straight marks.

HINTS & TIPS

Before embarking on this project, look at veneer samples of various grains and take photographs when you see interesting old oak gates, doors, and floors. The more wood you look at, the easier it becomes to develop a feel for the flow and beautiful structure of natural grain and figuring.

For more floor projects see:
Geometric Starburst Floor pp90–1;
Sponge-stamped Floor pp128–9.

Craquelure Lamp Base and Shade

PAINTED LAMP BASES like this one always look as though they are very expensive. Once you have mastered the *craquelure* technique, you will find it simple to do and you can delight in the large sum of money saved by doing it yourself. This cracked-porcelain effect is achieved by brushing on two different varnishes, a slow-drying oil varnish followed by a fast-drying water-soluble one, then rubbing in oil color to show up the cracks. The results are never quite predictable—the size of the cracks depends on how thickly you apply both layers of varnish. The thinner the layers, the smaller the cracks will be. The length of time between the application of the two coats also affects the size—the longer you leave them, the finer the cracks will be.

❖ YOU WILL NEED ❖

Household paintbrushes

White latex paint

Flexible masking tape

Acrylic glaze

Water

Acrylic paint

Stencil brush

Water-based varnish

Varnish brush

Two-part *craquelure*

Soft-bristled synthetic brush

Raw umber artist's oil paint

Mineral spirits

Paper towels

Satin oil-based varnish

1 Using a household paintbrush, paint the lamp with two or three coats of white latex paint, allowing each coat to dry thoroughly before applying the next. A plain white latex paint was chosen because it makes the cracks highly visible. At the end of the treatment, it will look cream-colored rather than white.

2 Mask above and below the bands around the lamp where you want a contrasting color. Use flexible masking tape to cover the curved surface of the lamp.

3 Mix a little acrylic glaze and water with some acrylic paint and stipple on the color with a stencil brush. Let it dry for approximately 4 hours and then seal the whole lamp base with a coat of water-based varnish. Allow it to dry thoroughly before you continue.

A plain lamp base was turned into a sophisticated piece using crackling techniques.

4 Brush the first part of the oil-based *craquelure* evenly over the lamp. Hold the lamp up to the light as you work to make sure that you have covered the entire surface. Allow this to dry (usually 2 to 4 hours) until it feels dry when you glide the back of your finger over the surface, but is still just tacky when you press your knuckle against it.

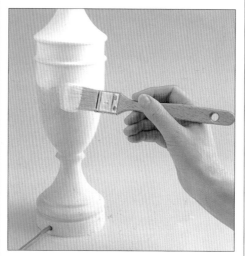

▲ Paint the lamp with latex paint.

▲ Stipple on the paint for the colored bands.

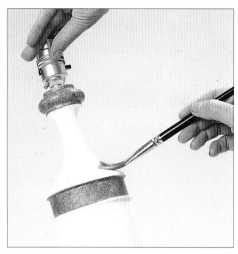

▲ Brush on the oil-based *craquelure* varnish.

5 Brush on the second part of the *craquelure* with a soft-bristled synthetic brush. Work lightly and quickly so as not to leave any brush marks. Cover over every part of the first coat. After about half an hour, check to see if there are any areas you have missed and cover them with more of the second coat.

6 The cracks should appear as soon as the second coat has dried, although they are hard to see at this stage. If they do not appear, leave the lamp base in a warm place or apply a gentle heat until they appear.

7 Dilute some raw umber artist's oil paint with a small amount mineral spirits until it reaches a creamy consistency, then rub this into the surface with paper towels. Take a clean piece of paper and wipe it off, leaving traces of the raw umber paint in the cracks.

▲ Wipe off the raw umber paint.

8 Stir a little additional mineral spirits into the raw umber paint and dip a stencil brush into it. Hold the brush up near the lamp and run your index finger over the ends of the bristles to spray the surface of the lamp base with fine spatters. Soften the effect by dabbing it with a paper towel. Allow the lamp to sit overnight until it is completely dry and then seal it with a coat of satin oil-based varnish.

9 The lampshade was first sealed with a layer of water-based varnish and then given the same *craquelure* treatment as the lamp base. In order to retain the matte appearance of the lampshade, however, it was sealed with a final coat of flat varnish.

For more lamp base projects see:
Tortoishell Lamp Base and Shade pp224–5.

For more lamp base projects see:
Tortoishell Lamp Base and Shade pp224–5.

HINTS & TIPS

• Remember that the second layer of craquelure is water soluble and care must be taken not to get it wet or touch it with damp hands.

• Avoid using this technique on a rainy or humid day as the cracks will need a lot of encouragement to appear! A hair dryer can assist the process but use it on a low setting or you will end up with an unnatural-looking pattern. This may also happen if you leave your work in front of a sunny window. Leaving your decorated piece near a radiator is usually effective.

• The effect can be used to create an antiqued appearance over hand-painted, découpaged, and stenciled designs.

• Practice this *craquelure* technique first on a piece of cardboard that has been sealed with water-based varnish.

• If you get into difficulty, you can remove the raw umber paint with mineral spirits, wash off the water-based varnish, and let it to dry before starting again.

▲ Spatter the lamp base with a mix of umber paint and mineral spirits.

Gilded Mirror Frame

THIS IS A NEW, inexpensive pine mirror that has taken on quite a different appearance by adding a few pieces of carved wooden molding bought cheaply at a flea market. Moldings can be used to give plain furniture a more decorative appearance. Many wonderful effects can be achieved using transfer metal leaf. Real gold and silver leaf are expensive, but aluminum, copper, and bronze are also available. Traditionally, either oil size or glue size is applied over several layers of gesso to receive the leaf, but gilding has become simpler with the introduction of acrylic gold size, which is ready to gild over in about 15 minutes and stays tacky indefinitely. Red ocher paint is used to imitate red bole—or clay—which is traditionally used as a base for gold leaf.

❖ YOU WILL NEED ❖

Molding

Wood glue or PVA glue

Wood filler

Palette knife

Masking tape

Red ocher and white latex or traditional paint

Household and artist's paintbrushes

Acrylic gold-leaf size medium

Transfer metal leaf

Scissors

Bronzing powder

Yellow shellac

Rottenstone

0000-grade steel wool

Methylated spirits

Clear or brown paste wax

Soft cloth

1 Decide where you want to position the moldings on your frame. Here they are concentrated on the upper part of the frame. Then, using wood glue or PVA glue, stick the moldings in place. Fill any gaps in the frame with wood filler.

2 Stick masking tape all around the mirror edge to keep it clean, then paint the whole frame with two coats of red ocher paint, allowing the first coat to dry thoroughly before applying the second one. Allow to dry.

3 Using a soft synthetic brush, apply acrylic gold-leaf size medium to the moldings on the frame. The size appears milky at this stage but it soon becomes transparent. After about 15 to 20 minutes, when the size is completely clear, it is ready to gild over.

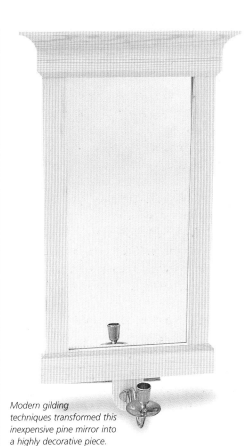

Modern gilding techniques transformed this inexpensive pine mirror into a highly decorative piece.

▲ Glue the molding pieces in place.

▲ Paint the frame in red ocher.

▲ Apply acrylic gold-leaf size to the molding.

▲ Use a brush to tamp the metal leaf down.

▲ Paint the frame with white latex paint.

4 Cut a sheet of transfer metal leaf in half with a pair of scissors and place this over the size. Tamp the leaf down with a firm-bristled brush so that it goes into the recessed areas as well as onto the surface. Lift the backing paper off and continue in this way, using all remaining scraps on the sheets to fill in small gaps. When you have covered the moldings as much as you can, dust with bronzing powder to fill any remaining gaps.

5 Gently brush a coat of yellow shellac over the gilded moldings to seal and "age" the metal leaf. You can add a little rottenstone to the shellac if you want to give the frame a slightly more aged effect.

6 Paint the remainder of the frame with two coats of white paint over the red, allowing the first coat to dry before applying the second. When this is dry, rub down the painted surface here and there with 0000-grade steel wool dipped in methylated spirits. If you have used a soft traditional paint, steel wool and water should create a sufficiently distressed appearance.

7 Mix some rottenstone with clear liquid wax and apply it to the frame, using a small brush to reach right up to the moldings. If you prefer, you can substitute brown paste wax for the clear wax. Allow the wax to dry, then polish the frame using a soft cloth.

For more gilding projects see:
Gilded Chair pp102–3.

▲ Brushing on a coat of yellow shellac.

▲ Apply rottenstone and wax with a brush to achieve an "aged" effect.

Dragged-effect Table

SCANDINAVIAN PAINTED FURNITURE is noted for its elegant, simple styling. The soft blue-gray used on this table is typical of the colors used on Swedish neo-classical furniture. The subtle dragged effect was achieved using a flat varnish brush and a transparent water-based glaze mixed with acrylic paint. This replaces the oil-based glazes used traditionally as it is faster drying and nonyellowing. The glaze takes two to four hours to dry, so avoid painting a surface adjoining one you have just worked on or you will spoil the finish.

❖ YOU WILL NEED ❖

Latex satin paint

Household paintbrushes

Artist's acrylic paint

Acrylic glaze

Flat varnish brush

Old measuring spoons

PVA medium or glue and rottenstone, or acrylic paint in raw umber

Paper towels

Gilt cream

Soft cloth

Matte water-based varnish

1 Paint the table with two coats of latex satin paint, allowing the first coat to dry before applying the second. Allow to dry.

The elegant lines of this delicate table lend themselves perfectly to this sophisticated painting technique.

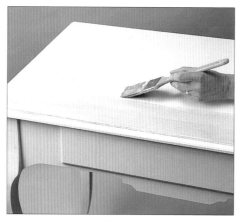
▲ Apply two coats of latex paint.

2 Mix the acrylic paint and glaze to the color required. Use a flat varnish brush to drag the glaze down the length of the top, a section at a time. Soften the effect with the brush. Next, drag the sides of the table. When completely dry to the touch, paint opposite surfaces on the legs, then the remaining ones. Allow to dry overnight.

3 Make an antiquing wash by mixing 1 teaspoon PVA medium or glue with 2 teaspoons rottenstone and 9 fluid ounces (250ml) water. Alternatively, dilute some raw umber acrylic paint with water. Brush the wash on the surface of the table a section at a time, then wipe it off with paper towels to give a soft, aged effect.

4 Paint the border around the tabletop and the drawer using your choice of acrylic color without added glaze. In this case, a mix of ivory black, Prussian blue, and titanium white latex satin was used.

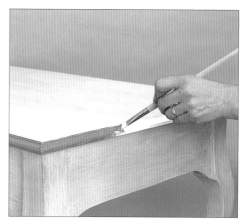
▲ Paint the border with an acrylic color.

5 Brush the gilt cream over the borders of the table. Let it dry completely and then buff it to a shine using a soft cloth. Varnish the whole table, except for the gold edges, with two coats of matte water-based varnish to protect it against everyday wear and tear. Allow the first coat of varnish to dry completely before you start to apply the second.

For more table projects see:
Tartan-band Dining Table pp100–1; Antiqued Table pp104–5; Freehand-painted Tables pp110–12; Marbled Dressing Table pp162–3; Spray-painted Table and Chairs pp204–5; Painted Tablecloth pp218–21.

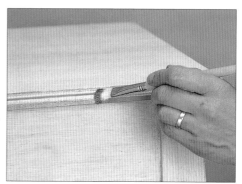
▲ Brush on the gilt cream.

Color-washed Wall

COLOR WASHING IS A TERM used so often to describe so many varied effects that it has almost become a generic term in the painting trade. It is actually a method for applying a thin glaze over the surface in such a way that the base color shows through a mottled surface. In this project the glaze is brushed on and spread out while it is still wet. Oil-based glaze is added to the paint to give it a slippery texture in order that the color will move about more easily on the wall as you soften and spread with the brush. Color washing must be carried out on top of a base coat of latex satin or eggshell rather than matte paint. The slight sheen of the base coat is extremely important for the softening to be effective.

❖ YOU WILL NEED ❖

1 pint (0.5l) oil-based paint

1 pint (0.5l) glaze

Approx. ½ pint (0.25l) mineral spirits

Household paintbrush

Natural-bristle softener brush

▲ Apply the glaze in broad crisscross sections.

▲ Soften with a natural-bristle brush.

1 To make the color-wash glaze, mix the oil-based paint with transparent glaze and stir well. Then add mineral spirits to thin the mixture until it is roughly the consistency of light cream.

2 Using a household paintbrush, apply the glaze over the wall, working quickly in broad crisscross strokes, in sections about 3 by 3' (1 by 1m) at a time. Leave some of the white base coat showing through and overlap many of the brushstrokes.

3 Spread the glaze with the same brush in crisscross directions as far as it will go. This requires some physical energy but is a very easy technique to master. Work fast and keep the edges of each section wet, overlapping as you go.

4 Before the glaze dries, sweep a softener brush over the crisscross marks in all directions. The soft bristles of the brush will obliterate most visible brushstrokes, but still leave behind the variations of shade.

HINTS & TIPS

• Occasionally, a thin glaze can become powdery when dry. This can be caused by a bad batch of ready-made paint but is usually the result of oil glaze that has not been stirred thoroughly before use. To remedy a powdery finish, apply a single coat of latex glaze when the wall is fully dry. This is very thin and should be applied with a brush, not a roller, for the best results. It dries clear and serves as a washable, protective coat, a varnish, and a cure for powdery glaze work. Latex glaze is very quick to apply and dries in about an hour.

• When softening the color-wash glaze, make sure you do not stop unless you are at a corner; otherwise, there will be a clear mark that will indicate the overlapping sections and spoil the effect.

For more wall projects see:

Checkered Walls pp94–7; Painted Panels pp133–5; A Kitchen Frieze pp148–9; A Bedroom Frieze pp172–4; Children's Balloon Stencils pp184–5; Marbled Bathroom pp200–1.

▲ Mix the color-wash glaze.

▲ Work fast to spread out the glaze.

Granite-effect Fireplace

REVIOUSLY RIPPED OUT and discarded in favor of modern-day heating, fireplaces are now coming back as a popular feature of many homes. Fireplaces provide a useful focus for any dining or living room, even if they are nonfunctioning. The granite effect creates a good rustic feel and disguises damaged wood. However, seek professional advice before restoring a fireplace that you want to work. Heat-resistant paint must be used and fixings must be secure. Similarly, chimneys must be professionally cleaned and checked before a fire is lit.

❖ YOU WILL NEED ❖

Warm, soapy water

Medium- and fine-grit sandpaper

Tack cloth

Eggshell paint

Household paintbrushes

Tablespoon

Paint can

Acrylic glaze

Artist's acrylic paint in two shades of green

Stirring stick

Dark green, fine silver, and fine black glitter

Paper

1 Wash the fireplace surround with detergent solution. Then gently sand the surface using medium- and then fine-grit sandpaper, before wiping with a tack cloth.

2 Apply the eggshell color (this should be paler than the chosen granite color) and allow to dry. Gently sand with fine-grit sandpaper and wipe off the dust with the tack cloth. Apply a second coat of eggshell and allow to dry.

3 Put a tablespoon of the acrylic glaze into the paint can and add two tube widths of the two shades of green artist's colors. Mix until smooth and keep adding small amounts of colors in this ratio until you achieve the desired granite color. Then add more acrylic glaze until there is a sufficient amount of mixture. Keep in mind that it is better to have too much than too little. Continue stirring until the consistency is like that of light cream.

4 Stirring all the time, gently tap in the contents of the small containers of silver, black, and green glitter. Continue stirring until all the glitter has been completely worked into the paint mixture.

5 Apply the glaze to the fireplace, taking care to cover all ridges, curves, and corners. Allow it to dry and then apply a second coat. To increase the glittery effect, put some fine glitter onto a piece of paper and gently blow this over the surface while the glaze is still wet.

HINTS & TIPS

Granite paint can be made in any number of colors. The fireplace here has been designed to have a two-tone look (using contrasting silver and green) but you can be as adventurous as you like.

For more stone effect projects see:
Porphyry Picture Frame pp106–7; Marbled Pot pp214–15.

▲ Use a base coat paler than the granite finish.

▲ Apply a mix of paint and glitter on a pale base.

Sponge-stamped Floor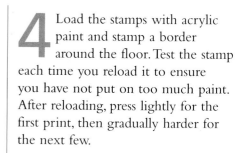

THE CHARMING PATTERN on this varnished wooden floor was created with nothing more complicated than a stamp made from kitchen sponges. It took only one day to paint the floor and varnish it, and the result is a bright and cheerful floor in an otherwise fairly somber room. The sponge texture works well to break up the solid lines of color. The turquoise-blue used to paint the design is the exact opposite color of the terra-cotta on the walls. The inspiration for this design originally came from a fabric design—this is particularly easy because you can cut the design out of the fabric and use it as a template to cut the sponges. See pages 84–5 for additional tips on how to use ideas from fabrics or, alternatively, design a pattern for yourself.

❖ YOU WILL NEED ❖

Wood stain

Floor varnish

Household paintbrushes

Scissors

Design to copy

Craft knife and cutting mat

Flat cellulose sponges

2 wooden base blocks

PVA adhesive

Artist's acrylic paint in turquoise-blue

Scrap paper

1 Apply the stain to the floor and then give it a generous single coat of varnish when dry. The varnish base prevents the acrylic paint from sinking into the woodgrain and allows you to wipe away any mistakes quickly. It can be expensive to rectify any mistakes made on an unvarnished floor.

2 With sharp scissors, cut out the motifs from the fabric. Using these as templates, cut out the sponge shapes using the craft knife and cutting mat. Two stamps have been used here: one for the stripes and one for the flower. Glue the pieces to the base blocks using the PVA adhesive.

3 To test the stamp, apply an even coat of artist's acrylic paint with the brush and press the stamp firmly onto some scrap paper. Make any necessary changes to the shape using the craft knife.

4 Load the stamps with acrylic paint and stamp a border around the floor. Test the stamp each time you reload it to ensure you have not put on too much paint. After reloading, press lightly for the first print, then gradually harder for the next few.

5 When the design is dry (about one hour for acrylic paints) apply two additional coats of varnish to the whole floor.

HINTS & TIPS

You can use any type of paint as long as it is sufficiently opaque to show up and thick enough not to run—it should be at least as thick as heavy cream.

For more stamping projects see:
Stamped Artichoke Chair pp102–3; Ivy-stamped Chair pp150–1; Stamped CD Box pp240–1.

▲ Cut out a fabric motif as a template.

▲ Apply acrylic paint generously to the stamp.

▲ Seal the floor with two coats of varnish.

Stenciled Balustrade

STENCILING DOES NOT have to be done on a small scale; a large architectural stencil can give subtle impact to a room. This balustrade is a simple design that works to great effect in a room with little furniture. It is painted with exterior paints that contain some sand and are gently shaded to give a three-dimensional quality. The paint is very durable, so the finished work needs no special care—it is washable and simple to repair if it ever becomes damaged. This design is an enlarged photocopy adapted to become a stencil by leaving gaps between the sections of the pillar. For the top and bottom of the design, which are straight runs along the wall, you will save time by using masking tape instead of cutting this section from the stencil.

❖ YOU WILL NEED ❖

Design for your stencil (see page 246)

Craft knife and cutting mat

Card stock, acetate, or stencil film

Low-tack masking tape

Metal ruler

Level

Pencil

Plumb line

Nonpermanent adhesive spray

Cellulose sponges or small paint roller

Scrap piece of paper (optional)

Fine-textured exterior paint (containing sand) in two colors, light and slightly darker

Artist's crayons, oils, or wax oils, in white and yellow ocher or raw sienna

---

1 Enlarge your chosen design to the required size on a photocopier, bearing in mind that if your room already has a chair rail in place your design will have to fit snugly between this and the baseboard.

2 Position the enlarged design on a cutting mat beneath a piece of stock card, acetate, stencil film at least twice as big as the design, and secure both in place with masking tape.

3 Carefully cut out the design in the stencil film, using a craft knife and a metal ruler for the straight edges. (Cut two stencils if you are working with a partner.) Remember to cut out the balustrade in separate sections, leaving a gap of about ¼" (0.5cm) between each one, which will remain unpainted.

4 Now mark the position of your stencils on the wall; do this by marking the top and bottom of each pillar with a straight line or piece

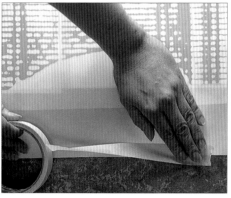
▲ Tape the stencil over the design.

of masking tape (use a level). Measure an equal distance between each pillar, so that they will be evenly spaced. Using a pencil lightly mark a vertical line, which will run through the center of each pillar, using a plumb line and ruler to guide you.

5 Spray the back of the stencil with nonpermanent adhesive spray and position it carefully on the wall, following the guidelines that mark the center. Secure the stencil further with small pieces of masking tape.

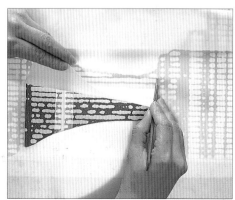
▲ Carefully cut out the stencil.

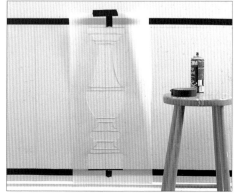
▲ Position the stencil over the penciled guides.

▲ Fill the whole area with the lighter color.

▲ Apply shading along the straight section.

▲ Add three-dimensional shading with crayons.

6 Using a chunk of cellulose sponge or a small paint roller, fill in the whole stencil with the lighter of your chosen colors of textured paint. Leave the stencil in place for the next step.

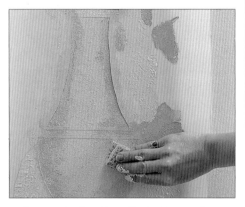

▲ Repeat shading along the bottom section.

7 Dip a small piece of sponge into your darker color and dab off any excess paint onto paper or the edge of the stencil. Dab the darker color through the stencil to shade it. Shade around the edges and at the bottom of each section of the pillar. Dab the two shades of wet paint together to blend the darker shade gently into the lighter shade. Peel away the stencil. Continue stenciling the pillars all around the room.

8 Mask off a straight section, along the top of your pillars, leaving no gap, as you can see in the picture above center. Using a sponge, fill it first with cream-colored paint, then apply the shading color along the edges.

9 Repeat step eight for the bottom section, painting the baseboard as well if you want your design to the floor.

10 When the paint is dry, carefully shade the pillars with crayons to create a three-dimensional effect. Run a thin line of yellow ocher or raw sienna around the edges where the shadows will fall, down the right-hand side and along the bottom of each section. Using a white crayon, add highlights where the light will catch your balustrade to complete the three-dimensional effect. You will see in the photograph below that a line of white has been run down the left-hand side of each section, following the curve of the outline, a fraction of an inch from the edge. A line of white has also been run along the top of each section.

HINTS & TIPS

• You can adjust the color of your balustrade by mixing artist's acrylic paints into the textured paint.

• Enlarged photocopies are not always perfectly symmetrical. For perfect symmetry in your design, cut the stencil in two halves. First, cut one half from the design, then turn it over and use it to cut out an identical shape in reverse for the second side.

For more stenciling projects see:
Frottaged and Stenciled Screen pp167–9; A Bedroom Frieze pp172–3; Children's Balloon Stencils pp184–5; Mexican-style Bathroom pp190–2; Repeating Border and Dragged Stripes pp208–11; Poppies Picture Frame pp236–7; Stenciled Mirror Frame pp242–3.

▲ A line of white down the left-hand side and along the top of each section completes the effect.

Painted Panels

THREE DIFFERENT paint effects—dragging, ragging, and bagging—work in harmony here to give an elegant and welcoming living room. The panels themselves are created simply by attaching wooden molding to the wall. They are easy to assemble; if you have used a saw before, you will be able to panel your room following the instructions given here. Before you start, decide how many panels you would like and how much molding you will need; you can buy this in lengths from a home-improvement store. In this room the colors are shades of the same color, selected from the paint-mixing color strips displayed in stores. By choosing all your shades from the same strip you can be sure that your colors will go well together.

❖ YOU WILL NEED ❖

Wood primer paint

Household paintbrush

Sufficient lengths of molding to make panels, plus one extra length to allow for cutting loss

Tenon saw and miter box

2½ quarts (2.5l) of latex satin paint in your 2 chosen base colors

Border and panel adhesive

Masking tape

1 quart (1l) of transparent oil glaze

1 pint (0.5l) of eggshell paint in your 3 chosen glaze colors

3 large plastic plant saucers

Mineral spirits

Stippling brush (optional)

Cotton cloths

Dragging brush

3 or 4 plastic grocery bags

1 Apply a coat of primer paint to the wooden molding if it is raw when you buy it. Allow the molding to dry thoroughly.

2 Cut the molding into accurate lengths, using the tenon saw and miter box as shown in the photograph below left. Take care that your pieces will all be angled correctly, and reverse the angle of the cut for the second of two of the corner cuts so that they can fit together. You will soon get the hang of how the angles should be cut.

3 Paint above and below the chair rail with two coats of latex satin in the colors you have chosen for your base coats. In the panel demonstrated here, a very pale blue-green has been used for the top section and a deeper blue-green for the bottom section—both were chosen from the same paint-mixing color strip.

4 Using a pencil, mark the inside line of each panel on the wall for guidance. Stick the molding into position on the wall to create the panels, using blobs of glue on the backs of the pieces or putting blobs onto the wall. Keep a close eye on the panels you have glued, as they sometimes slip. Secure them with masking tape if they start to move. Fill any gaps where the corners join with more panel adhesive.

5 Then mix three trays of glaze in your chosen colors, using the plastic plant saucers as containers. Your colors should be about two or three shades apart on a paint-mixing card, and darker than your base paint. Use 1 part transparent oil glaze, 1 part paint, and 1 part mineral spirits. Keep the lightest and darkest glazes quite thick, but dilute the medium glaze with a drop more mineral spirits so that it has the consistency of milk.

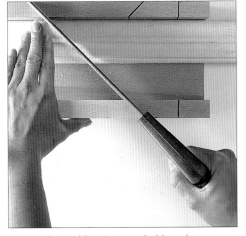

▲ Cut the molding into angled lengths.

▲ Paint above and below the chair rail.

▲ Attach the molding to the wall with glue.

▲ Brush the glaze over the inside of the panel.

6 Brush your lightest-colored glaze evenly all over the inside of one panel, then immediately stipple away the brushstrokes with light jabbing motions using a stippling (or household) brush. This stippling is optional, but it prevents any of your brushstrokes from showing up on the finished work, and so gives a more pleasing result.

▲ Draw the dragging brush evenly down the glaze, applying firm and even pressure.

▲ Dab a crumpled cloth over the glaze.

7 Immediately, dab quickly and evenly all over the glazed area with a piece of cloth, crumpled into a ball. This is known as ragging.

8 Apply the thinner, medium-color glaze around the outsides of the panels. Lay the dragging brush onto the wet glaze, starting at the top or side of each section, and pull it down through the glaze, pressing firmly as you go to create a delicate striped effect. Use it vertically between the panels and horizontally along the top and bottom.

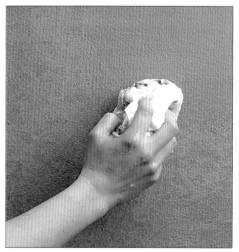

▲ Use a crumpled bag for a "leather" look.

9 Apply the darkest glaze, which can be quite thick, to the painted area below the chair rail. Turn a plastic grocery bag inside out (to keep printing ink from coming off on your work) and crumple it up in your hand. Dab this firmly all over the glaze.

10 Finally, give the chair rail and molding two coats of paint in a complementary color. Using a deep shade from the same color-mixing strip as your other colors creates a dramatic effect.

▲ Paint the molding in a contrasting color.

HINTS & TIPS

• Work quickly with glazing techniques or the glaze will start to dry and there will be a mark where you apply the next section.

• If the stripes fade out toward the end of the stroke when you are dragging, try applying more glaze. If this doesn't work, thin the glaze with mineral spirits.

For more wall projects see:
Checkered Walls pp94–7; Color-washed Wall pp124–5; A Bedroom Frieze pp172–4; Children's Balloon Stencils pp184–5; Marbled Bathroom pp200–1.

THE KITCHEN TENDS TO BE ONE OF
THE BUSIEST AND MOST SOCIABLE
ROOMS IN THE HOME. WHETHER IT
IS A NEIGHBOR DROPPING IN FOR A
CUP OF COFFEE OR GUESTS HELPING
WITH THE PREPARATIONS FOR AN
INFORMAL DINNER, YOUR KITCHEN
HAS TO BE ABLE TO MEET EVERY
SITUATION'S NEEDS. FURNITURE
AND ACCESSORIES HAVE TO EARN
THEIR PLACE HERE, BUT THERE IS
NO REASON WHY THEY SHOULD
NOT BE EYE-CATCHING AS WELL.
THIS CHAPTER PROVIDES PLENTY
OF IDEAS FOR PAINTED PIECES THAT
WILL ADD WARMTH AND BEAUTY
TO THE HEART OF YOUR HOME.

Kitchen Projects

Kitchen Accessories

WHEN WANDERING AROUND a yard sale or secondhand store, objects such as these seem to be everywhere, and even if you have discarded something similar yourself only a couple of weeks before, the urge to buy can be overwhelming. It must be the lure of pine, which always looks attractive, but particularly when you evoke its Scandinavian connections. This is exactly what has been done with these pine pieces, which are decorated with a soft, dusty turquoise—a color that turns up time and time again on old Swedish furniture.

Pine Shelf

❖ YOU WILL NEED ❖

Wood filler

Palette knife

Medium- and fine-grit sandpaper

Tack cloth

Gouache paints in ultramarine, lemon yellow, and raw umber

Glass jar

Old tablespoon

White latex paint

Two 1½" (4cm) household paintbrushes

Clear matte polyurethane varnish

Paper

Pencil

Artist's paintbrush

Gouache or acrylic paints, in various shades, for applying the design

1 The amount of preparation you need to do will depend on the condition of your shelf. This shelf was obviously once painted white and has survived a half-hearted attempt to strip it. It has also been kicked around and there are several little cracks and holes. Fill these in with a fast-drying wood filler using the flexible blade of the palette knife, making it as smooth as you can. If your shelf is in better condition than this one, it may need no more than a wiping down to remove any dust and dirt.

2 Once the filler has completely dried, rub it down first with medium- and then with fine-grit sandpaper. Then wipe the entire surface with a tack cloth to leave it smooth and dust-free.

3 To mix this subtle shade of turquoise, squeeze about 1" (2.5cm) of ultramarine gouache paint into the bottom of a glass jar, then add a little dot of lemon yellow. Mix together with an old tablespoon—at this stage you will have a very bluey green. Add just a touch of raw umber and a little water, then gradually spoon in white latex paint, mixing it in until the shade begins to look right.

4 Once you are happy with the color, add more water until the paint is about the consistency of light cream—this will give the shelf a faded look when the paint dries.

▲ Fill any cracks and sand before painting.

5 Apply a coat of the turquoise paint mixture over the whole shelf. If your shelf is in fairly good condition, one coat will be enough, and the color will look effective with some of the woodgrain showing through. If your shelf is quite rough, however, or if you have had to fill it extensively, you will need to give it a second coat, after the first one has dried, to cover up its worst features.

6 Bookshelves can be difficult to decorate, since most of the surfaces are normally covered by books and the ends are often obscured by being positioned up against a wall. With this shelf, however, you can decorate both ends so that the design is visible even if one end is hung against a wall. Trim the front edges in a complementary shade to add some color to the overall design, wherever the shelf is to be placed.

▲ Paint a contrasting border along the edges.

7 If you not very confident about painting your design freehand directly on the latex coat, apply a coat of clear matte varnish to your shelf at this point. Later, if you do happen to make a mistake, you can easily wash the paint off, using a little liquid detergent and some steel wool, without disturbing the base coat underneath. However, if you are skilled and confident enough to take freehand painting in stride, you can paint directly on the latex base coat with gouache or acrylic paints.

8 Practice your design on paper first until you feel reasonably confident about putting the design on the shelf freehand. Pine objects look great when decorated with simple folk art designs, so aim for a spontaneous, unsophisticated look. If you are taking your design from a plate or other object, you will need to make some scale drawings on paper in order to work out exactly how it will fit into the space at the end of the shelf.

9 Once you have found an arrangement that you like, lightly pencil a few basic guidelines on the shelf and then copy the design from the plate freehand, using simple brushstrokes. If you have varnished your shelf first, you will need to use acrylic paints for this stage; gouache paint does not cover well over varnish and is easily removed by subsequent washing.

10 Once you have decorated both ends of the shelf to your satisfaction (remember, they do not have to be identical because they cannot be seen at the same time), choose one of the dominant colors from the design and use it to paint a contrasting border along the front edges of the shelf.

11 Set aside until the paint has dried thoroughly. Finally, give the shelf a coat of clear matte polyurethane varnish all over to protect your design from wear and tear.

HINTS & TIPS

• When sketching guidelines on the shelf, keep them to a minimum or you will lose the fluidity of your design.

• Make sure you mix enough of the latex base coat to do the whole shelf twice if necessary; you may find it difficult to match the shade if you have to mix extra paint up.

For more freehand projects see:
Color-washed Oak Sideboard pp98–9; Tartan-band Dining Table pp100–101; Freehand-painted Tables pp110–12; Cups and Saucers Chair pp146–7; Painted China pp152–4; Hand-printed Blanket Chest pp164–6; Hand-painted Chest pp206–7; Painted Frames pp232–3.

Pine Spice Rack

Hand painting this plain pine spice rack will add a touch of individuality to your kitchen.

❖ YOU WILL NEED ❖

Materials as for pine shelf on page 138.

1 This spice rack was in good condition and only needed a light sanding with fine-grit paper. Paint it with the latex mixture as before, but leave the drawers and jars unpainted, except for their knobs and a little trim around the tops. Varnish before applying the design.

▲ Adapt the design to fit the space available.

2 Take the design from the same source as the pine shelf, practicing it on paper as before. It will need adapting for the long, narrow space available. Once you are satisfied, pencil some guidelines on the rack and paint the design. Once dry, give the whole thing a final coat of matte polyurethane varnish.

For more freehand projects see:
Color-washed Oak Sideboard pp98–9; Tartan-band Dining Table pp100–101; Freehand-painted Tables pp110–12; Cups and Saucers Chair pp146–7; Painted China pp152–4; Hand-printed Blanket Chest pp164–6; Hand-painted Chest pp206–7; Painted Frames pp232–3.

Pine Spoon Holder

Fine steel wool

Hot, soapy water

Cotton swabs

Bleach

Lint-free cloth

Wood filler

Palette knife

Medium- and fine-grit sandpaper

Tack cloth

Gouache paint in ultramarine, lemon yellow, and raw umber

Glass jar and old tablespoon

White latex paint

Two 1½" (4cm) household paintbrushes

Clear matte polyurethane varnish

Paper and pencil

Artist's paintbrush

Acrylic paints in various colors, for applying the design

1 This spoon holder needed a lot more preparation than the shelf or the spice rack because it was greasy and stained with ink. To remove the grease, scrub it well with fine steel wool and hot, soapy water. However, if you have to give a wooden item a thorough cleaning in this way, try not to make the wood too wet as this will raise the grain and leave you with a great deal of sanding to do.

2 To remove the ink, use a cotton swab dipped in bleach—this will take time and patience. Once the spoon holder is sufficiently clean, wipe the whole thing down with a cool, damp lint-free cloth and set it aside until dry.

3 Fill any holes with wood filler and a palette knife. Then rub the spoon holder down with some fine- or medium-grit sandpaper and remove the dust with a tack cloth.

4 Apply two coats of the latex mixture as for the shelf and spice rack on pages 138–9. Leave some of the pine showing so it matches the spice rack. Map out the design and varnish the spoon holder before applying the design. Finally, paint it to match the other two items and apply a coat of clear matte varnish.

For more freehand projects see:
Color-washed Oak Sideboard pp98–9.

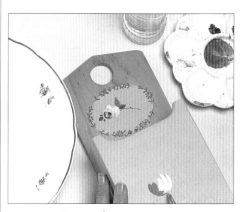

▲ Use single brushstrokes to apply the design.

Key Holder

Fine steel wool

Methylated spirits

Fine-grit sandpaper

Tack cloth

Two 1" (2.5cm) household paintbrushes

Brunswick green enamel paint

Piece of chalk

Paper and pencil

No. 3 artist's brush (sable or synthetic)

Small pots of enamel paint in crimson, bright red, yellow, white, lime green, and tan

Gloss polyurethane varnish

3 screw-in brass hooks

1 Remove the mirror and hooks from the key holder and wipe the base with fine steel wool and methylated spirits to clean it. If the varnish on the base is shiny and undamaged, lightly sand it with fine-grit paper to roughen it enough so that the enamel will adhere well.

2 Go over the key holder with a tack cloth. Apply two coats of Brunswick green enamel paint, allowing 6 hours between each coat.

3 Work out your design on a piece of paper. Use the chalk to mark circles on the dry enamel as a guide to where the flowers will go. Use the artist's paintbrush and bright enamel colors to paint the roses, then carefully paint the leaves and the daisy centers. Add petals to the roses and allow to dry overnight.

4 Varnish the key holder, let it dry for 24 hours, then apply another coat. After the varnish is dry, clean and replace the mirror and treat the revamped key holder to three shiny, new brass hooks.

For more freehand projects see:
Color-washed Oak Sideboard pp98–9; Tartan-banded Dining Table pp100–1; Cups and Saucers Chair pp146–7.

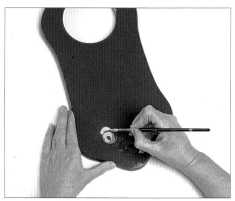

▲ Paint each petal with a single brushstroke.

Lined Clock Case

THIS ATTRACTIVE CLOCK CASE has been made from old pine floorboards. The cardboard clock face is transformed using a *craquelure* technique. A simple découpaged pear motif has been used for the door and three tones of yellow chosen to complement this. The middle tone is a creamy yellow—white has been added to the central panel and raw umber pigment to the darker panel surround. A lining technique has been used here. A sword liner brush is ideal for this because it holds the right amount of paint for a continuous flow. It can also produce a variety of line sizes, depending on the pressure used when applying paint. Sword liners are available from art-supply and craft stores, or you can use a 1/4" (6mm) long-haired flat artist's brush instead.

❖ YOU WILL NEED ❖

Medium-grit sandpaper

Wood filler

Palette or putty knife

Latex or traditional paint in three shades

Household paintbrushes

Pencil

Ruler

Sword liner or 1/4" (6mm) artist's brush

Fruit print, for découpage

Manicure scissors

Paper glue

Glue brush

Sponge

Satin water-based acrylic varnish

Varnish brush

Two-part *craquelure*

Paper towels

Raw umber pigment

Matte oil-based varnish

Brown wax

Soft cloth

The clock's simple lines call for unfussy decoration.

1 Rub down the clock case with medium-grit sandpaper, then fill all cracks with wood filler. Apply a coat of the middle tone of paint to all the surfaces except the door panel, then paint the central panel with the lightest tone. When dry, paint the panel surround with the darkest color.

2 Using a pencil and ruler, lightly mark the clock where you want to position the narrow lines. Load a sword liner with the dark paint color and drag the brush along the pencil line, applying an even pressure the whole time.

▲ Apply the darkest tone to the panel surround.

3 Cut out the print with manicure scissors. Glue it to the panel and wipe off excess glue with a sponge. When dry, go over any white edges on the cutout with the pencil.

4 Apply two coats of acrylic varnish over the entire case. Then apply 8 to 10 more coats over the découpaged panel, letting each coat to dry before applying the next. Use one coat on the clock face, then apply the two-part *craquelure*.

5 When the second coat is dry, use paper towels to rub in the raw umber pigment. Seal the surface with a matte oil-based varnish the next day. Then apply a brown wax, again using paper towels, over the entire surface, including the clock face. Let dry, then polish with a soft cloth.

For more case projects see:
Color-washed Oak Sideboard pp98–9.

▲ Disguise any white edges with a pencil.

Painted Chairs

TRANSFORMING A CHAIR can make a refreshing change to a kitchen. Simplicity is the key to success for both of the techniques shown below as they follow the rule—do not cover a chair in fussy details. In the first project, little pigs in a pale shade are painted on a strongly colored background, making an ideal rustic stencil design for a chair in a country-style kitchen. Choice of color is important when planning the second project, a crackle effect. This eye-catching, elegant design in French blue and pale cream is suitable for a sophisticated setting.

Stenciled Pigs Chair

❖ YOU WILL NEED ❖

Sandpaper

Tack cloth

1" (2.5cm) household paintbrush

Gouache paint in teal and oyster pearl

Card stock, acetate, or stencil film

Fine-point permanent marker

Craft knife and cutting mat

Masking tape

Stencil brush

Paper towels

Satin varnish and brush

1 Sand the chair to remove any old paint or varnish and create a smooth surface. Wipe with the tack cloth to remove all dust.

2 Using the household paintbrush, apply two coats of teal paint and allow it to dry.

3 Tape the acetate over the patterns on page 246 and carefully trace the designs with the marker. Using the craft knife and cutting mat, cut out the design.

4 Position the pig stencil in the center of the chair back and use masking tape to hold it in position. Dip your stencil brush into the oyster pearl paint and then dab it onto the paper towels to eliminate any excess paint. Apply paint over the stencil, working in a circular motion to build up as much color as required.

5 Repeat step 4 on the front of the seat and add hearts to the rungs of the back and the front legs.

6 Allow to dry for 24 hours. Apply two or three coats of varnish and allow to dry.

For more stenciling projects see:
Stenciled Cane Chair pp160–1; Frottaged and Stenciled Screen pp167–9; Stenciled Newspaper Rack pp238–9.

Crackled Chair

❖ YOU WILL NEED ❖

Sandpaper

Tack cloth

1" (2.5cm) household paintbrush

Gouache paint in oyster pearl and French blue

One-part crackle glaze

Satin varnish and brush

1 Sand the chair to create a smooth surface. Wipe it with the tack cloth to remove all dust particles.

2 Using the household paintbrush, apply two coats of oyster pearl paint and allow it to dry.

3 Then, use a clean household paintbrush to apply a smooth, even coat of the one-part crackle glaze over the dry oyster pearl base coat. Let it dry until it is smooth and no longer tacky to the touch (this will take approximately 20 minutes to 1 hour).

4 Use French blue paint to apply an even coat of paint over the dry crackle glaze. It will begin to take effect right away. Do not re-work the final coat of paint because this will ruin the effect.

5 Allow the paint to dry for at least 24 hours. Then apply two or three coats of satin varnish, letting each coat dry before applying the next. For a smooth finish, lightly sand after each of the first two coats.

For more crackle projects see:
Aged Rustic Chair pp212–13.

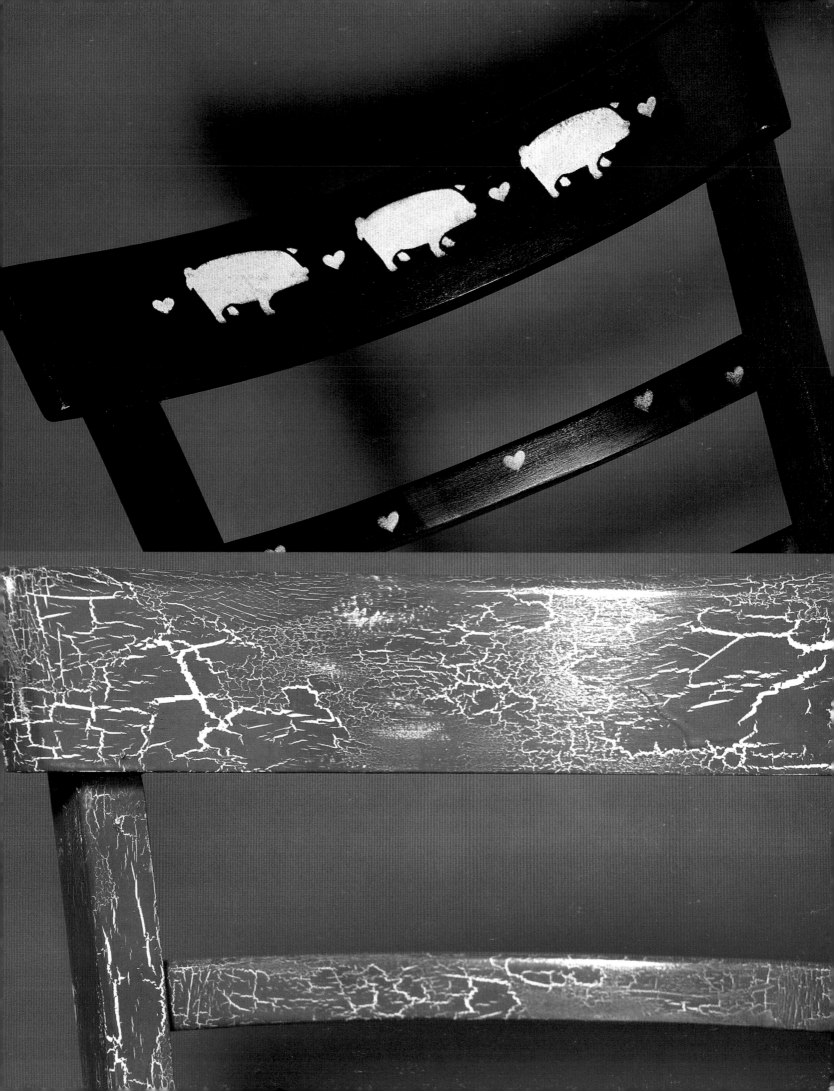

Cups and Saucers Chair

THIS IS THE PERFECT KITCHEN chair with its cup and saucer design. All you need to re-create this work of art is a sturdy chair that has been stripped down to the raw wood, some paints, and the patterns in this book (see page 246). If desired, the chair can be varnished or waxed to give a sturdier, more hard-wearing finish. This cup and saucer design was inspired by 18th-century Minton pattern books, which depicted designs for tea bowls and saucers. After about 1800, the tea bowls were replaced by the new fashion of the time—cups with handles.

❖ YOU WILL NEED ❖

Medium-grit andpaper

Tack cloth

Household paintbrushes

Latex paint in smoked pearl, warm white, carbon black, yellow oxide, and ultra deep blue

Cloth

Tracing paper

Design for your stencil (see page 246)

Pencil

Carbon paper

Stylus or ballpoint pen

Crackle glaze

Sword liner brush

Satin varnish or beeswax

1 Sand the chair with sandpaper to create a smooth surface and then wipe it with the tack cloth. Paint the chair with watery, warm white paint. Apply one section at a time and wipe with a cloth to give an uneven effect.

2 Trace the outline of one of the cups and saucers (see page 246) onto tracing paper. Then, using carbon paper and the stylus or ballpoint pen, transfer it to the back of the chair. Paint the cup and saucer shape in smoked pearl. Next, apply the crackle glaze to the cup and saucer shapes and let it dry. Paint warm white paint (with a little water added) over the crackle glaze in order to activate it.

3 Place the traced design back on to the chair, slip the carbon paper under it, and again trace the cup and saucer shape. Mix smoked pearl with a touch of yellow oxide and carbon black, and add shading to the cup and saucer. Add the lines and decoration in ultra deep blue with a sword liner brush.

4 Using ultra deep blue, draw freehand lines around the back struts and the edge of the top of the seat. The chair can be varnished with a clear varnish or waxed with beeswax or furniture wax.

For more chair projects see:
Decorative Chairs pp102–3; Spray-painted Table and Chairs pp204–5; Aged Rustic Chair pp212–13.

A Paint the shape in smoked pearl.

B Apply the crackle and let it dry.

C Activate the crackle with warm white paint.

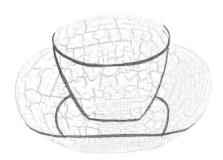

D Trace the shape with carbon paper.

E Add the shading to the relevant areas.

F Add the decoration in ultra deep blue.

A Kitchen Frieze

SINCE IT IS RARELY advisable to hang wallpaper in an area where steam and heat are produced, the hard-wearing finish of stenciling is ideal for adding some life and interest to the kitchen. However, restrict stencils to surfaces that are receptive to paint if you want the designs to survive. Paint on modern laminates will not look good for long, and painting on ceramic tiles should only be attempted with specialist tile paint, which is unsuitable for stenciling. Most wood-faced cabinets will, however, take stenciled designs that will hold up well if properly varnished. The stenciled kitchen shown here uses an appropriately culinary stencil with a bold outline and simple shapes. The technique and design appear both around the walls and on objects in the room.

❖ YOU WILL NEED ❖

Design to copy

Artist's acrylic paint in assorted colors

Household paintbrushes

Tracing paper

Pencil

Card stock, acetate, or stencil film

Craft knife and cutting mat

Nonpermanent adhesive spray or masking tape

Bathroom sponge

Heat-resistant varnish

---

1 When you have chosen your stencil design, photocopy or draw it to the size required. Paint the design in the colors that you wish your final stencils to be. Follow this "master" design when applying the stencils.

2 Trace the master onto a piece of card, acetate, or stencil film and use a craft knife and cutting mat to cut the outline shape of the design.

3 Hold the stencil firmly in position with nonpermanent adhesive spray or masking tape. Then, using a slightly damp bathroom sponge, apply a rough-textured coat of pale ocher acrylic paint.

4 When the base coat is dry, add the detail freehand with a paintbrush. Following your master, color the various different elements in the design using watered-down acrylic paint over the ocher base. Do not worry about being too precise when painting in the detail— the rustic look of this design is actually improved and enhanced by some irregularity and roughness.

5 Stencils on a kitchen wall should always be varnished. Here, the stenciled baskets received several coats of varnish, and the stencil design on the tray was treated with several coats of a heat-resistant varnish to protect it from hot mugs or plates.

For more stenciling projects see:
Stenciled Balustrade pp130–2; Stenciled Pigs Chairs pp144–5; Stenciled Cane Chair pp160–1; Frottaged and Stenciled Screen pp167–9; A Bedroom Frieze pp172–4; Cherub Wardrobe pp180–3; Children's Balloon Stencils pp184–5; Mexican-style Bathroom pp190–2; Fish Stencil Shower Glass pp193–5; Repeating Border and Dragged Stripes pp208–11; Poppies Picture Frame pp236–7; Stenciled Newspaper Rack pp238–9; Stenciled Mirror Frame pp242–3; Monogrammed Box pp244–5.

▲ Sponge on the ocher base coat.

▲ Follow the master design.

▲ Apply heat-resistant varnish to a tray.

Ivy-stamped Chair

THIS RUSTIC CHAIR was given an aging paint finish before the stamps were applied. The design was taken directly from nature—a sprig of ivy was picked from the garden and the stamp was made out of a potato. The chair was purchased flat-packed and assembled prior to painting. When an item like this is painted after it has been assembled, the paint helps to fill some of the gaps between the pieces of wood. Do not prime the chair because you do not want the white or pink color of the primer to show through when you rub away the paint. Oil-based paint will not dry well without a primer base, so add few drops of drying oil to the paint.

YOU WILL NEED

Spirit-based wood stain

Household paintbrushes

Medium- and fine-grit sandpaper or sanding block

Ivy leaf

Craft knife

Potato

Small artist's brush

Brown paint

Oil-based varnish

1 The assembled chair was stained all over with a spirit-based wood stain. This is purely a stain and not a colored varnish. The stained chair was allowed to dry overnight and then painted with two coats of green-gray eggshell-finish paint. As the paint is applied, it begins to take on an aged appearance as some of the stain mixes with the paint. This mixing of the stain cannot be controlled other than by applying additional coats of paint. Use a lighter shade than required on the finished item.

2 When the paint is dry, continue the aging process by rubbing back the paint to the stained bare wood first with medium and then fine sandpaper or a sanding block. Concentrate on areas where the chair would have worn if it were old, such as on the edges of the legs and seat. Don't worry at this stage if you rub right through the stain to the new wood.

3 The final aging is achieved by brushing more wood stain onto the chair and then stroking over the wet stain with a clean, dry brush, working in the direction of the grain.

4 To make the ivy stamp, cut around the outline of an ivy leaf with a craft knife onto half a potato. Then cut away the background so that the design is raised. Vegetables give off water so blot the potato with tissue. This chair was printed with three different-sized leaves and the stems were hand painted using a small artist's brush and brown paint.

5 Finally, varnish the chair with a couple of coats of oil-based varnish to protect the wood and to maintain the distressed look.

For more stamping projects see:
Stamped Artichoke Chair pp102–3; Sponge-stamped Floor pp128–9; Stamped CD Box pp240–1.

▲ Stain the chair with wood stain.

▲ Sand the chair to make it look old.

▲ Apply wet stain with a clean, dry brush.

Painted China

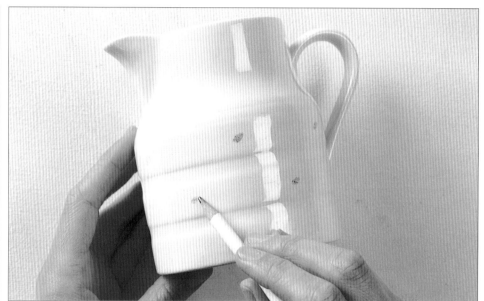

THINK TWICE BEFORE abandoning your old, dull crockery in favor of something bright and new, because you can completely rejuvenate your ceramics using special paint. As with painted glasses (see pages 155–7), simple designs usually look most effective. For example, bold spots and stripes work well, as do simple flowers and leaves. You could even choose a design that echoes those found around the kitchen or dining room already—on patterned curtains, tiles, or ceramics. These designs are applied to white china, but painting on any plain pastel-colored crockery would also give attractive results. However, be sure that the color scheme you choose matches the base color of the china. You can check this by experimenting with a test piece.

❖ YOU WILL NEED ❖

Warm, soapy water

Methylated spirits

Soft cloth

Paper or test piece of china

Pencil

Paintbrush

Old plate

Ceramic paint in various colors

Damp cloth

▲ Use a pencil to lightly draw marks that will serve as a guide.

1 Wash and wipe dry the china that is to be painted. Then wipe it with a cloth soaked in a little methylated spirits in order to remove any traces of grease.

2 On a piece of paper or with a test piece of china, work out your design before you begin to paint. Then, mark the design onto the china very faintly with a pencil to act as a guide as you work. The pencil marks will be covered over when you apply the painted design.

3 In order to achieve the desired colors, use a paintbrush to mix the various paints on an old plate, of the same color as the china that is to be decorated. You can also use the plate to practice painting your design. This experimenting will allow you to judge the success of your design and make any adjustments. It will help you to decide how much paint you need to apply in order to achieve the effect you would like.

▲ Choose ceramic paint in various colors.

▲ Mix the paints on an old plate.

▲ Do not overfill your brush when applying paint circles to your ceramics.

• Ceramic paints that are baked in the oven will be more durable than those that are simply left to dry.

• Painting is a great way to personalize a piece of china, such as a child's breakfast bowl or mom's special mug. Items such as these make very special gifts.

• You could use different paint colors to indicate different contents in kitchenware; blue for salt, red for pepper, and yellow for vinegar in a cruet set, for example.

For more freehand projects see:
Color-washed Oak Sideboard pp98–9; Tartan-band Dining Room Table pp100–1; Freehand-painted Tables pp110–12; Kitchen Accessories pp138–41; Cups and Saucers Chair pp146–7; Hand-printed Blanket Chest pp164–6; Hand-painted Chest pp206–7.

4 Apply the paint sparingly if you are painting circles, or with long, even strokes if you are using stripes as decoration. Do not apply additional paint to an area you have just painted because this may cause smudges or smears. Instead, wait for the paint to dry completely and then apply another coat.

5 If you make a mistake or you are not happy with the result of your design, simply wipe the paint away using a damp cloth, then try again.

6 Once the design is complete, allow the piece to dry, or bake it in the oven according to the paint manufacturer's instructions.

▲ Wipe away any unwanted areas of paint.

Brilliant Painted Glass

MANY KITCHENS house various shelves and ledges that, unless you are incredibly self-disciplined, can end up covered in all sorts of cooking equipment and general household clutter. The best way to avoid this problem is to put the kitchen surfaces to work for storage and display. So, make a determined effort to clear away all those odds and ends from your kitchen shelves and replace them with this useful and attractive glassware, which will brighten up the room and keep clutter at bay. The simplest patterns are often the most effective and will add decorative splashes of color to a dull shelf or the kitchen table. Choose colors and a pattern or design that coordinate well with your kitchen decor or your table setting.

❖ YOU WILL NEED ❖

Warm, soapy water

Methylated spirits

Soft cloth

Colored pens

White paper

Piece of old glassware (optional)

Old plate

Translucent glass paints

Fine artist's brush

Cotton swabs

Damp cloth (optional)

▲ Work out the design on a piece of paper.

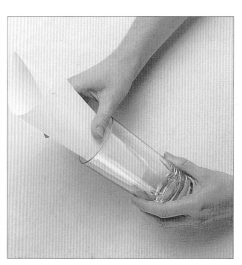

▲ Put a piece of white paper into the glass.

1 Wash and dry the glasses thoroughly, then wipe them gently with a soft cloth and a little methylated spirits to remove any stubborn traces of grease.

2 Work out your chosen design and color scheme with colored pens on a sheet of white paper. You do not need to be a great artist to do this because you will find that even simple, random designs will produce quite stunning effects. If possible, it is also a good idea to practice on an old piece of glassware before you begin.

3 Before you start to paint, put a piece of white paper or a crumpled white tissue into the glass—this will allow you to see your design more easily as you work. You may also find it helpful to work on a plain white surface, such as white paper or cardboard.

4 Using an old white plate as a palette, mix up small amounts of the glass paint in order to achieve the colors that you need for your designs. However, do not mix too much paint at once because it will dry quite quickly while you work and will be wasted.

▲ Mix the desired paint colors.

155

5 Apply the paint carefully using a fine paintbrush. Take care not to apply too much paint as this will cause it to dry unevenly or to drip (you can dab the paintbrush on a piece of scrap paper first to remove any excess). However, too little paint will cause brushstrokes to show.

6 Do not worry if you make a mistake. You can simply neaten edges with a damp cotton swab. If all else fails and you need to start again, you can wipe off the wet paint with a damp cloth.

▲ Apply the paint with a fine paintbrush.

▲ Remove unwanted paint with a damp cotton swab.

For more glass painting projects see:
Painted Decanter and Glasses pp92–3;
Fish Stencil Shower Glass pp193–5.

The bedroom should be
a sanctuary—calm, quiet,
and relaxing. It is also a place
where you should feel free
to reflect your personal style
and turn your dreams into
reality. Add some touches of
comfort and luxury with a
few exquisite accessories, or
take a flight of fantasy and
transform an uninspiring piece
of furniture into a thing of
beauty and elegance.

Bedroom Projects

Stenciled Cane Chair

THIS LITTLE CHAIR is covered in the kind of weave often mistakenly labeled as Lloyd Loom. Whatever its real name, its smooth surface is far more amenable to stenciling than the genuine article. Unfortunately, this specimen had been smothered in black paint, which was painted on rather than sprayed, so the weave was completely clogged. If you find something in this weave that is still in its original state, it will look a lot better if you spray it or brush on several diluted coats of paint rather than brushing on two or three layers straight from the can.

❖ YOU WILL NEED ❖

Oil-based paint in color of your choice

Tape measure

Drawing paper

Pencil

Design from fabric or source of your choice

Masking tape

Tracing paper

Technical drawing pen or fine-tip permanent maker

Card stock, acetate, or stencil film

Craft knife and cutting mat

Acrylic craft paints

Saucer

Stencil brush

Scrap paper

Warm, soapy water

The chair had been thickly painted in black, and needed several coats of cream paint to cover it up.

1. Measure the area that you want the design to occupy on the chair. On a piece of drawing paper, draw a shape slightly larger than you want the finished stencil to be and then draw the design within the shape, copying from your source and simplifying the shapes.

2. Tape a piece of tracing paper over your drawing and, using a technical drawing pen, trace the design, refining and simplifying it as you go. Tape the tracing onto a work surface, then tape the stencil film over it, matte side up. Using the same pen, trace the design onto the film.

3. Lay the plastic shiny side up on the cutting mat. Using a craft knife, and working as accurately as possible, cut out the stencil. When you are finished, check to make sure that there are no jagged edges. Try the stencil out on a piece of scrap paper to see if it needs any final adjustments.

4. Measure the back of the chair and lightly mark the center. You will need to use the stencil twice on the chair back (the right way on one side of the midline and flipped over on the other). Fix the stencil in position with masking tape.

5. Pour a little of the acrylic craft paint into a saucer and take some of it up on the end of the stencil brush. Dab the brush onto a piece of scrap paper until you have worked most of the paint off—the less paint you have on the brush, the better.

6. Dab the brush onto your stencil, using your free hand to hold the adjacent edges of the stencil down. You can graduate the color on the roses and leaves by using different shades of green and pink.

7. Remove the stencil and wash off the paint with warm, soapy water. Dry it and tape it opposite the first design, in reverse. Complete the second side to match the first. You can also use part of the stencil to make a motif at the base of the chair.

For more chair projects see:
Decorative Chairs pp102–3; Painted Chairs pp144–7; Ivy-stamped Chair pp150–1.

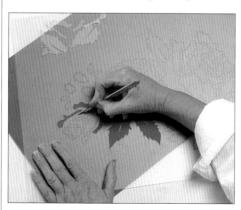
▲ Use a very sharp knife to cut out the stencil.

▲ Hold the stencil firmly in place as you paint.

Marbled Dressing Table

THIS CLASSIC KIDNEY–SHAPED dressing table came from a flea market. It was covered in layers of thick white paint, which needed to be professionally stripped. When the dressing table returned from the strippers, the mirror frames had been reduced to a bundle of sticks, which then had to be repinned by a picture framer. The main body was then painted in white eggshell, and a range of soft pinks were used to create the faux marbling effect on the top. Frills and curtains in a floral print were added to complete the feminine effect.

❖ YOU WILL NEED ❖

Fine- and super-fine-grit sandpaper

Tack cloth

White primer

White eggshell paint

Mineral spirits

Two 1½" (4cm) household paintbrushes

Artist's oils in rose madder, cadmium yellow, and raw umber

3 small nonplastic containers

Transparent oil glaze

Piece of white paper

Lint-free cloth

Artist's paintbrush (sable or synthetic mixture)

Natural-bristle softener brush

Clear polyurethane satin varnish

Clean cloth

1 Rub down the table with fine-grit sandpaper to as smooth a finish as possible. Remove any dust with a tack cloth, then apply a coat of white primer and allow to dry.

2 Lightly rub down the primer with the fine-grit sandpaper and tack the surface again. Slightly thin some eggshell paint with mineral spirits. Apply three or four coats of eggshell, letting each coat dry, rubbing down with super-fine-grit sandpaper and removing dust with a tack cloth between coats.

3 Using artist's oil paints and white eggshell paint, mix up three color shades (pink in this case) to match the fabric. The darkest shade will be used for the marble veins.

4 Mix the first two colors in separate containers and dissolve them with enough mineral spirits to give a creamy consistency. Gradually add the transparent oil glaze and stir it into the mixture. Finally, stir in the rest of the mineral spirits to produce a mix that is fluid and looks transparent when brushed onto white paper, but that is not so thin that it does not hold its pattern and shape when ragged onto a surface.

5 Paint irregular patches of one color glaze on the top of the table. Partially fill the open areas with similar patches of the second glaze. Leave some of the white base coat showing through. While the glaze is still wet, take a crumpled piece of lint-free cloth and press it firmly and quickly all over the glazed area.

6 Using an artist's paintbrush, loosely add the darkest color to make the veining. For a more realistic effect, be sure that the veins

▲ Paint on the "marble" veins.

travel diagonally and either begin or finish on the edge of the piece or where they connect with each other. Use a softener brush to dust the veins lightly and soften the effect. Allow to dry for 24 hours, then apply a coat of clear polyurethane satin varnish.

7 Paint the mirror frames with irregular patches of the first two glazes. Dab firmly with a clean cloth to leave the glaze mainly in the molding. Varnish when dry.

For more marbling projects see:
Marbled Bathroom pp200–1; Marbled Pot pp214–15.

▲ Rag the tabletop to create a random effect.

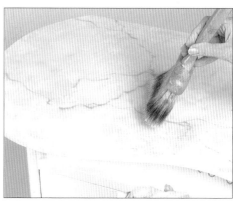
▲ Soften the effect with a softener brush.

Hand-printed Blanket Chest

PAINTED BETROTHAL CHESTS were traditional in Europe for centuries and they would often include the bride's initials and the date of marriage. Although the design of this project is not traditional, the use of a painted panel, the oak-leaf motif, and the printing technique are. Today, a blanket chest would make an original personalized wedding gift or could be adapted to make a lovely birth

or christening present, by varying the coloring and decorating the chest with the child's initials and date of birth. Draw around paint cans to get the curves for the template and make the oak-leaf print by drawing the shape onto a sponge and cutting it out with a craft knife. You can make the gold paint yourself—use a deep gold bronzing powder and an artist's acrylic medium to get the shade and degree of luster that you want.

❖ YOU WILL NEED ❖

Rubber gloves

Soft cloths

Dark brown French enamel varnish or water-based wood stain and clear shellac

Liquid wax

Brush for applying wax

Latex or traditional paint in 2 colors

Household paintbrushes

Water-soluble pencil

Cardboard

Ruler

Craft knife and cutting mat

Flexible masking tape

00-grade steel wool

Medium-grit sandpaper

Template for design (see page 246)

Small, soft bath sponge

Plate

Gold paint

Transfer paper

Brown paste wax

This stenciling project will enable you to personalize furniture such as this chest.

1 The first thing that you need to do is stain and seal the chest. Make sure that the chest is clean and dry before you begin. Wearing rubber gloves to protect your hands

▲ Rub French enamel varnish over the chest.

and using a soft cloth, stain the chest by rubbing French enamel varnish over the surface. This is shellac based and therefore seals the wood at the same time as staining it. On the other hand, a water-based wood stain and a coat of clear shellac would make an equally successful alternative. If you do choose to use a wood stain, make sure that you go over it thoroughly with clear shellac.

2 The next step is to apply liquid wax with a paintbrush over the areas that would naturally wear. This will ensure that the wood has a perfect finish. Then, when the chest is completely dry, paint it with your primary choice of color.

▲ Draw around the template to create the panel.

▲ Paint inside the panel in a different color.

▲ Dip the sponge in the paint and press on chest.

3 Draw your panel shape onto a piece of cardboard using a ruler to check your measurements. Cut the template using a craft knife, then put it in the center of the chest, and draw around it with a pencil.

4 Mask the panel, using flexible masking tape where necessary, and paint inside it with the second color of paint. Remove the tape and rub back the whole chest with steel wool and sandpaper.

5 Cut out an oak-leaf shape from the sponge using the template on page 246. Brush some of the darker-colored paint onto a plate, dip the sponge into this, and press it down flat along the edge of the blanket chest. Continue in this way until you have formed a border all the way around the edges. Print in gold over the existing oak leaves using the same process.

6 Transfer the initials and dates onto the central panel using transfer paper. Then, using a fine brush, paint a gold line over the darker color around the edge of the panel. Afterwards, carefully fill in the lettering and the date.

7 Apply a coat of brown paste wax to the blanket chest with a cloth; set it aside for about half an hour before you start to buff it. If you have used chalky paints, buffing will completely transform the appearance of the blanket chest and bring out all the richness of the paint colors.

HINTS & TIPS

• If you prefer, you can make a stencil of three or four oak leaves and cut them out to form a border. You will then need to mark horizontal and vertical lines onto the blanket chest with a pencil where you want to position the border. Begin stenciling by placing the center of the stencil in the middle of a penciled line and working outward from there.

For more freehand projects see:
Color-washed Oak Sideboard pp98–9, Tartan-band Dining Table pp100–1; Kitchen Accessories pp138–41; Hand-painted Chest pp206–7; Painted Tablecloth pp218–19; Painted Frames pp232–3.

▲ Carefully fill in the initials, date, and panel outline with gold paint.

Frottaged and Stenciled Screen

THE IDEA OF DECORATING a three-paneled screen can be quite daunting. Such screens are often decorated with fabric and the combination of paint effects used here will give the impression that it has been covered in trompe-l'oeil antique damask and surrounded by a ribbon border. Although there are numerous layers, each one is quick and simple. However, for the effect to be a success, it is absolutely essential that you mark the vertical lines accurately and make sure that the horizontal ones line up on each of the panels. The pattern here is adapted from an embossed wallpaper design and will fit screens of various sizes.

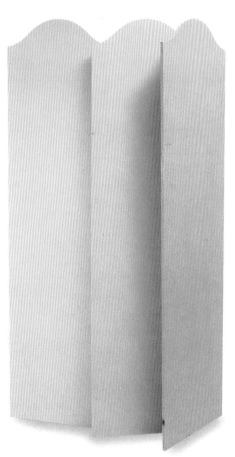

You can build a screen out of plywood or chipboard.

1 The first thing you need to do is create texture for the screen by applying two coats of yellow paint over the surface with a paint roller. Allow the first coat of paint to dry thoroughly before you start to apply the second. Yellow is a good color to use because it helps to disguise any thin area in the final gold layer, but can use another color if you prefer. Using a paintbrush, apply two coats of gold paint over the yellow, allowing the first coat to dry thoroughly before applying the second.

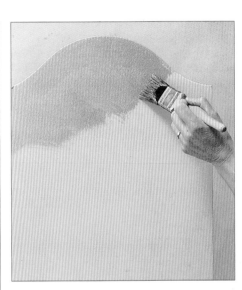

▲ Apply two layers of gold paint to the screen.

2 When the gold paint has dried thoroughly, paint the color that you have chosen over approximately one-third of one of the screen panels. You will find it easiest if you use a large, wide paintbrush for this.

▲ Use a wide paintbrush to apply the color.

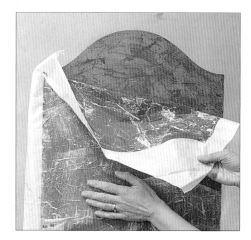

▲ Use tissue paper to create this textured effect.

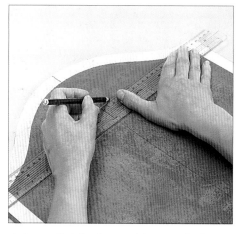

▲ Ensure that the lines match up perfectly.

▲ Paint a border of gold paint around the edge.

3 Immediately press a sheet of tissue paper against the wet surface of the screen, pressing it flat with your hand, then peel it off. This creates a textured effect, which will cover all the brush marks. This paint effect is known as frottage. Complete the rest of this panel and the other two panels in the same way.

4 Trace the pattern on page 247 onto stencil film with a pencil and mark the line down the middle of the stencil. Cut out the design, including the registration marks (the little diamond on each corner) with a craft knife, using a cutting mat or thick cardboard to protect your work surface. Stick masking tape around each panel, using flexible tape for the curved area at the top.

Draw a line down the center of each panel exactly in the middle. To do this, make a series of dots at regular intervals down the length of each panel, checking that the distance between the dot and the edge of the panel on one side is equal to the distance on the other side. Join up all the dots with a light pencil line using a long ruler or straightedge. You will find it easier if you lay each panel on a flat surface for measuring and marking.

5 Draw a line across one of the panels near the top. Make sure that it is horizontal by checking its position in relation to the line down the center, using a steel square. Place another panel level next to it and continue the line in exactly the same

position on this one, then finally do the same on the third panel.

6 Place the stencil in the position for starting, aligning the center of the stencil with the line down the middle of the screen. Secure with some masking tape and then draw a horizontal line on the stencil film to match that on the panel. This will allow you to ensure that the starting point is the same for each panel.

Dip the stencil brush into the gold paint and wipe off the excess on a paper towel. Dab the paint through the stencil, varying the amount that you use in order to give the design a faded appearance. Make sure that you dab a little paint through the diamond registration mark. You will need this in order to line up the next stencil. Do not worry that these registration marks will spoil your design because they will be lost in the overall effect of the paint. Move the stencil down the screen, lining up

▲ Dab gold paint through the stencil.

the diamonds at the top with the gold ones at the bottom of the previous stencil. Continue all the way down the panel and on the sides, matching up the registration marks. Stencil the pattern on all the panels in the same way.

7 Place a second row of masking tape just inside the existing tape before removing it and then brush gold paint around the edges of the screen. Use the paint sparingly, with the brush fairly dry, so that the red paint still shows through.

8 Rub the surface of the screen gently with a medium-grit sandpaper, then seal the screen by applying a coat of matte water-based varnish.

HINTS & TIPS

• The stenciled area is quite big and you will find it much faster to work with a large stencil brush. Try to find one that is not too close-textured for greater flexibility and ease of use. Alternatively, you can use a natural sponge or a brush. It is important to have plenty of paper towels handy for removing the excess paint.

• The color used here is red ocher, which looks very good with the gold, but deep shades of green or blue would also look extremely striking.

For more stenciling projects see:
Stenciled Balustrade pp130–2; A Kitchen Frieze pp148–9; Stenciled Cane Chair pp160–1; Stenciled Headboard pp170–1; A Bedroom Frieze pp172–4; Stenciled Animal Prints pp175–6; Children's Balloon Stencils pp184–5; Poppies Picture Frame pp236–7; Stenciled Newspaper Rack pp238–9.

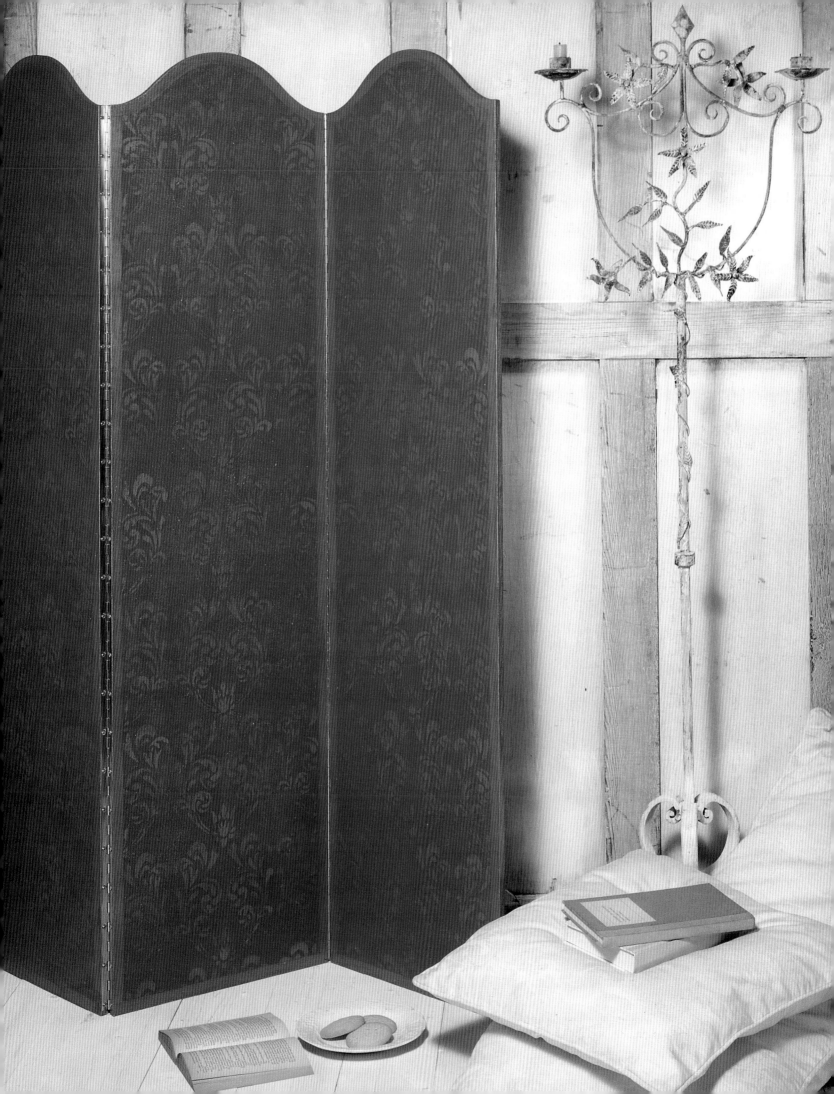

Stenciled Headboard

THE DESIGN USED FOR THIS old-fashioned headboard is a pretty, modern version of the French 18th-century pattern known as toile du Jouy. It is an intricate and delicate pattern, but the strong lines and emphatic shapes, together with the variety of separate motifs, have a great deal of scope. To add more interest to the design, a "drop shadow" effect was created by a lightly sponged application of a pale, warm gray. When this had completely dried, the design was stenciled in terra-cotta latex to match the fabric. The large design here offered plenty of opportunity for a range of techniques. Different densities of paint add interest and life to a pattern. Notice how effective using the same stencil twice can be in adding depth to the design.

❖ YOU WILL NEED ❖

A piece of plywood or chipboard

Screws

Paint in color to match wall

Tape measure

Plumb line

Pencil

Design for your stencil (see page 247)

Card stock, acetate, or stencil film

Craft knife and cutting mat

Warm-gray acrylic paint

Terra-cotta latex paint

Sponges

Fine paintbrush

Clear polyurethane varnish with yellow ocher

1 This headboard was made by cutting a piece of chipboard into a shape that complemented the motif. It was then screwed into the plaster and painted to match the wall.

2 Measure the central point of the headboard and suspend a plumb line from the top at this point and lightly mark a vertical line running down the center.

3 Note the height of the pillows and position the design around them. Losing the end of a design behind pillows looks informal, but if too much is obscured, it may just look messy.

4 Trace the template on page 247 onto acetate and cut out with a craft knife. Align the stencil with the center mark and then move it down and to the left. Apply warm-gray acrylic through the stencil using a sponge.

5 When the paint is dry, align the central line of the stencil to the center mark of the headboard and apply terra-cotta latex with a sponge.

6 Sharpen up the shapes with a fine paintbrush to give a highly polished finish.

7 Add a little yellow ocher to the varnish to give a mellow, antique effect. Apply two coats of varnish to protect the headboard from bumps and scrapes. If you are feeling adventurous, you can repeat the jug motif on the walls.

For more stenciling projects see:
Stenciled Balustrade pp130–2; A Kitchen Frieze pp148–9; Stenciled Cane Chair pp160–1; Frottaged and Stenciled Screen pp167–9; A Bedroom Frieze pp172–4; Stenciled Animal Prints pp175–7; Children's Balloon Stencils pp184–5; Poppies Picture Frame pp236–7; Stenciled Mirror Frame pp242–3; Monogrammed Box pp244–5.

▲ The jug motif was repeated on the walls.

▲ Check the alignment of the stencil.

▲ Position the design so it is not obscured.

A Bedroom Frieze

CONTINUING THE PATTERN of the curtains onto the plain walls by painting a stenciled border beneath the cornice is a good way of integrating the space in your bedroom. The colors of this stencil were taken from the curtains: beige, dark pink, light pink, and greenish gray. The design for the stencil was an amalgamation of several of the elements found in the curtain pattern. The upper half of the fruit bowl made a good starting point for the border. The grapes were left out because their pattern was too dense, which left a gap in the bottom corner. This was then filled by repeating a few of the flowers from the top of the design. The elegant curved bow was then added and the whole design simplified.

❖ YOU WILL NEED ❖

Tracing paper

Design for your stencil from fabric or source of your choice

Pencil

Latex paint in beige, dark pink, light pink, and greenish gray

3 small, nonplastic containers

Scrap paper

Card stock, acetate, or stencil film

Craft knife and cutting mat

Level

Nonpermanent adhesive spray

Sponges

1 Trace the elements in the curtain design that you want to incorporate into your stencil. Adapt and simplify as necessary.

2 Make the three paint colors you have chosen. Start by putting some of the base color (the beige color in the curtains in this case) into each of the three containers. To the first, gradually add a light pink and mix thoroughly until you achieve the shade you require; to the second, add greenish gray; and to the third, add a tiny amount of a dark pink paint.

3 Plan the colors of the design by painting onto a full-size photocopy of the stencil design. As well as marking where the colors will go, clearly mark the areas where the wall color is to be used as an element of the design. Some of the pattern elements here, such as the rim of the grapefruit and the highlights on the apple and the leaves, were created by leaving the beige base color blank. Bear in mind that light stenciling allows much of the base wall color to show through, which produces subtle variations of shade. Mark these areas on the design plan. For example, light shades of green and pink were created by applying them lightly over the base color. Other colors can also be created by applying one color on top of another.

▲ Plan the colors of the design on paper.

▲ Take your design from the curtain pattern.

▲ Trace and adapt the design.

▲ Mix the tints and try them out.

▲ Trace the outline of each color.

▲ Check the effect on a piece of paper.

• When mixing the wall paints, use the small color registration circles, found inside the seams of your curtain fabric, as a guide so that you can match the tones perfectly.

• If you work cleanly and methodically, there is no real limit to the amount of color you can use through one stencil.

For more stenciling projects see:
Stenciled Balustrade pp130–2; A Kitchen Frieze pp148–9; Stenciled Cane Chair pp160–1; Frottaged and Stenciled Screen pp167–9; A Bedroom Frieze pp172–4; Stenciled Animal Prints pp175–7; Children's Balloon Stencils pp184–5; Poppies Picture Frame pp236–7; Stenciled Mirror Frame pp242–3; Monogrammed Box pp244–5.

4 Break the final design down into three separate color stencils by tracing the outline of each area of color onto a separate sheet of tracing paper. Make sure that the center lines are accurately marked on each of the color tracings.

5 Transfer each color stencil and its center lines from the tracing paper onto a piece of card stock, acetate, or stencil film. Then, using a craft knife on a cutting mat, cut out the stencil pattern from each piece of card. Start by removing the smallest areas first to keep the stencil firm—always remember to cut away from your body.

6 Cut a V-shaped groove at either side of each piece of card along the horizontal center line. These grooves will enable you to line up the stencils accurately.

7 Check that the finished effect works before applying it to the wall—try each stencil out on a piece of paper and practice lining them up on top of each other.

8 Plan the position of the stencils on the wall. Draw a light pencil line to follow, using a level, and mark the position of each stencil.

9 Apply the first color with a sponge and mark the center of the stencil in pencil on the wall. This will enable you to position the other stencils accurately.

10 Allow the paint to dry completely before applying the next stencil color. When the stencils are completely dry, rub off the pencil lines.

▲ Make pencil marks on the wall to help you line up the stencils correctly.

Stenciled Animal Prints

ANIMAL PRINTS are very popular in today's fashion and are found more and more in the interiors of people's homes. They can be used on curtains, pillow cases and cushion covers, or throws to bring a sophisticated look, or an element of kitsch, to your bedroom. Combine them with themed accessories such as pictures of a sunset over the savannah or elephant ornaments to evoke an exciting African or Indian atmosphere. You can find leopard, zebra, giraffe, and tiger prints on many fabrics. Look around to find the texture and color of material that you like best. Imitation suede, mock satin, and even velvet are all suitable fabrics for stenciling animal prints. To fill a large area, simply work in sections, washing the stencils carefully between uses.

❖ YOU WILL NEED ❖

Fabric of your choice

Iron

Design for your stencil (see page 247) or design from source of your choice

Paper

Pencil

Fabric paint in sienna natural and black

Nonpermanent adhesive spray

Card stock, acetate, or stencil film

Permanent marker

Craft knife and cutting mat

Blotting paper

Two No. 2 stencil brushes

Palette

Paper towels

Clean cloth

1 Wash your chosen fabric in order to remove any residues that might react with the paint, then dry and iron the fabric so that it is free of creases.

2 To stencil the leopard print design, use a photocopier to enlarge the two templates on page 247 to the required size. Or, use another source such as a piece of material or a picture in a book as the starting point for your design.

3 Draw a template of the shapes on white paper and color as you want the final design to look using black and sienna fabric paint. When dry, spray nonpermanent adhesive onto the back of a piece of card stock, acetate, or stencil film and place it over the leopard design. Trace the outlines of the black shapes on the stencil film with a permanent marker.

4 Repeat with a second piece of card stock, acetate, or stencil film, this time tracing the sienna-colored elements of the design.

5 Peel each piece of stencil film off the paper, place it on a cutting mat and cut out the stencil design following the marker outlines with a craft knife. Cut away from your body as you work. Push out the cut pieces carefully (the film tears easily).

6 Place the fabric down flat on a piece of blotting paper and secure the first stencil on top using nonpermanent adhesive spray.

7 Dip the stencil brush into a small amount of sienna natural-fabric paint in your palette and dab off any excess onto paper towels. Apply the paint through the stencil, working gently in a circular motion.

▲ Copy the design from a piece of fabric.

▲ Cut out the stencil carefully.

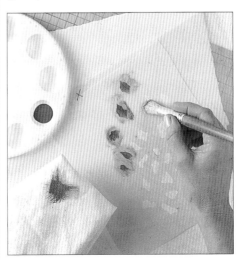

▲ Apply the paint through the first stencil.

For more stenciling projects see:
Stenciled Balustrade pp130–2; A Kitchen Frieze pp148–9; Stenciled Cane Chair pp160–1; Frottaged and Stenciled Screen pp167–9; Children's Balloon Stencils pp184–5; Poppies Picture Frame pp236–7; Monogrammed Box pp244–5.

▲ Apply the second color through the stencil.

8 Allow the paint to dry for a couple of hours, then carefully peel off the first stencil.

9 Place the second stencil on the painted fabric, aligning it carefully. Use black fabric paint and a clean stencil brush to apply the paint in the same way.

10 When you have finished, allow the paint to dry for a couple of hours and then peel the film away carefully.

11 Position the first stencil below or at the side of the completed section, leaving space for the black of the first stencil to show around the edges.

12 Paint the fabric in sections until it is completely covered with the pattern. To fill in small gaps, use just the dots from the first stencil. Allow the paint to dry— refer to the manufacturer's recommended drying times.

13 Most fabric paints have to be fixed by heat before they can be washed or dry-cleaned (check the label). Simply place a clean cloth over the completed stencil and heat-seal with a hot iron.

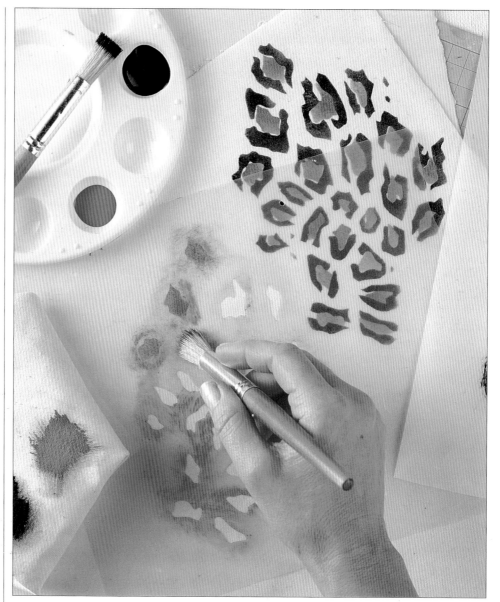

▲ Repeat the stencil until you achieve the desired pattern.

Antiqued Iron Bed Frame

Y OU MIGHT THINK that it is all very well to be tempted to buy an old jug from a secondhand store, because you know that prior to taking up pride of place on your dresser it will have a thorough dusting and washing. However, if the piece you intend to purchase is likely to be the weight of a pony and rusty besides, the idea of cleaning such a large object might not be so appealing. This project shows that with a little determination and some elbow grease, it is quite possible to rescue and revamp a large cast-iron bed frame, thus combining the elegance of a bygone era with the comfort and convenience of today's lifestyle.

❖ YOU WILL NEED ❖

Warm, soapy water and cloth or stiff brush

Cloth or scrub brush

Coarse- and medium-grit sandpaper

Household paintbrush

All-purpose acrylic primer or rustproofing primer

Latex paint in white, pink, and pistachio

2 fine artist's paintbrushes

Soft cloth

Raw umber paint pigment

Acrylic varnish

Long-haired soft dragging brush

Silver metallic paint

1 Remove the surface dust and dirt with a large bowl of warm, soapy water and a cloth or a stiff brush. Sand off any rust and old paintwork with coarse-grit sandpaper. Using a household paintbrush, apply a coat of all-purpose acrylic primer. If the frame is rusty, use a rustproofing primer. Allow to dry.

2 Paint a coat of white latex over the bed frame, watching out for any runs or drips. Let dry and apply a second coat if needed.

3 Using a fine artist's brush, pick out any details or ornamental features of the bed frame's design in pale pink latex paint. Then, using a soft cloth, rub away some of the pink paint on the details to create the look of wear and tear.

4 Paint fine lines of pistachio-colored latex over the ornamental details to highlight the intricate metalwork. Allow to dry.

5 Using medium-grit sandpaper, rub down the paintwork on the bed frame to reveal patches of previous paint layers and bare metal. This will add to the aged and worn feel that an old bed would have.

6 Make some aging glaze by mixing a tablespoon of raw umber paint pigment in a can

▲ Rub down the paintwork for an aged effect.

of acrylic varnish. Brush a coat of this aging glaze over the frame, using a long-haired soft dragging brush. Allow the glaze to pool in some areas, but do not allow it to run.

7 Using a fine artist's brush, carefully apply silver metallic paint in order to pick out and highlight any intricate moldings. Allow to dry thoroughly.

For other aging projects see:
Antiqued Table pp104–5; Distressed Chest pp198–9; Aged Rustic Chair pp212–13.

▲ Sand off any old paintwork and rust.

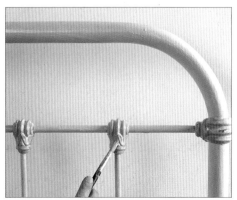

▲ Apply pink latex to the details.

▲ Varnish with a coat of glaze.

Cherub Wardrobe

THIS WARDROBE, which has been rag-rolled and stenciled with a light, bright, whimsical cherub theme, was originally a gentleman's wardrobe. It is made from good, solid wood, with shelves in one half and a clothes rod in the other, and would be ideal for a child's bedroom or a guest room. The flat doors lend themselves well to the paint techniques of stenciling and rag-rolling. If the door handles are unsuitable for painting, or do not blend in, replace them with silver or glass knobs. Two inexpensive silver tassels can add a stylish finishing touch.

❖ YOU WILL NEED ❖

Screwdriver

Wood filler

Palette knife

Medium- and fine-grit sandpaper

Tack cloth

Primer

Eggshell base coat

Paint tray

Paint roller with sleeve for oil-based paint

Household paintbrushes

Old tablespoon

Transparent oil glaze, or acrylic or ready-made acrylic mix

Paint bucket

Black artist's oil paint

Mineral spirits

Pink eggshell paint

Stippling brush

Clean lint-free cotton cloths

Card stock, acetate, or stencil film

Design for your stencil (see page 248)

Fine-tipped permanent marker

Craft knife and cutting mat

Nonpermanent adhesive spray

Acrylic paintbrush

Black and white stencil crayons

Medium-size stencil brush

Acrylic satin glaze

Two glass knobs (optional)

Two silver tassels (optional)

1 Remove the handles with a screwdriver to make sanding and painting easier. Fill any holes with wood filler. Allow to dry and then rub down with medium-grit sandpaper, following the grain of the wood. Wipe with a tack cloth, then apply a coat of primer and allow to dry completely.

2 Pour the eggshell base coat into the paint tray. Use a roller, fitted with a sleeve for oil-based paint, to apply paint to the wardrobe. Finish edges with a small paintbrush and let dry. Rub down any uneven areas with fine-grit sandpaper, tack, then apply a second coat.

3 Place a tablespoon of transparent glaze into the paint bucket, then squeeze in a tube width of black artis't' oil paint and stir until smooth. Add more transparent glaze plus mineral spirits in the ratio of 2 to 1, finally adding one spoon of pink eggshell paint, until you have enough to cover the whole wardrobe. The

A dark solid piece of wooden furniture can easily be brightened up.

consistency of the mix should be similar to that of light cream.

4 With a well-loaded stippling brush, apply the glaze over one section of the wardrobe.

▲ Roll on the first coat of eggshell base coat.

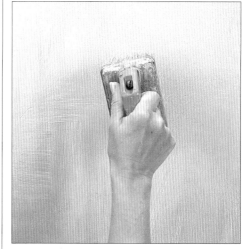

▲ Use a stippling brush over the glaze.

Work quickly and do not overbrush. While the glaze is still wet, apply the stippling brush with a moderate up-and-down stabbing motion in order to remove the brushstrokes and create a fine-speckled effect. Move on to the next step immediately.

5 Cut up the cotton material into large pieces. Screw up a piece of cloth, twisting it into a sausage shape. Place the cloth at a top corner and roll it down to the bottom of the wardrobe, using your fingertips and applying even pressure. Return to the top of the wardrobe door and position the cloth next to the side of the last section. Repeat the movement, making sure that you overlap the last "run" to avoid hard edges. Then repeat steps 4 and 5 on the next panel, and gradually work around the wardrobe.

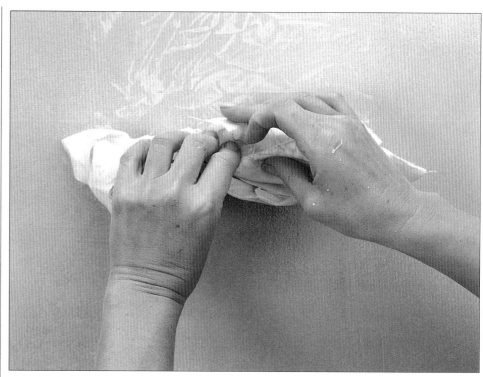

▲ Roll a cloth, place it on top of the glaze, and work down the wardrobe gradually.

▲ Stencil part one of the design in pale gray.

6 To make the cherub stencil, position the film over the template for part one of the cherub stencil on page 248, and trace the outline with a fine-tipped permanent marker. Allow extra stencil film around the edges to mix colors, and for the positioning marks. Cut along the lines with a craft knife and cut out the circular guide dots, which will enable you to position the second stencil correctly. On a separate piece of film, repeat the same for part two of the stencil.

7 Apply adhesive spray to the reverse side of the part one stencil and stick it into place on the wardrobe door. Check the position and adjust if necessary before applying the color. Break the seals of the stencil crayons (manufacturers' instructions are given on the packaging) and work black and white on the spare area of the film. Mix the colors together until you produce a pale gray shade. Working the stencil brush into this mix, cover all of the cutout areas of part one, using a circular and stippling motion. Add positioning marks to the surface to help you when you are ready to align the next stencil, before carefully peeling part one away.

▲ Stencil part two of the design in dark gray.

▲ Detail of the darker parts of the stencil.

For more dragging projects see:
Painted Panels pp133–5;
Repeating Border and Dragged Stripes pp208–11.

8 Apply adhesive spray to the reverse side of part two of the stencil, then position it correctly over part one of the stencil by aligning with the position marks.

9 Mix the stencil crayons as before but make a darker gray color, and keep some plain black beside this to use for highlighting small areas. Color all the cutout areas of part two with dark gray, accentuating some intricate parts and features by stippling with a small amount of black.

10 Peel the stencil off and wipe away the guide marks. Then clean the stencil with a cloth moistened in mineral spirits, and allow to dry. Repeat the stenciling process on the other door by reversing the stencil. Wipe off the marker lines and set aside both doors for at least 24 hours to dry thoroughly.

11 Using the acrylic brush, finish the wardrobe by applying two coats of acrylic satin glaze. This glaze will initially give the appearance of a milky finish but it will dry clear, so do not be tempted to overwork the medium. Finally, replace the door knobs or use glass replacements instead.

▲ Detail of a finished cherub.

Children's Balloon Stencils

O F ALL THE ROOMS in the house, the stenciled nursery has become an enduring favorite. This is probably due to the fact that most nursery stencils are simple and bright. Although complicated stencils of figures or locomotives accurately reproduced down to the last piston are undeniably lovely, it's a matter of debate whether such sophistication is appreciated by the room's inhabitants. While the children are still young, it is much better to go for bright, saturated colors, which tiny newborns' eyes do seem to notice and enjoy. This type of random project is ideal for tackling a little at a time. More than one nursery has remained incomplete at the arrival of its new occupant; the beauty of this scheme is that there is no definitive finish line.

❖ YOU WILL NEED ❖

Ruler

Paper and pencil

Card stock, acetate, or stencil film

Black permanent marker

Craft knife and cutting mat

Nonpermanent adhesive spray

Scrap paper for masking

Craft spray or acrylic paint in assorted colors

Face mask

Masking tape

Straight pin or needle

1 For the balloon shape, draw a straight line of a suitable length and connect the top and bottom ends with a curve. Trace the shape onto card stock, acetate, or stencil film and then flip it over from the central line and trace a mirror image to give a symmetrical balloon shape. Cut out the balloon shape with a craft knife.

2 Mask the area around the stencil. Spray the base color through the stencil. When the base color is dry, tape a pin or needle in front of the nozzle of a can of contrasting colored paint so that it interrupts the spray, producing larger spots of color.

3 Add a highlight to each balloon stencil with a short burst of the white spray. Draw in the curling balloon string using a black permanent marker.

For more stenciling projects see:
Stenciled Balustrade pp130–2; A Kitchen Frieze pp148–9; Stenciled Cane Chair pp160–1; Stenciled Headboard pp170–1; Stenciled Animal Prints pp175–7.

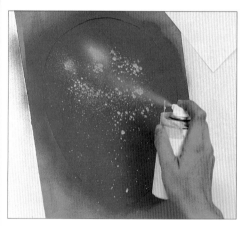

▲ Spray on the contrasting color.

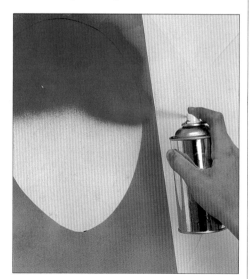

▲ Spray on the base coat.

▲ Detail of the finished overlapping balloons.

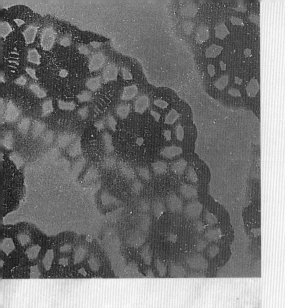

OFTEN CROWDED WITH

UNATTRACTIVE BUT NECESSARY

ITEMS SUCH AS LAUNDRY BASKETS

AND TOWEL RACKS, THE BATHROOM

CAN BE A CHALLENGE FOR EVEN THE

MOST EXPERIENCED DECORATOR.

HOWEVER, A LITTLE PLANNING WILL

DEAL WITH THE CLUTTER, AND THE

FOLLOWING IDEAS FOR BRIGHTLY

PAINTED PROJECTS WILL INSPIRE YOU

TO TRANSFORM THOSE OTHERWISE

DULL ODDS AND ENDS. WHEN YOU

HAVE FINISHED, RUN A HOT BATH,

LIE BACK FOR A LONG SOAK, AND

ADMIRE YOUR HANDIWORK.

Bathroom Projects

Verdigris Mirror and Door Handles

HERE ARE VARIOUS paint effect techniques that make things look worn and neglected. Of all the antiquing methods, however, verdigris is among the most striking and the most popular. This is the effect that you get when certain metals, such as copper and brass, are left to their own devices and eventually become discolored and corroded with age. The metal of this mirror and door handles was definitely not worth cleaning up but it was very decorative and lent itself well to a verdigris paint finish.

❖ YOU WILL NEED ❖

Hot, soapy water and cloth

Masking tape

Glass jars

Latex paint in dark green, peppermint green, pale blue, pale turquoise

1½" (4cm) household paintbrush

Old tablespoon

Methylated spirits

Sieve

Whiting

Several boar-bristle artist's brushes

Cloth

PVA glue

1 Wash the metal in hot, soapy water to get rid of any dust and grease, and then dry everything thoroughly with a clean cloth. Mask off the mirror to protect it while painting the frame.

2 Make up half a jar of diluted dark green latex paint (1 part latex paint to 3 parts water). Apply a coat of the diluted latex to the mirror frame and stand. Do the same to the door plates and knobs. Let them dry.

3 To make up the verdigris pastes, place a tablespoon of the pale blue and pale green latex paint into separate jars and stir two tablespoons of methylated spirits into each color. Add enough sieved whiting to each of the jars to make a firm mixture.

4 Start with the mirror only and, using a boar-bristle brush, go over the whole frame and base in all three paint colors. Try to make the distribution of color and texture as random as possible. When the verdigris paste is completely dry, which should not take very long, go over the mirror again, lightly dabbing it all over with water on a clean brush.

5 While the frame is still damp, sprinkle on some additional sieved whiting—dab and push this gently into the molding of the frame with your fingers. Take a little of the diluted green base color and trickle a very small amount here and there, but be careful not to overdo this because it could end up spoiling the final effect.

6 As the frame begins to dry out go over it with a dry cloth, rubbing some of it back to the green base coat and some small raised areas back to the metal. However, make sure that you leave most untouched.

7 While the frame is drying, give the door plates and doorknobs the same treatment.

8 When they are all dry, seal with a coat of diluted PVA glue (2 parts water to 1 part PVA).

HINTS & TIPS

If you have trouble getting hold of small containers of dark green latex paint, you will probably find that the little trial cans of latex, which some manufacturers produce, will give you plenty of paint.

For other aging projects see:
Antiqued Table pp104–5; Antiqued Iron Bed Frame pp178–9; Distressed Chest pp198–9; Aged Rustic Chair pp212–13.

▲ Mix up the verdigris paste.

▲ Dab on the whiting with your fingers.

Mexican-style Bathroom

BATHROOMS ARE BEST APPROACHED with a degree of whimsy and fun. Many can have a very cold feel, due to the large expanses of shiny ceramic and direct overhead lighting. A strong, perhaps daring, approach to color offers instant improvement, and an ideal opportunity to explore a particular theme.

In this bathroom, the bright warm colors and folk-art patterns of Mexico have been used as a starting point. This theme is continued throughout, from the mellow terra-cotta walls and the traditional Mexican patterns on the hanging shelf, walls, and windows to the small details on the eye-catching, brightly colored plant pots.

❖ YOU WILL NEED ❖

Tracing paper, newspaper, or scrap paper

Pencil or felt pen

Card stock, acetate, or stencil film

Craft knife and cutting mat

Warm terra-cotta flat latex paint

Nonpermanent adhesive spray

Acrylic paint in assorted colors

Sponge

Coarse-grit sandpaper

Clear polyurethane and gloss varnishes

Upholstery nails

Matte spray varnish

Protective face mask

Matte spray lacquer

1 Make the Mexican-style stencils by designing or tracing a ziggurat and star shapes. Transfer them onto stencil material and cut them out using a craft knife and mat.

2 Color wash the walls with a terra-cotta flat latex paint and then attach the ziggurat stencil to the wall using nonpermanent adhesive spray. Apply the paint in the color of your choice using a sponge. Allow to dry and then apply the paint through the star stencil. Distress the surface with coarse-grit sandpaper. When dry, apply a layer of clear polyurethane varnish.

3 The shelf was suspended from the ceiling to clear the sloping wall in this attic bathroom. Design and cut a simple symmetrical stencil design and apply to the shelf using bright colors. The edge of the shelf can then be stenciled with a bright pattern. First, apply a layer of diluted warm terra-cotta latex straight into the grain of the untreated wood of the shelf and overstencil using bright primary colors. Provide additional detail with upholstery nails. Keep the stenciled motif as rough as possible to give a

rustic feel. The colors used here were chosen to match the Mexican pottery on the shelves.

4 The colorful collection of terra-cotta flower pots was stenciled with brightly hued acrylic paints. The colors were chosen with the traditional pottery of Mexico in mind. The pots could just as easily have been hand painted because acrylics are opaque enough to allow you to cover up any mistakes. First, give the pots a latex base coat.

5 It is far easier when stenciling a curved and tapering object to make a stencil that fits it like a glove so that the paint is less likely to smudge or seep. To make the stencil, roll a large cone shape from a sheet of tracing paper, newspaper, or scrap paper. Follow the top and bottom edges of the flower pot with a pencil or felt pen. Make light marks in pencil to show the position of the stencil, then

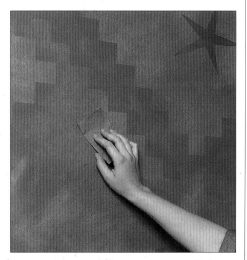
▲ Use sandpaper to distress the wall.

▲ Make the stencil to fit the flower pots.

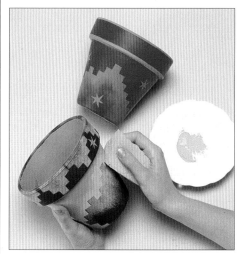
▲ Apply the paint using a sponge.

carefully unwrap the paper and you will have an exact template of the flower pot from which you can derive your stencil. Using the pencil marks as a guide, draw the stencil pattern onto some card stock, acetate, or stencil film. Use the craft knife and mat to remove the sections where you want the paint to come through onto the pot. Place the flower pot inside the stencil and apply the paint, using a sponge with a dabbing motion. When the paint is dry, add a little freehand detailing and let it dry. To protect your ceramics, finish with a couple of coats of gloss varnish.

▲ Spray the window with matte spray lacquer.

6 Textured glass is rarely attractive, and sandblasted glass tends to be extremely expensive. On the other hand, matte spray lacquer, when sprayed directly onto glass, gives a very plausible and attractive sandblasted effect. It is also durable and practical enough for most windows. Various effects similar to sandblasted glass can be achieved to give a good-looking alternative to textured or opaque glass bathroom windows. The stenciled window also solves a common problem found in bathrooms—how to have glass that both lets in light, while still being opaque enough to prevent you from being seen. One of the joys of this technique of stenciling on window glass is that when direct sunlight streams through the stenciled glass, the unsprayed areas creating the motif are projected perfectly onto the opposite wall. You can reuse the stencils that you made to decorate the bathroom wall. Mask the window frame and stick the motifs to the glass with nonpermanent spray adhesive. Wearing a protective face mask, gently spray the window with matte spray lacquer.

HINTS & TIPS

• Many interesting finishes and effects can be achieved by using a variety of household items as a mask for your spray stencil pattern. If you prefer a Victorian-inspired bathroom, ordinary paper doilies will give a lace-like finish while leaves attached to the glass with a PVA adhesive will give you a ready-made forest glade—even large paper clips can create interesting effects.

• Panes of glass and mirrors can be bordered with the simple use of masking tape and a straight line. For example, a particularly elegant window above a front door can be stenciled with the number of the house. To do this, simply trace the existing brass number from the front door and make a mask from stencil film. Then use a masking tape border to create a clear frame around the pane.

For more stenciling projects see:
Stenciled Balustrade pp130–2; A Kitchen Frieze pp148–9; Stenciled Cane Chair pp160–1; Frottaged and Stenciled Screen pp167–9; Children's Balloon Stencils pp184–5; Poppies Picture Frame pp236–7; Monogrammed Box pp244–5.

▲ Doilies can be used as stencils to create interesting effects.

Fish Stencil Shower Glass

THE FISH STENCIL was not specifically intended to bring a marine theme to this bathroom, rather it was selected because of its simplicity and its unusual appearance. Inspired by a more complicated Art Deco design, it has been simplified and is used modestly in order to break up one or two of the straight lines in the bathroom and soften the effect.

There are two methods for frosting glass yourself, both very effective, using materials readily available from craft stores, and more cost effective than buying etched glass. One method is to use sheets of sticky-backed plastic in a frosted finish and to cut pieces carefully with a knife and apply them to clean glass. The second method, shown here, is a touch more professional and longer lasting.

❖ YOU WILL NEED ❖

Design to copy

Card stock, acetate, or stencil film

Marking pen or crayon

Craft knife and cutting mat

Repositionable spray mount

Scrap paper for masking

Frosting spray

1 Either make your own design or select a design from a book or piece of wrapping paper, making sure that it can be simplified into sections. Enlarge it on a photocopier if necessary. The fish design used here is already in sections and is extremely easy to work with.

2 Trace the image onto the stencil material, simplifying the design, if necessary, as you go. You will see here that the eye and face area have been reduced into one part each.

3 Cut the stencil using a craft knife and cutting mat. Cut the smaller pieces out first then the larger ones so that the stencil remains firm. Take care not to split the stencil as this will cause leaks when the frosting spray is applied.

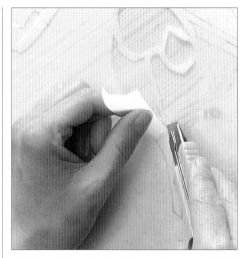

▲ Cut out the stencil with a craft knife.

4 Apply the stencil to the glass and hold it firmly in place using repositionable spray mount. Make sure that it is correctly positioned on the glass and press it flat against the surface, smoothing out any wrinkles or bubbles that could spoil the effect.

▲ Select a design that can be easily simplified.

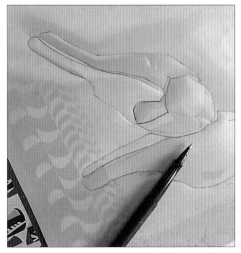

▲ Trace the image onto the stencil material.

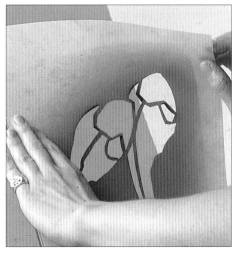

▲ Smooth the stencil flat on the glass.

▲ It is important to mask all around the stencil.

• The spray goes on almost clear and dries to a frosted finish. Let it dry for a few minutes before removing the stencil fully.

• You could also use the fish stencil to decorate your bathroom walls. Spray paints are perfect for a soft and misty stencil. Practice working them on a piece of scrap paper or board first because every spray can acts differently in terms of how much paint is released when you press the button. Spray lacquer is superb for painting directly onto tiles because the cellulose ingredients are long-lasting and water-resistant

For more stenciling projects see:
Stenciled Balustrade pp130–2; A Kitchen Frieze pp148–9; Stenciled Cane Chair pp160–1; Frottaged and Stenciled Screen pp167–9; Children's Balloon Stencils pp184–5; Poppies Picture Frame pp236–7; Monogrammed Box pp244–5.

5 To protect the surrounding area from stray spray, mask it off with scrap paper. Wearing a mask, spray the frosting solution through the stencil in short sharp bursts as lightly as possible. Let it dry, then repeat.

6 Peel back a small corner of the stencil after a couple of minutes to check the depth of frosting you have produced. You may need to apply another coat, so don't remove the stencil completely until you have achieved the effect that you want. Any errors can be removed by carefully scraping them away with a flat blade, but take care not to scratch the glass.

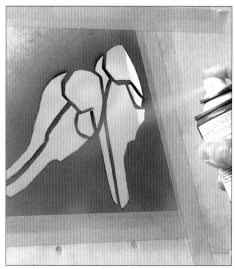

▲ Spray the paint in short bursts.

▲ Peel back the stencil and check the depth of the frosting.

Lime-washed Bath Panels

THE SUBTLETY of the paint finish on the tongue-and-groove bath panels helps to soften and understate your bathroom's color scheme. You would be forgiven for thinking it looks as though the painter is running out of paint because that is exactly how this technique is carried out—using a half-loaded paintbrush. The pale color used here is the same color as the walls of the bathroom. Once the base coat of paint is complete, this effect takes very little time and is dry in minutes. It is therefore convenient for those forced to put the new-look bathroom back into service quickly. Of course, dry-brushing is not a technique reserved exclusively for wall panels and can be used on any surface. It works just as well on paneled doors.

❖ **YOU WILL NEED** ❖

2" (5cm) household paintbrush

2 quarts (2l) of primer

2 quarts (2l) of base color paint

1¼" (3cm) wide paintbrush

8 oz (250ml) of a lighter-colored paint for the streaks

Piece of scrap wood

---

1 It is very important to prime the wood with a good quality waterproof primer before you start to paint it. Carefully prime right up to the edges, because raw paint will absorb moisture and eventually cause dry rot.

2 When the primer is dry, apply a good coat of paint in the chosen base color. One coat will be sufficient if it is well-applied. Water-based latex satin will work well if you are confident of the quality of the priming. Otherwise use an oil-based eggshell paint.

3 For the soft-brushed effect, dip the tip of the small paintbrush into a shallow tray of the lighter color paint. (The lid of the can is ideal for this purpose.) Wipe off any excess drips on the side of the paint can.

4 Gently move the brush up or down one of the planks of wood, following the direction of the grain. The brush will leave thin streaks. Turn it over and exhaust the paint on the other side as well before stroking it up and down gently to

▲ Use the can lid as a paint tray.

spread the paint streaks that you have just applied. You may like to test this step on a piece of scrap wood before working on the actual bath panels so that you can perfect your technique.

For more liming projects see:
Limed Picture Frame pp230–1.

▲ Prime right up to the edges of the wood.

▲ Apply the base coat color.

▲ Lightly streak the panels with your brush.

Decorative Bathroom Chests

 Either of these chests would grace any bathroom and provide practical storage space for towels or toiletries. Their beauty lies in the subtlety of the paint effects that are used. In the first project, checks in cream and two tones of pink were painted on and allowed to dry before they were rubbed down with sandpaper to produce the distressed finish. In the second project, a meandering ivy-stenciled pattern in soft green adds an elegant touch to the small chest of drawers. The materials used here are available from most craft stores.

Distressed Chest

❖ YOU WILL NEED ❖

Wet and dry medium-grit abrasive paper

Tack cloth

1" (2.5cm) base-coat brush

Gouache paint in oyster pearl and blush

Ruler

Chalk

Masking tape

1" (2.5cm) and ½" (1cm) paintbrushes

Light- and dark-pink latex paint

Extender medium

Palette or old plate

Varnish

1 Sand the chest and remove any dust with the tack cloth. Remove the drawer knobs. Using the base-coat brush, apply two or three coats of oyster pearl. Allow to dry.

2 Mark out the design with a ruler and chalk. Mask off the areas that are to be dark pink. With one of the 1" (2.5cm) brushes, paint the dark-pink checks with blush. Allow the paint to dry and then remove the tape.

3 Mask the areas that will be light pink. Mix light-pink latex paint with oyster pearl and blush paints and apply with a 1" (2.5cm) brush. Allow to dry and remove the tape.

4 Place some extender and blush paint on a palette. Load extender onto the ½" (1cm) brush, wipe the brush over the paint, then blend the extender and blush paint on the palette. Paint this transparent pink on the routed edges of the drawers, as well as the top of the chest and knobs.

5 Distress the chest by rubbing it with wet abrasive paper. Allow to dry. Remove any dust with a tack cloth, then replace the knobs. Apply two or three coats of varnish.

For more aging projects see:
Antiqued Table pp104–5; Old Oak Woodgrain Floor pp113–15; Aged Rustic Chair pp212–13.

Stenciled Chest

❖ YOU WILL NEED ❖

Sandpaper

Tack cloth

1" (2.5cm) base-coat brush

Gouache paint in oyster pearl and colonial green

Card stock, acetate, or stencil film

Fine-point permanent marker

Craft knife and cutting mat

Masking tape

Stencil brush

Extender medium

Palette or old plate

Varnish

1 Sand down the chest well and remove any dust with a tack cloth. Remove the knobs. Using the base-coat brush, apply two or three coats of oyster pearl, and allow the chest to dry between coats.

2 Draw the pattern freehand onto a stencil material or trace from a source of your choice. Using the craft knife, cut out the design.

3 Work out the position of the stencil, and tape it in position with masking tape. Start at the top drawer, and try to create an effect that looks natural.

4 Load a stencil brush with colonial green and dab off any excess. Apply paint in a circular motion.

5 To highlight the routed edge, drawers, and top of the chest with a transparent green, place some extender and colonial green on the palette. Dab a flat brush into the extender, then wipe it over the green.

6 Allow to dry for 24 hours. Replace the drawer knobs. Apply two or three coats of varnish.

For more stenciling projects see:
Stenciled Headboard pp170–1.

Marbled Bathroom

SIT BACK IN YOUR BATHTUB and enjoy the flowing and relaxing movements of this simple paint effect that seems to swish and cascade down the walls. Low cost, easy to prepare, and quick to finish, this is a super treatment for walls that are already painted or have paper on them that is still in good condition. This is not a lesson in how to imitate marble—good marbling takes more than a weekend to master. It is a decoration inspired by the look of natural marbles, but uses no glazes or special brushes. It is not even a very messy job.

❖ YOU WILL NEED ❖

Three 1 quart (1l) cans of eggshell finish paint in your chosen three colors

3 flat paint trays

Wide natural-bristle decorating brush

Scrap paper

Masking tape

1 Prepare the room for painting by making sure that the walls are clean. Mask off any fixtures such as faucets, light switches, and the point at which the walls meet the ceiling. Prepare three flat trays of paint with only ¹/₂"(1cm) of paint in each. Eggshell paint is used here because it is water-resistant when dry (and is therefore excellent for bathrooms) and it dries more slowly than latex, offering extra time for blending.

2 Starting with the darkest paint color, dip the tip of the dusting brush into the tray. Do not overload the brush—if any paint drips

from the brush, dab it off on some paper before you start stippling.

3 Working in patches about 2' (60cm) across, hold your brush with the long side following the direction of the intended "flow." Stipple the paint onto the wall with a sharp but light jabbing motion. Follow a general, wiggly diagonal flow. Go easy on the darkest shade. Avoid making any large or noticeable X shapes. If you make any of these by mistake, quickly blend them in using the other shades.

4 When you have run out of paint on your brush, immediately dip the tip into the medium shade and apply some diagonally flowing lines to the wall, next to the dark lines. Blend the two colors together where they meet by dabbing the brush into the dark lines, which will still be wet, then back into the lighter shade.

5 Repeat the process with the lightest shade of paint (here it is white), filling in all the spaces and blending into both colors.

▲ Stipple on the lightest shade, blending it in.

6 Finally, stand back from the wall and check that your colors are blended well. Add extra lines in any shade where you think it necessary. Look out for any obvious marks left by the jabbing motion of your brush and gently stipple them away. Repeat steps 4 and 5, regularly stepping back to check your work and blending until all the walls are covered. When you are satisfied with the effect, wash out the brush and remove the masking tape.

For more marbling projects see:
Marbled Dressing Table pp162–3; Marbled Pot pp214–15.

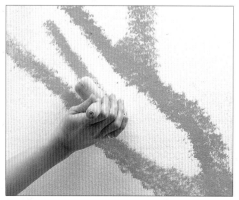
▲ Stipple the darkest color onto the wall first.

▲ Move onto the medium shade immediately.

▲ Adjust the finish as necessary.

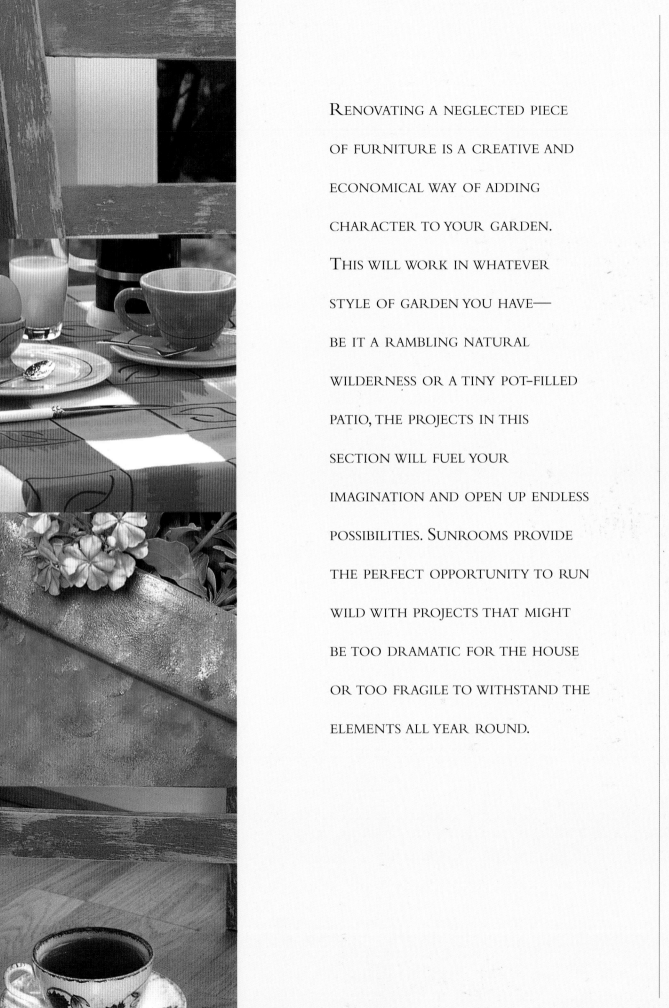

RENOVATING A NEGLECTED PIECE OF FURNITURE IS A CREATIVE AND ECONOMICAL WAY OF ADDING CHARACTER TO YOUR GARDEN. THIS WILL WORK IN WHATEVER STYLE OF GARDEN YOU HAVE— BE IT A RAMBLING NATURAL WILDERNESS OR A TINY POT-FILLED PATIO, THE PROJECTS IN THIS SECTION WILL FUEL YOUR IMAGINATION AND OPEN UP ENDLESS POSSIBILITIES. SUNROOMS PROVIDE THE PERFECT OPPORTUNITY TO RUN WILD WITH PROJECTS THAT MIGHT BE TOO DRAMATIC FOR THE HOUSE OR TOO FRAGILE TO WITHSTAND THE ELEMENTS ALL YEAR ROUND.

Garden & Sunroom Projects

Spray-painted Table and Chairs

GARDEN AND SUNROOM furniture can get into quite a state if it is not well-maintained. However, renovation can save and rejuvenate pieces such as this old tattered garden table and chair set. These white chairs were also rather uncomfortable, so a set of pretty cushions were added not only to help with the visual effect but also to make the chairs a more practical feature of the patio. The garden table was made partly of metal and partly of wood, but luckily the rustproofing spray paint could handle both.

❖ YOU WILL NEED ❖

Hot, soapy water and cloth

Fine steel wool

Rust remover

Paint stripper and stripping tool

Medium- and fine-grit sandpaper

Tack cloth

Wood primer

1½" (4cm) household paintbrush

3 cans of green rustproofing spray paint

Old newspapers

This table and chairs will be out in the elements so they will have to be treated with protective paint.

1 Start by washing the metal on the table thoroughly in hot, soapy water. Rub off any loose paint with steel wool.

2 When the metal is completely dry, treat the rust spots with rust remover and steel wool until the bare metal is gleaming.

3 Strip the tabletop and then rub it down, first with some medium-grit and then with fine-grit sandpaper. Go over the surface with a tack cloth to remove any dust. Prime the wood, painting as smoothly as possible and working in the same direction as the woodgrain.

4 When the primer is dry, sand it lightly and tack once more. Then give it four or five applications of rustproofing paint. It is best to use spray paint because of the curly nature of the wrought iron.

5 If the metal chairs are dirty or in bad condition, wash them in the same way as the metal table legs in step 1. Once the rust has been removed, apply the same spray paint. First, turn the chairs upside down and spray all the surfaces you can see from that angle, then turn them the right side up and repeat the process.

HINTS & TIPS

• A word of caution regarding spray paints, especially if you have had little or no experience of them—follow the instructions carefully and don't attempt to put too much paint on at any one time or you will get runs or drips. Even so, with this type of paint the layers do have to be built up in fairly quick succession so that they can meld together before the paint begins to cure.

• If possible, work outside on a calm day to paint, and protect the area around where you are working by laying down plenty of old newspapers.

For more table and chair projects see:
Tartan-band Dining Table pp100–1; Decorative Chairs pp102–3; Antiqued Table pp104–5; Freehand-painted Tables pp110–12; Dragged-effect Table pp122–3; Painted Chairs pp144–7; Ivy-stamped Chair pp150–1; Stenciled Cane Chair pp160–1; Aged Rustic Chair pp212–13.

▲ Rub down the wooden tabletop.

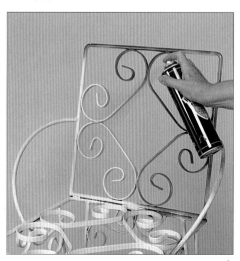

▲ Spray the wrought-iron chair thoroughly.

Hand-painted Chest

THIS CHEST would make a very attractive addition to any sunroom and would be ideal for storing small items of garden equipment, such as gloves or scissors. The drawer arrangement on the chest is unusual and attempting individual decoration of each drawer could look uneven. One solution is to treat the piece as a whole and this design, with the help of a photocopier, fits neatly between the top and bottom of each drawer. It was adapted from a traditional Indian embroidery design and the red and white colors give it an appealing freshness. The design was transferred to the chest using a transfer paper, which comes in various colors. The red paper used here was close in color to the paint and completely invisible once the chest had been lightly sanded. This project can be time-consuming but is not difficult—all you need is a steady hand.

❖ YOU WILL NEED ❖

Latex paint in deep red and white

Household paintbrushes

Fine-grit sandpaper

Masking tape

Pencil

Tracing paper

Transfer paper

Fine-point artist's paintbrush

Deep red acrylic paint

Steel wool

Matte water-based varnish

Clear wax

Soft cloth

This chest came from a popular home furnishings store.

1 Paint the entire chest with two coats of red latex paint, allowing the first coat to dry thoroughly before applying the second. Then, when this is dry, paint two coats of white latex paint over the whole of the chest.

▲ Sand the chest until the red shows through.

2 Rub the white paint lightly with sandpaper so some red shows through, particularly around the edges of the chest. Link the two middle drawers with masking tape, avoiding the surface to be decorated. Repeat for the three top drawers. You will then be able to treat them as one surface.

3 Trace the design from the template (see page 248) and place the tracing paper in position on the chest. Slide a piece of transfer paper underneath and secure the design in place with masking tape. Transfer the design by drawing over it with a pencil. Do not remove the tracing paper until you have transferred the whole design, as it is difficult to reposition accurately. Continue for the remaining areas of the chest.

4 Using a fine-point artist's brush, carefully fill in the design with deep red acrylic paint.

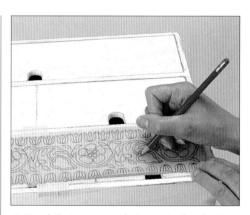

▲ Carefully trace your design onto the chest.

▲ Use a dark red paint to fill in the design.

5 When the paint has dried thoroughly, rub it down lightly with steel wool to distress it. Finish the chest by brushing it with a coat of matte water-based varnish and applying a clear wax over this when it is dry. Buff to a shine with a soft cloth.

For more freehand projects see:
Color-washed Oak Sideboard pp98–9; Kitchen Accessories pp138–40; Cups and Saucers Chair pp146–7; Painted Frames pp232–3

Repeating Border and Dragged Stripes

UNUSUAL WALL FINISHES below a chair rail can be extremely effective, and a decorative border can be used to look like a chair rail. Used here to decorate the inside wall of a sunroom, this design is a simplified "egg and dart" motif, once common in wallpaper designs. Its close repeat means that awkward corners can be accommodated easily, without showing up any missed or botched repeats. Broad vertical stripes look attractive and can also be used as an effective device for increasing the height of a room but can sometimes be a little too bold if used over an entire wall. Restricted to the area below a chair rail, however, they add a note of old-world elegance and increase the feeling of space without overpowering the rest of the scheme.

❖ YOU WILL NEED ❖

Design to copy

Tracing paper

Card stock, acetate, or stencil film

Craft knife and cutting mat

Level

Pencil

Tape measure

Warm-gray acrylic paint mixed with a little latex

Household paintbrushes

White acrylic paint

Palette

Clear matte varnish

Stiff mounting card

Steel square

Plumb line

Low-tack masking tape or card stock

Nonpermanent adhesive spray

Oil-based glaze

Refined linseed oil

Raw umber oil pigment

Mineral spirits

Dragging brush

1 The first thing you need to do is to trace your chair rail design. The one used here was taken from a book of classical architectural moldings. Photocopy it to a size that works well within the space available—in this case, it was 2" (5cm) high. The straight lines along the upper and lower edges prevent the border from looking messy or isolated on the wall.

2 Transfer the tracing onto card stock, acetate, or stencil film, shade in, and then cut out the "negative" areas with a craft knife. Then cut a second stencil the same shape as the egg, but about 1/4" (5mm) smaller all round.

3 Select the position on the wall where you want the chair rail to run. The traditional height of a chair rail is one third of the height of

▲ Trace your stencil design.

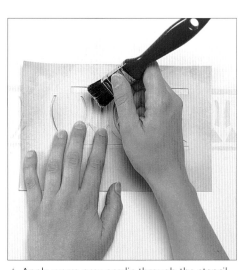
▲ Apply warm-gray acrylic through the stencil.

the room. Adjust this to suit your particular room. Low ceilings will seem higher with a lower chair rail, and a high ceiling can seem lower with a higher rail. Ensure that the chair rail clears any radiators and does not pass over the mantle shelf, or over the windows. Mark a line around the whole room in pencil using a level and tape measure to draw perfectly straight lines.

4 Because of the close repeat of the design, you can start applying the stencil at any point on the wall. Mix some warm-gray acrylic with some of the background color of the wall and apply with a stiff, dry brush leaving a light finish. After about five minutes go back to the beginning of each stencil and apply additional paint to the top to give a flat, darker area between the moldings, which will look like shadow.

▲ Highlight the bottom right area of each egg.

5 Mix some white acrylic with the wall color latex to make the light-colored paint that will form the highlights in the stencil pattern. Using a dry paintbrush, apply the paint through the second stencil, working from the bottom right to the top left, and leaving less and less paint on the wall as you go. Finally, apply a coat of matte varnish.

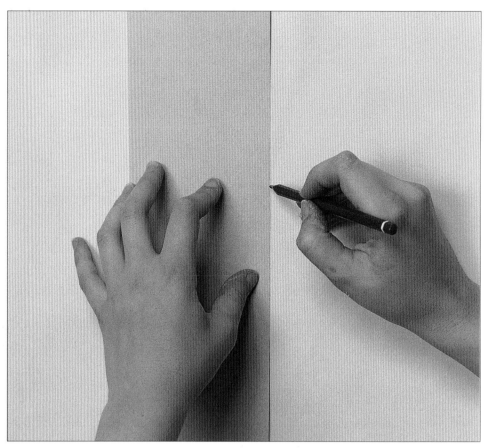

▲ Using the card template as a guide, lightly mark in the position of the stripes on the wall.

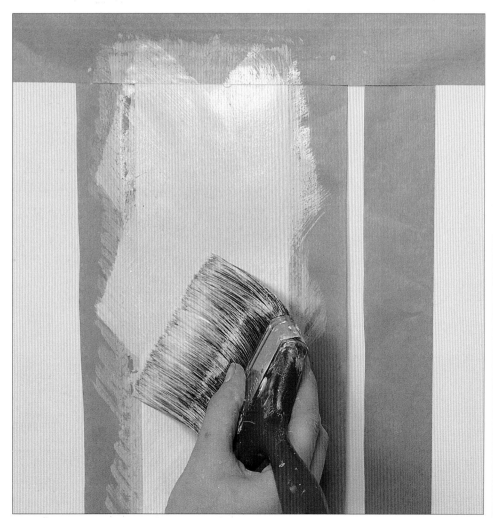

▲ Mask off the area around the stripes and apply the paint with a large paintbrush.

6 Calculate what size of stripe will fit best on to each wall. If the stripes are a subtle shade, they can accommodate being split on corners, though bolder colors where the stripes are very defined might require greater consideration.

7 Cut a piece of stiff mounting card to the width and height of the stripes. Use a steel square to ensure that all the corners are right angles. Then use this as a template to mark out the stripes in pencil around the room, starting from the middle of the wall that will be most visible. Use a level and plumb line as you work.

8 Mask off the edges of a few stripes using either low-tack masking tape (trimmed in half so as not to obscure neighboring stripes) or card and nonpermanent adhesive spray.

9 Mix an oil-based glaze, combining half a small can of matte varnish with a dash of refined linseed oil, and some raw umber dissolved in mineral spirits.

▲ Drag a coarse, dry brush down through the glaze to give a worn texture.

the brush at a right angle to the wall. This dragging technique will produce lovely mellow stripes that have an attractive, delicately worn texture. If latex is used, seal with varnish.

HINTS & TIPS

• The easiest stripes are those that are equidistant or that have the same width for both the stripe and the space between.

• Ordinary masking tape, whatever the manufacturers may claim, can unfortunately be very good at pulling off existing paintwork. Low-tack masking tape is not difficult to find in a good paint store, and is not only reusable but also very easy to apply in a straight line.

• Latex paint could obviously be used but, if you want to disguise a radiator by including it in the paint scheme, you will need to use an oil paint or spray. No amount of coaxing will keep latex on a radiator for long.

• You could use other techniques with cloths, sponges, or plastic bags to create texture in the paint.

• If, when you remove the tape or card mask, you find the glaze has seeped underneath and smudged, quickly remove the unwanted paint with a cotton swab soaked in mineral spirits.

• It is always a good idea to start painting in an area that you know will be hidden by a piece of furniture. This will give you an opportunity to gain confidence before tackling the more visible areas, such as alcoves on either side of the chimney breast.

• Because a varnish-based glaze was used on this project, an additional coat of varnish was not needed. But bear in mind that latex stripes are easily scuffed unless they are sealed with a tough matte or satin varnish.

---

10 Apply the glaze in short diagonal strokes working from the middle of the stripe outwardsto that the brush is drier as it hits the tape.

11 While the glaze is still wet, go over the stripes again with a coarse, dry brush, this time literally dragging the paint downward over the surface. While you work hold

For more wall projects see:

Checkered Walls pp94–7; Color-washed Wall pp124–5; Painted Panels pp133–5; A Kitchen Frieze pp148–9; A Bedroom Frieze pp172–3; Marbled Bathroom pp200–1.

Aged Rustic Chair

IT IS EASY TO IMAGINE this rustic Greek chair, with the worn paint cracked by the heat, being sat upon year after year by customers enjoying a glass or two of retsina outside a whitewashed taverna. Lovely Mediterranean blues were used for the chair—the colors were created by mixing cerulean blue and ultramarine powdered pigments with white latex paint. The chair would make a cheerful addition to a garden room or sunroom. Good results are achieved with both ordinary latex and traditional paint, but there can be a variation in the extent of cracking between different brands of paint and even different colors from the same manufacturer. Whichever paint you choose, be sure it is not too thick and has a good flow.

❖ YOU WILL NEED ❖

Latex or traditional paint in 2 contrasting shades, or white latex paint and 2 shades of powder pigment

Household paintbrushes

One-part crackle glaze

Medium-grit sandpaper

Sanding block

Matte water-based varnish

Bright colors give this chair a Mediterranean look.

1 Paint the lighter of the two colors on the chair rather patchily so that both bare wood and paint will be revealed beneath the cracks to add to the illusion of age. Allow to dry.

2 Brush on the crackle glaze. The thicker you apply it, the larger the cracks will be. Allow the chair to dry before applying the next coat of paint. The medium becomes more stable and easier to handle if you leave it for at least four hours or overnight.

3 Brush on the second, darker, paint color, again in a random fashion, but covering most of the first color. Try to work quickly and confidently and do not go over an area you have just painted more than once or you will reactivate the glaze and the paint will start to skid and slide. Wait for the paint to dry thoroughly, then fill in any spots you have missed with more paint. Allow to dry.

4 Using medium-grit sandpaper wrapped around a sanding block, rub back the paint to reveal more of the base coat and soften any hard edges. Seal with one or two coats of water-based varnish, working quickly so as not to activate the crackle

▲ Brush on the crackle glaze.

medium. Allow the varnish to dry between coats. If you do not seal the surface properly and the chair gets wet, the paint surface will be disturbed.

For other aging projects see:
Antiqued Table pp104–5; Antiqued Iron Bed Frame pp178–9; Distressed Chest pp198–9.

▲ Paint on the paler of the two colors first.

▲ Sand the paint to produce a worn look.

Decorated Pots

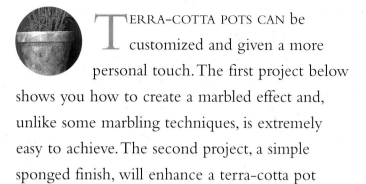

Terra-cotta pots can be customized and given a more personal touch. The first project below shows you how to create a marbled effect and, unlike some marbling techniques, is extremely easy to achieve. The second project, a simple sponged finish, will enhance a terra-cotta pot without drawing the eye away from the plant that it holds. Pots that are used outdoors should always be finished with an oil-based or weatherproof varnish so that all your hard work will not be ruined by the rain. Remember, oil-based products can be used over water-based products, but you must never use a water-based product over an oil-based one.

Marbled Pot

❖ YOU WILL NEED ❖

All-purpose water-based sealer

Household paintbrushes

Acrylic gouache paint in oyster pearl, warm beige, pearl white, and carbon black

Palette

Glaze

Stencil brush

Plastic wrap

Water-based satin varnish

1 Seal the pot both inside and out with the all-purpose sealer and allow it to dry completely.

2 Using a paintbrush, apply one or two coats of oyster pearl paint to the inside and outside of the pot, and allow to dry.

3 Next, you need to apply one generous coat of glaze to the outside of the pot.

4 On your palette, place warm beige, pearl white, and carbon black. Be generous with your portions of paint, as this helps to maintain the same color throughout.

5 Using the stencil brush, dab each color randomly over the pot while the glaze is still wet.

6 To create the marbled effect, cover the pot with plastic wrap. Press it to the pot, then remove it. Use the same plastic to rewrap the pot and press it again. Repeat until the desired effect has been achieved.

7 Allow the paint to dry for 24 hours and then apply two or three coats of satin varnish to protect the pot.

For more marbling projects see:
Marbled Dressing Table pp162–3.

Sponged Pot

❖ YOU WILL NEED ❖

All-purpose water-based sealer

Household paintbrushes

Acrylic gouache paint in ocean blue, ultramarine light, and pearl white

Palette

Sponge

Paper towels

Water-based satin varnish

1 Seal the pot both inside and out with the all-purpose sealer and allow it to dry completely.

2 Using a paintbrush, apply one or two coats of ocean blue to the inside and outside of the pot. Allow it to dry.

3 On your palette place some ocean blue, ultramarine light, and pearl white paint. Be generous with your portions of paint, as this helps to maintain the same color mix for the whole project.

4 Dab your sponge into the three colors, starting with the darkest color. Blot onto paper towels before starting on the pot.

5 Dab the pot with the sponge. When reloading your sponge, blot it before applying it to the pot.

6 Allow the pot to dry for 24 hours, then apply two or three coats of satin varnish to finish.

For more sponging projects see:
Sponge-stamped floor pp128–9.

Brightly Colored Pots

As TERRA-COTTA is an absorbent, porous surface, latex paint can be painted directly onto it. Bold colors have been used to jazz up these terra-cotta pots. The crackle-glazed effect is an easy and fun way to use strong colors together – red under pink or blue under bright yellow, for example. It also creates an impression of age. Because latex paint dries quickly, it can always be repainted in a different color if you are not happy with the final look. Once the pots have been varnished, they will be wipeable and durable.

❖ YOU WILL NEED ❖

Latex paint in blue and yellow, or your two chosen colors

Household paintbrush

One-part crackle glaze

Artist's paintbrush

Flat varnish

---

1 Apply a coat of latex paint in your chosen base color. Allow to dry and apply a second coat. The cracks will appear in the same direction as you apply the paint. Here, the paint has been applied in brushstrokes around the pot.

2 Once the base coat is dry, apply the crackle glaze in the same direction as the base coat. For strong cracks, as shown here, allow the first coat of glaze to dry completely, then apply a second coat.

3 Once the crackle glaze has completely dried, apply the top coat of latex paint in a contrasting color in the same direction as before. Apply the paint in one sweeping motion and do not go back over an area that has just been painted—this will pull the glaze off and ruin the effect. If this does happen, let it dry, then start again. Use enough paint just to cover the area and allow to dry. Large cracks will start to appear.

▲ Apply the crackle glaze.

4 Line the rim of the pot once it is dry—apply a new base coat, then a coat of crackle glaze, followed by the top coat. Use a small artist's brush to create an even finish. Let the pot dry, then apply two coats of flat varnish to the whole pot, allowing each coat to dry.

For more crackle projects see:
Aged Rustic Chair pp212–13.

▲ Paint the first base coat.

▲ Paint on a contrasting color.

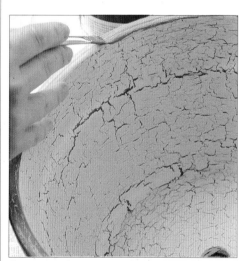
▲ Line the rim of the pot with an artist's brush.

Painted Tablecloth

A RED-AND-WHITE check tablecloth brings a cheerful touch to dining alfresco. Made from medium weight canvas, this tablecloth is marked with a grid pattern and then painted with fabric paint. This is a no-sew tablecloth—the edges are turned under with double-sided bonding tape, or, for an even simpler method, you could fray the edges. Eyelets are hammered in on the corners so that you can hang weights to ensure the cloth will stay put in a strong wind. Stones with natural holes worn in them will keep the cloth still. A string of shells is decorative and also gives the right sort of weighting. Or, you could buy some heavy beads and use them instead. Keep the cloth in the car for the times you come upon one of those unexpected picnic spots.

❖ YOU WILL NEED ❖

12¼ oz (350g) cotton duck canvas

Scissors

Tape measure

Pencil

Straightedge

Fabric paint

Glass jar

Household paintbrush

Iron

Clean pressing cloth

Double-sided bonding tape

Black felt pen or fabric marker

Stamp or appliqué motif (optional)

Grommets

Grommet tool

Hammer

String or raffia

Stones

1 Cut the cotton duck canvas into a square. The easiest way to do this is by folding the cloth diagonally, to make a triangle, then cutting along the raw edge.

2 Mark the cloth along the edge every 4" (10cm). Then use a straightedge to draw lines across the cloth, lightly joining the marks with a pencil. This will produce the checked pattern and gives you a guide when painting.

3 Use the fabric paint container as a measure to water down the fabric paint in a glass jar, 1 part paint to 6 parts water. Diluting the paint in this way will make it easier to use, and the pain will also go farther. Using a thinned-down paint mix also means that you can create interesting shades where two blocks of color overlap.

▲ Mark outlines with a pencil.

4 Use a wide paintbrush and follow the pencil guidelines to apply the paint in rough stripes, working first in one direction across the fabric. The paint will sit on the surface of the canvas to begin with, so you may need to work it in to the fabric a bit with the brush.

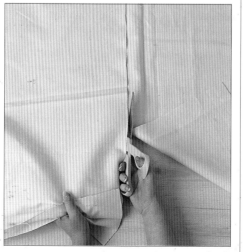

▲ Cut the cloth to the right size and shape.

▲ Paint one set of stripes across the cloth.

▲ Paint the second set of stripes on.

5 When you have finished all the stripes in one direction, allow them to dry completely, then paint the rest of the stripes at right angles to create a checked effect.

6 Seal the paint with a hot iron when it is dry, following the paint manufacturer's instructions. Place a clean pressing cloth over the tablecloth so as not to scorch it. Ensure that you iron the whole tablecloth.

▲ Iron the entire cloth, using a pressing cloth, to seal the paint.

▲ Iron a hem in place using double-sided bonding tape.

7 Turn under a 1" (3cm) hem all around the edges onto the wrong side of the tablecloth and press in place with double-sided bonding tape to give a neat edge that will not fray. Then turn the tablecloth the right side up and use a felt pen or fabric marker to outline the squares where the two lines of paint cross; this outline does not have to be precise. A rough look will fit in with the intended final effect of rustic simplicity.

▲ Outline the squares where the stripes meet.

▲ Insert a grommet in each corner of the cloth.

8 Draw a freehand leaf in the center of each marked square. Or, if you are not confident when drawing freehand, use a stencil or stamp, or appliqué a fabric design on the cloth. Next, insert a grommet in each corner of the tablecloth with a hammer. Mark the position of the grommets with a pencil and use the grommet tool to cut the hole. Thread string or raffia through the grommets and hang stones collected from the beach that have natural holes, large beads, or any other small heavy objects that will anchor the tablecloth in the wind.

HINTS & TIPS

• On some fabrics, diluting fabric paint will give an attractive watery edge to the paint, similar to that of watercolor paint on paper.

• If the fabric is too thick to insert the grommets, snip it away with a pair of scissors until the holes are big enough to take them.

▲ Thread stones through the grommets to act as anchors.

For more fabric painting projects see:
Stenciled Animal Prints pp175–7.

Details matter, and each of the small items featured in this chapter will add a finishing touch to your home that has more impact than anything you could buy ready-made. Most of the projects can be completed in a relatively short time, and the basic objects can be picked up at flea markets and yard sales for little cost. Why not make one as a unique and personal gift to let a friend know how special they are? Your thoughtfulness will be long remembered.

Gift & Accessory Projects

Tortoiseshell Lamp Base and Shade

THERE ARE MANY wonderful ways of using varnishes to make tortoiseshell effects that are almost indistinguishable from the real thing. This method is blatantly faux, but it is great fun to do and gives a smart new finish to the elderly base and the brand new lampshade. The lamp base was beautifully turned and had a fascinating, red Bakelite switch, but it was also covered in layers and layers of green paint that had to be stripped off. If you don't like the rich effect of gold on tortoiseshell, you could try a dark brown or even a white trim.

❖ YOU WILL NEED ❖

Fine-grit sandpaper

Tack cloth

Primer

Two 1½" (4cm) household paintbrushes

Warm light-yellow eggshell paint

Artist's oil paints in raw umber, burnt sienna, light red, and black

Transparent oil glaze

Palette or old plate

Artist's paintbrushes

Mineral spirits

Palette knife

Natural-bristle softener brush

Gold bronzing powder

Acrylic varnish

Clear polyurethane satin varnish

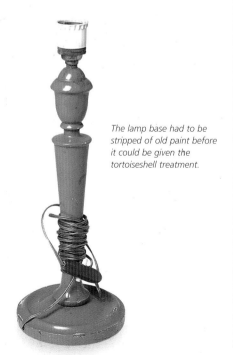

The lamp base had to be stripped of old paint before it could be given the tortoiseshell treatment.

1 Strip the lamp base and, when it is dry, rub it down with fine-grit sandpaper and dust it with a tack cloth. Paint the base and lampshade with primer and allow to dry. Apply three coats of eggshell paint, leaving 24 hours between coats and rubbing down and tacking after each application.

2 Lay out each of the oil paints and a tablespoonful of transparent oil glaze on the palette. Using an artist's brush, mix a little of the raw umber oil paint with some mineral spirits, then add some transparent oil glaze with a palette knife. When this mixture is well integrated, add a few more drops of mineral spirits until the glaze is the consistency of milk. Paint this onto the lampshade in random squiggly lines, moving in a diagonal direction and leaving a few patches of the base color showing through.

3 Make up the other glazes in the same way. Apply burnt sienna glaze along the same diagonals as the raw umber but in separate, broad, curly strokes. Dab on the light-red glaze sparingly in little groups of two or three brushstrokes. Then, using the black glaze again, paint small groups of curly, comma-shaped brushstrokes. Use the natural-bristle brush to soften the overall effect and blend the colors into each other, brushing the glaze gently up and down the diagonals, just allowing the bristles to touch the glaze. Imagine another set of diagonals in the other direction, and lightly brush up and down these until the colors begin to merge.

4 Allow to dry for 24 hours and then mix some of the gold bronzing powder into a little acrylic varnish. Paint this mixture around the binding of the lampshade and highlight some of the molding on the base. When the gold is dry, give the whole piece a coat of satin varnish.

For more lamp projects see:
Craquelure Lamp Base and Shade pp116–17.

▲ Apply small black comma-shaped marks.

▲ Soften the effect with a softener brush.

Malachite Painted Box

SMALL WOODEN BOXES are quite easy to find at a reasonable cost. Often gifts such as wine and cigars are packed in wooden boxes and these can be totally transformed. Boxes can be finished in many ways—such as stenciling, hand-painted designs, découpage, paint techniques, and distressing—to personalize them as gifts for your family and friends. This project shows you how to produce a wonderful satin finish simulating the polished-stone effect of malachite. The technique requires some work but the end result is well worth the effort.

❖ YOU WILL NEED ❖

Screwdriver

Fine-grit sandpaper

Tack cloth

Hide glue

Pot that fits into the saucepan

Saucepan

Sieve

Gilder's whiting

Small paintbrush

Soft brush or mop for applying gesso

Sealer or primer

Varnish

Raw linseed oil

Mineral spirits

Pale sea-green oil-based eggshell paint

Pencil

Straightedge

Transparent oil glaze

Artist's oils in viridian and burnt sienna

Drying oil

Piece of stiff card stock

Cloth

Fine glasspaper

A roughly finished wooden box is ideal for transforming from its raw state into a beautiful gift.

1 If possible, take the lid and the hinges off the box before you start so that it is easier to work on. If it has a lock, you may be able to remove that too. Thoroughly rub down the surfaces with sandpaper and wipe over with a tack cloth to remove any dust.

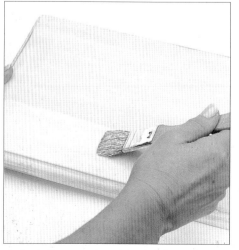

▲ Apply the gesso in quick, straight strokes.

2 Gesso is the key ingredient for this technique. The recipe for gesso is 1 part hide glue to 16 parts water. Whiting is added later. Place the size in a suitable container with 6 parts of water. Let this stand for two hours. Add the remaining water, then place the pot in a saucepan of hot water on a low heat until melted. Take off the heat, put aside a small amount of the size, and then sieve gilder's whiting into the remaining warm size. Keep adding whiting until it is about $1/4$" (6mm) below the surface of the size, and gently stir (the consistency should be that of light cream). Put in the refrigerator overnight.

3 Using a brush, apply the size (the original mixture that you put aside before adding whiting to the rest) to the whole of the box. Allow to dry. Warm the gesso in a saucepan of hot water again and, using a soft brush, apply the gesso in straight brushstrokes.

▲ Sand the gesso surface.

Look along the surface and, as soon as the sheen has disappeared, apply the next coat by stippling it on with the soft brush, still maintaining the gesso at a warm temperature. Apply more coats of gesso as the sheen disappears, stippling every other coat until you have applied at least five coats. Allow to dry for 24 hours.

▲ Apply at least two coats of pale sea-green eggshell paint.

4 Carefully rub down the surfaces with fine-grit sandpaper until you are left with a smooth finish—this makes a mess, so do it somewhere that is easy to clean and away from where you are going to do any painting.

5 Apply a coat of sealer or primer with a mixture of varnish (1 part), mineral spirits (1 part), and raw linseed oil ($\frac{1}{2}$ part). Set the box aside and allow it to dry completely overnight.

6 "Denib" all surfaces (lightly rub down with fine-grit sandpaper). Apply at least two coats of pale sea-green oil-based eggshell paint, allowing each coat to dry overnight. You need to lightly sand the surface and tack between coats to remove any dust.

7 Using a pencil and a small straightedge, mark irregular sections covering each surface of the box.

▲ Draw uneven sections with a pencil.

▲ Use a piece of card to emulate malachite.

▲ Define the edges of the shapes by wiping with a clean cloth.

10 Wipe the box with a clean, dry cloth. Apply a coat of gloss varnish; allow to dry overnight and then gently rub the surface with a fine finishing glasspaper. Repeat until you have a high gloss shine (this may take several coats). Do not rub down the final coat.

HINTS & TIPS

• The inside of the box can be finished with a contrasting color such as deep red or a complementary color such as black. Alternatively, you could line it with a fabric of your choice.

• It may be a good idea to have a piece of genuine malachite, or a photograph of the stone, next to you as you work. This will help you to create a realistic effect.

For more stone-effect projects see:
Marbled Dressing Table pp162–3; Verdigris Mirror and Door Handles pp188–9; Marbled Bathroom pp200–1; Tortoiseshell Lamp Base and Shade pp224–5.

8 Mix a rich green color, using oil glaze and viridian pigment or artist's oils with a touch of burnt sienna to keep the green from being too blue. If using pigment, make a thinning glaze with 1 part linseed oil, 2 parts mineral spirits, and 5 drops of drying oil. Then thin the glaze slightly with this.

9 Using a paintbrush, apply glaze to alternate sections that have no adjoining edges. Take a piece of stiff card stock and, using a straightedge, tear off a piece slightly larger than the section marked. Drag this piece of card through the glaze with a shaky movement to emulate the lines and swirls that are so characteristic of malachite. Vary the direction of each separate section when dragging through the glaze to create a realistic effect of malachite stone. Use a straightedge and clean cloth to wipe the excess glaze down to the drawn shape. Let the glaze dry thoroughly overnight. The following day continue to fill in the remaining shapes, wiping back the excess glaze as before. Allow to dry overnight again. Continue until all the sections have been filled in.

▲ Varnish the painted box until you have a high gloss shine.

Limed Picture Frame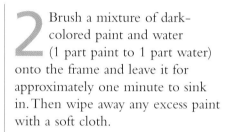

THE TECHNIQUE OF LIMING, or pickling, has been used on furniture for centuries, originally to protect it from fungus and insects, then later purely as a decorative effect. The caustic properties of lime make it unkind to skin, so today we use a white pigment added to wax instead. It is possible to buy a water-based liming paste and, if you can find this, follow the same instructions as below but apply the clear wax after you have removed the excess paste. Liming is a traditional way to treat oak, which is often dark and has a marked, open grain. But, the technique can be used effectively on pine if it is brushed with a wire brush and then color washed with paint or stained with wood dye. Choose a dark color to contrast with the white liming wax.

❖ YOU WILL NEED ❖

Wire brush

Dark-colored latex or traditional paint

Household paintbrush

2 soft cloths

Liming wax

0000-grade steel wool

Clear wax

Liming will give this pine picture frame an attractive decorative finish and a more aged appearance.

1 Open up the grain on the wood by brushing the surface of the picture frame vigorously with a wire brush, always brushing in the direction of the grain. This could take about 15 minutes.

2 Brush a mixture of dark-colored paint and water (1 part paint to 1 part water) onto the frame and leave it for approximately one minute to sink in. Then wipe away any excess paint with a soft cloth.

3 When the paint has completely dried, apply the liming wax to the surface using steel wool. This will tone down the color of the paint. Set it aside for at least half an hour or until it is dry.

4 Using steel wool, rub the surface of the frame with clear wax to remove the excess liming wax. Allow the wax to dry for about half an hour and then buff the frame to a shine with a soft cloth.

For more liming projects see:
Lime-washed Bath Panels pp196–7.

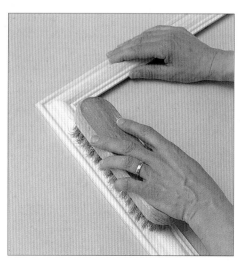

▲ Rub down the wood with a wire brush.

▲ Remove the excess paint with a cloth.

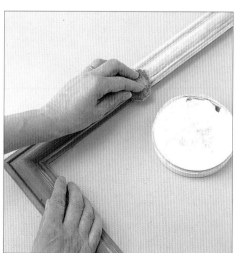

▲ Apply the liming wax over the paint.

Painted Frames

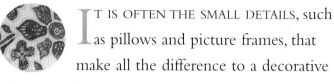 IT IS OFTEN THE SMALL DETAILS, such as pillows and picture frames, that make all the difference to a decorative scheme. Picking out a pattern or theme throughout a room can create a feeling of continuity and harmony. If you have a couple of hours to spare, and a fabric design that you would like to reflect in other areas of your home, then decorating simple picture frames may be the answer. Plain, flat picture frames are easiest to work with and they are readily available. Choose small frames that are not too daunting in size because they will not take too long to complete. Before you start work, spend some time studying the fabric and picking out the detail of the design. If you want to use it at a different size, use a photocopier to reduce or enlarge it.

Checkered Frame

❖ YOU WILL NEED ❖

Fine-grit sandpaper

Tack cloth

Fabric to copy design

Latex paint in the colors of your choice to match the fabric

Small household paintbrush

Masking tape

Ruler

Artist's paintbrush

Blue marker

Clear varnish

1 Rub down the frame with fine-grit sandpaper, then remove any dust with a tack cloth. Paint it using a color that matches the fabric. Then use the masking tape to create straight lines. The fabric will provide a template so that you can position the tape at intervals of the correct width.

2 Allow to dry, then draw in the dark blue lines with a marker and ruler. Finish with a coat of varnish.

For more frame projects see:
Porphyry picture frame pp106–7.

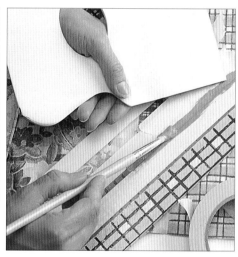
▲ Copy the fabric pattern onto the frame.

Periwinkle Frame

❖ YOU WILL NEED ❖

Fabric to copy design

Latex paint in color of fabric background

Small household brush

Scissors

Carbon paper

Small and very fine artist's paintbrushes

Artist's acrylic in the color of your choice

1 Paint the frame to match the fabric and allow to dry. Cut out sections of fabric and trace the design onto the frame with carbon paper.

2 First, paint the pale blue outlines of the flowers with a small, soft artist's brush. Next, fill in the center of each flower with a deep blue acrylic color. Finally, copy the detail onto each flower and leaf using a very fine-point brush.

For more frame projects:
Poppies picture frame pp236–7.

▲ Trace the pattern directly onto the frame.

Golden Pear Picture Frame

THE TRADITIONAL TECHNIQUES of folk art painting (see "Hints & Tips" below) can be used to great effect to create beautiful painted picture frames. Some of the techniques are complicated, but with practice they can be mastered even if you have no prior painting experience. The golden pear design on a deep red background used here will make a luscious frame for a mirror or painting. You can choose colors that fit in with your decor and suit the picture that will eventually sit in your customized frame.

❖ YOU WILL NEED ❖

Fine-grit sandpaper

Artist's acrylic paint in Indian red oxide, yellow oxide, Turner's yellow, pine green, moss green, warm white, burnt umber, and naphthol red light

All-purpose sealer

2 sponges

Tracing paper

Carbon paper

Stylus

Piece of chalk

Flat paintbrush

Old toothbrush

Liner brush

Masking tape

One-part crackle glaze

Water-based satin varnish and brush

1 Lightly sand the frame and mix 1 part Indian red oxide with 1 part sealer. Apply one coat with the sponge. Sand again and apply one unmixed coat of Indian red oxide.

2 Draw the pear pattern freehand and apply it to one side of the frame with carbon paper and a stylus. Add the pattern to the opposite side, top, and bottom of the frame.

3 Using a piece of chalk, draw a line to divide each side of the frame in half lengthwise. With the flat brush, float (see "Hints & Tips") burnt umber on the inside edge of this line. Then float around the edge of the pear motif with burnt umber. Double load the flat brush with pine green and moss green, and paint the leaves on either side of the pears. Do not paint the leaves in between the pears at this stage.

4 Base coat the dark pears with yellow oxide and the light pears with Turner's yellow. To shade the pears, load the flat brush with the base color, then pick up a small amount of Indian red oxide on one corner. Blend them by brushing up and down on the palette until you have a soft graduation of color from dark to light that can be painted onto the pears. Highlight the pears by loading the brush in the base color and then picking up warm white on one corner and blending.

5 Reinforce the shading and highlighting by dry brushing some base color and Indian red oxide over shaded areas and some base color and warm white on highlighted areas.

6 Dry brush on napthol red light to add a blush to the light pears and add moss green to the dark pears. Use an old toothbrush to spatter Indian red oxide over the pears lightly.

7 Paint the pear stems with the liner brush loaded with yellow oxide and Indian red oxide, lightly blended but not thoroughly mixed. Add small liner brushstrokes with burnt umber to the bottom of the light pears.

8 Mask the inner half of the frame and use a sponge to apply a coat of crackle medium to the outer

▲ Give the pears a rosy glow with shading.

part, avoiding the pears. When the crackle is dry, use the sponge to apply another coat of Indian red oxide. Remove the tape, allow the crackle to dry, and then apply two or three coats of satin varnish with the varnish brush.

HINTS & TIPS

Folk art paint techniques will enable you to create exquisite paint finishes:

• Loading: Stroke the brush through the paint on the palette and then stroke the brush on a clean part of the palette until the paint has worked through the brush.

• Double loading: Load the brush fully with one paint color, then stroke the brush through the second color.

• Floating: Allows you to add shading to your design. Dip the brush in water and then dip one corner of the brush into the paint. Stroke the brush along your palette so that the paint gradually fades out across the bristles.

For more frame projects see:
Porphyry Picture Frame pp106–7; Gilded Mirror Frame pp119–21; Limed Picture Frame pp230–1.

Poppies Picture Frame

POPPIES CONJURE UP the quintessential hazy feeling of a warm summer's day. In this project, the combination of deep red and fiery orange creates a harmonious warm atmosphere. Spiky leaves, curvaceous poppy flowers with dark seductive centers, rounded seed heads, gently bending buds, and bumblebees fuse to form a sympathetic union of shapes. Together the colors and shapes convey the feeling of walking through the countryside, dotted with the richness of red and orange wildflowers.

❖ YOU WILL NEED ❖

Primer/sealer

Yellow ocher latex paint

Acrylic paint in burnt umber, orange, deep red, and fiery orange

Latex glaze

Stencil brush

Paper cutouts of poppies

Designs for your stencil (see page 249)

Tracing paper

Pencil

Card stock, acetate, or stencil film

Craft knife and cutting mat

Nonpermanent adhesive spray

Small household paintbrush

Clear varnish

1 Paint the frame with primer/ sealer. Allow it to dry completely and then paint two layers of yellow ocher latex.

2 Mix up a wash, the consistency of light cream, using a burnt umber acrylic and latex glaze. Gently apply the wash with big brushstrokes, working across the frame to give it just a hint of color.

3 Plan the position of the poppy and leaf stencils over the frame using paper cutouts. Move the shapes around until you are happy with the design. Apply the large poppy stencils in the corners of the frame and add the other elements in a random pattern. Start with the larger shapes to get the pattern going and fill in the gaps with the smaller ones.

4 Trace the designs for the pattern and transfer to the card stock, acetate, or stencil film. Use a craft knife to cut them. Hold in place over the frame with nonpermanent adhesive spray and apply the paint.

5 For the largest poppy stencil, make three separate stencils, one for each color used in the design. Stencil the colors one at a time. To position the stencils accurately on the frame, slide them into position under a tracing of the whole poppy shape, then remove the tracing paper.

6 Finish the frame by painting the inner and outer edges in a rich red color to give the sides definition. Allow the paint to dry, then apply two protective coats of varnish.

HINTS & TIPS

When using two colors within the same shape, work from opposite ends of the stencil. Combine the colors in the middle with a different brush to keep the tones clean and clear.

For more stenciling projects see:
Stenciled Balustrade pp130–2; Cups and Saucers Chairs pp146–7; A Kitchen Frieze pp148–9; Stenciled Cane Chair pp160–1; Frottaged and Stenciled Screen pp167–9; A Bedroom Frieze pp172–4; Cherub Wardrobe pp180–3.

▲ Use paper cutouts to plan the design.

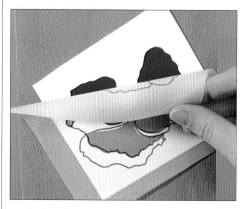

▲ Line up the poppy stencils using a tracing.

▲ Use a stencil brush to apply the paint.

Stenciled Newspaper Rack

THIS EVERYDAY PIECE was given a makeover in no time at all. It should take no more than a couple of hours to complete the work (plus drying time). Stenciling is used as the main technique with a little pen work added to give the design extra definition. Glued-on pieces of newspaper are added as a finishing touch to complete the overall effect. This newspaper rack is intended to be less flowery and feminine than many stencils can be, so it would be suitable as a gift for a man or a woman. For a truly individual touch, you can choose items such as charts and headlines from newspapers that the person who will receive the gift actually reads. Of course, the same techniques could be adapted for any container.

❖ YOU WILL NEED ❖

Piece of paper

Pencil

Pile of books or other design to copy

Artist's acrylic paint in the colors of your choice

Household paintbrushes

Tracing paper

Card stock, acetate, or stencil film

Craft knife and cutting mat

Nonpermanent adhesive spray

Stencil brush

Permanent marker

Old newspapers or magazines

PVA glue and glue brush

Clear varnish

1 Plan your design on paper. Then either draw your stencil design yourself by copying a pile of real books or photocopy an image from a book or magazine to the size you want it. Color the final photocopy as you want the stencil to look so that you can refer to this while you work.

2 Use tracing paper to transfer the design onto a piece of stencil film. Carefully cut out the stencil design using a craft knife on a cutting mat. Start by removing the smaller areas to keep the stencil as firm as possible. Hold the stencil in place on the newspaper rack with nonpermanent adhesive spray. Apply the paint with a stencil brush in a dabbing motion. Carefully peel away the stencil.

3 Outline every section using a permanent marker to make them stand out more.

4 Cut out headlines or charts from a newspaper or magazine and glue them onto the rack.

5 Once the glue and paint are dry, varnish the entire surface. Apply several coats to prevent the newspaper from peeling off.

HINTS & TIPS

• Make the pages of the books look dirty by adding a little darker paint from a stiff almost-dry brush, on top of the white and following the line of the pages.

• You could use a commercial stencil, but it is much cheaper and more satisfying to design one yourself.

For more stenciling projects see:
Stenciled Balustrade pp130–2; A Kitchen Frieze pp148–9; Stenciled Cane Chair pp160–1; Frottaged and Stenciled Screen pp167–9; Children's Balloon Stencils pp184–5; Monogrammed Box pp244–5.

▲ Cut out items from newspapers.

▲ Detail of the book stencil.

Stamped CD Box

STAMPING IS AN EXCELLENT WAY of creating repeating patterns over surfaces. A block stamp is particularly well suited to a simple, rustic look. The decorative effect should come from repeating motifs, rather than from complex shapes. This CD box was customized as a gift for a friend, basing the stamp design on a piece of the fabric that was used in their living room. A stamp was made for each of the two basic elements of the fabric design—one checked with a zigzag border, the other a sinuous curving plant stem. The curvy part of the design was used to accent the top and sides of the box. The colors used exactly echo the dyes on the fabric, and attractive little brass handles were added to each drawer as a finishing touch.

❖ YOU WILL NEED ❖

Design to copy or create your own

Tape measure

Pencil

Tracing paper

2 pieces of sheet rubber

Craft knife and cutting mat

PVA adhesive

2 pieces of rigid foam plastic

2 wooden base blocks

Scrap paper

Sponge

Artist's acrylic paint in burnt sienna and black

Select a simple pattern to use as a starting point.

1 You can either design your own stamp or look for ideas that you can incorporate in your pattern from books or fabric. Plan how large the stamp will need to be to cover the CD box. It may help if you lightly mark the positions of the stamps with a tape measure and pencil.

2 Photocopy your design to the correct size if necessary. Then make a tracing of it and transfer each separate pattern to a different sheet of rubber. Cut out the designs with a craft knife and mat. Use PVA adhesive to apply two pieces of foam to two wooden blocks. Stick the cutout pieces of rubber onto the bits of foam, press firmly in place, and allow to dry.

3 Test each stamp on a piece of scrap paper before you use it. Use a piece of sponge to coat the stamp with artist's acrylic paint. Adjust the amount of paint and pressure applied if necessary. Once you are satisfied with the pattern, cut away the extra foam on each block. Then use the same technique to stamp the box.

For more stamping projects see:
Sponge-stamped Floor pp128–9; Ivy-stamped Chair pp150–1.

▲ Cover the stamps evenly with paint.

▲ Detail of stamped drawer.

Stenciled Mirror Frame

THIS MIRROR FRAME is an excellent project for beginners who have not attempted many paint-effect projects before. It is quick and easy to make and will delight the recipient if it is given as a gift. The starting point is a very simple mirror frame made of unfinished pine. Before buying the mirror, check that it hasn't been treated or varnished in any way.

For such a down-to-earth object, the rough finish of stenciling can be used to create a "rustic" look. The simple outline of the ivy leaf is ideal for a stencil, and the long undulating stems are perfect for decorating tall, narrow areas. Mellow colors were used for a subtle effect. The position of each leaf and the regular curves of the stem were calculated to fit in the rectangular frame.

❖ YOU WILL NEED ❖

Fine-grit sandpaper

Tack cloth

Pale stone latex satin paint

Yellow ocher acrylic paint

Paint bucket or saucer

Sponge

Template for your stencil (see page 248)

Pencil

Card stock, acetate, or stencil film

Craft knife and cutting mat

Ruler

Nonpermanent adhesive spray

Household paintbrush

Clear matte polyurethane varnish

1 Lightly sand the frame with the sandpaper to remove any roughness. Remove any dust with a tack cloth, then apply two coats of latex satin.

2 Mix a little yellow ocher with the latex and apply to the frame with a sponge. When the new color is completely dry, gently distress it by rubbing down lightly with sandpaper to achieve a subtle, clouded finish. Remove any dust with a tack cloth.

3 Trace the ivy-leaf design from page 248 on acetate and cut out the shape with a craft knife. Divide the length of the frame by the length of a leaf and stem to calculate the number of leaves and stems that will fit. Lay the design on the mirror frame and pencil in each leaf, then connect them with a curved stem.

4 Apply yellow ocher through the stencil with a sponge. Flip the stencil to create a mirror image on the other side of the frame. Allow to dry for at least 12 hours, then apply a couple of protective coats of matte varnish, allowing each to dry before applying the next.

HINTS & TIPS

• Take care when cutting out and handling the stencil; if the acetate or stencil film tears, the paint could leak out beyond the outline of the stencil.

• Do not overload the sponge with paint when stenciling.

For more stenciling projects see:
Stenciled Balustrade pp130–2; Cups and Saucers Chair pp146–7; A Kitchen Frieze pp148–9; Stenciled Cane Chair pp160–1; Frottaged and Stenciled Screen pp167–9; A Bedroom Frieze pp172–4; Cherub Wardrobe pp180–3; Children's Balloon Stencils pp184–5; Poppies Picture Frame pp236–7.

▲ Apply yellow ocher with a sponge.

▲ Draw the ivy-leaf design.

▲ Sponge yellow ocher through the stencil.

Monogrammed Box

 **T**HIS IS AN IDEAL personalized present and it is particularly appropriate as a wedding gift, since the bride's and groom's initials can be combined in the monogram. The starting point was a very ordinary little box to which a few coats of dark oak varnish had been applied. Because the box lid was quite small, simple classic letters were used. But the design became more interesting by having the "S" curve around the straight lines of the "H." A wreathed circle of reeds and long, pointed leaves was chosen for the border detail, which prevents the letters from looking isolated. The masking required in such cases is time-consuming (particularly since each side can be sprayed only when the previous stencil is dry) but the effect is well worth it.

❖ YOU WILL NEED ❖

Dark-oak tinted varnish

Paintbrush

Piece of paper

Ruler

Pencil

Piece of string

Straight pin

Selected capital letters for monogram, cut from a newspaper

Tracing paper

Template for your design (see page 249)

Card stock, acetate, or stencil film

Craft knife and cutting mat

Nonpermanent adhesive spray

Spray paint in yellow ocher and dark umber

Pinking shears

1 Apply two or three coats of dark oak varnish. Then make a plan of the top of the box using paper, pencil, and ruler. Find the midpoint by connecting the diagonals from each corner. Mark the midpoint, then, using a piece of string and a straight pin placed in the midpoint to form a compass, draw a circle on the paper.

2 Take the chosen initials and enlarge them to the required size on a photocopier. Combine them on tracing paper to form a decorative monogram. Trace the wreath of leaves from the template on page 249, following the circle that you outlined in step 1.

3 Having combined the border and the monogram, transfer them to the card stock, acetate, or stencil film and cut the stencil. Mask all areas of the box that you are not spraying and lay the stencil in position, holding it in place with nonpermanent adhesive spray.

▲ Spatter on some dark umber.

4 Apply a thin coat of yellow ocher spray paint and allow to dry. Spatter on some dark umber.

5 Cut a piece of card stock with pinking shears to make a border stencil. Attach to the box with nonpermanent adhesive and spray with yellow ocher paint. When dry, apply a coat of dark-oak tinted varnish (the same as that used originally).

For more box projects see:
Hand-printed Blanket Chest pp164–5.

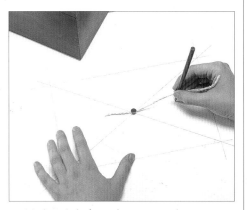
▲ Mark a circle from the center point.

▲ Combine the initials and wreath.

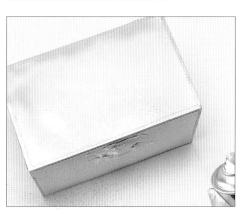
▲ Spray on the zigzag border.

Templates

Painted Decanter and Glasses pp92–3
(Photocopy at 58%)

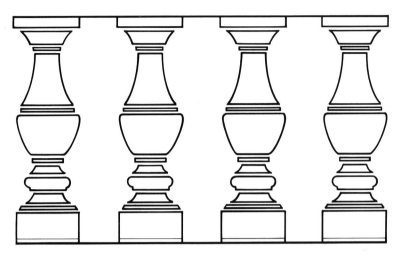

Stenciled balustrade pp130–2
(Photocopy to fit your wall)

Cups and Saucers Chair pp146–7
(Photocopy at 125%)

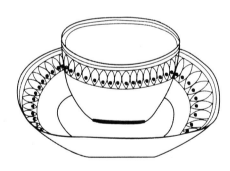

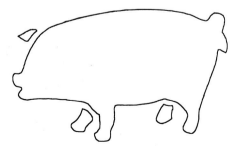

Stenciled Pigs Chair pp144–5
(Actual size)

Hand-printed Blanket Chest pp164–6
(Photocopy at 74%)

Stenciled Headboard pp170–1
(Photocopy at 200%)

Frottaged and Stenciled Screen pp167–9
(Photocopy at 200%)

Stenciled Headboard pp170–1
(Photocopy at 200%)

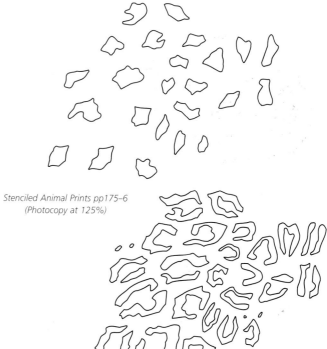

Stenciled Animal Prints pp175–6
(Photocopy at 125%)

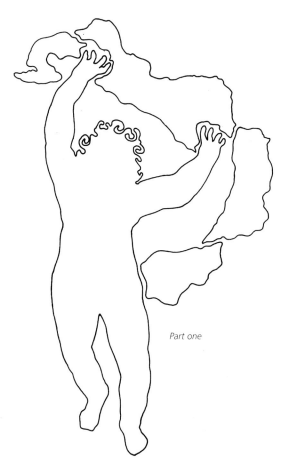

Part one

*Cherub Wardrobe pp180–3
(Actual size)*

*Hand-painted Chest pp206–7
(Photocopy at 125%)*

Part two

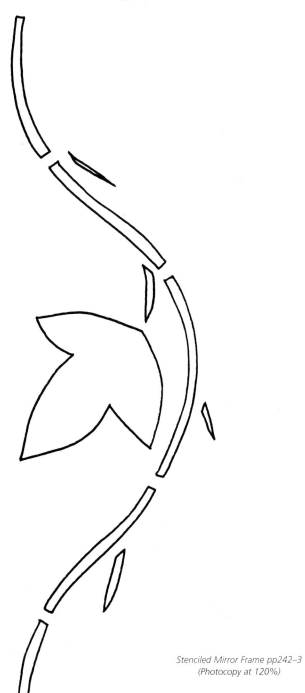

*Stenciled Mirror Frame pp242–3
(Photocopy at 120%)*

Poppies Picture Frame pp236–7
(Photocopy at 105%)

Monogrammed Box pp244–5
(Photocopy at 110%)

Glossary

THE RANGE OF ARTIST'S materials that can be used for basic repairs and decorative techniques is large. Whatever equipment, tool, or product you plan to use, be sure to follow manufacturer's guidelines. Always wear appropriate safety equipment and work in ventilated areas.

ACETATE
Used in stenciling as an alternative to manila card or card stock. Designs must be traced onto acetate using a permanent marker.

ACRYLIC GOLD SIZE
A water-based size often used for gilding and metal leaf application. Although it appears milky on application, it dries transparent.

ACRYLIC PRIMER
A quick-drying primer that can be used to seal wood. Some brands may also be used on metal and masonry.

ACRYLIC SCUMBLE
A slow-drying, water-based glaze medium, which can be mixed with color and used for stippling and sponging.

ANTIQUING, OR AGING
Making an object look older than it really is. There are various techniques, including the use of color and stains, *craquelure*, and distressing.

ARTIST'S ACRYLIC PAINT
Quick-drying and durable, these paints are suitable for many types of surface decoration, and can be used to color acrylic glazes.

ARTIST'S BRUSHES
Finer tipped than household decorating brushes, artist's brushes can be used for painting intricate designs and are available in a variety of sizes and qualities.

ARTIST'S OIL COLORS
More slow-drying than acrylics, these paints can be mixed to a range of subtle colors and are suitable for most techniques, providing the surface is oil-based. The paints can also be used to color oil-based glazes.

BASE COAT
The initial, base application of paint to a surface.

CHEESECLOTH OR STOCKINETTE
Ideal for polishing and mopping up, these cloths can also be used to create texture on a painted surface and for eliminating brush marks.

CHINA FILLER
Used to fill missing edges, cracks, and chips on china, this filler dries to a fine, hard finish on most types of chinaware.

CHIPBOARD
Coarse-grain board made of wood chips that are bound together. It is cheaper than timber but not as strong.

CRACKLE GLAZE
A water-soluble glaze that is applied as a sandwich between two layers of paint or between wood and paint. Crackle glaze dries clear but causes the paint applied over the top to crack, giving the appearance of peeling paint.

CRAFT KNIFE
Needed for cutting stencils, cardboard templates, and découpage cutouts. Replace blades regularly and use in conjunction with a self-healing cutting mat.

CRAQUELURE
Craquelure is the French name for the fine cracks that often cover old oil paintings. These cracks are formed by the layers of paint beneath the varnish surface gradually shrinking over time. The effect can be imitated by using two-part *craquelure* varnish.

DÉCOUPAGE
The French art of cutting, pasting, and varnishing paper or fabric images to form a decorated finish.

DISTRESSING
The action of sanding and battering a surface to imitate age and wear and tear.

ENAMEL PAINT
Very smooth and fairly fast-drying, these paints are suitable for projects such as barge painting. They have their own cellulose thinners to act as a solvent, but mineral spirits can be used as an alternative.

GESSO
Made from animal hide size and gilder's whiting, gesso is used as a preparation before water gilding. It can also be used to fill the grain on unpainted wood, before being rubbed down to a smooth finish.

GILDING
A decorative technique involving transfer leaf, gilding cream, or gilding powder to imitate a metallic finish such as gold.

GILDING POWDER
Painted on to tacky size, gilding powder creates a gold, silver, bronze, or copper finish.

GILT CREAM
This cream can be used as a highlighting agent, or to touch up gilding on frames and furniture. It is applied either by brush or finger and then buffed to a shine when dry.

GLASS PAINT
Made with resins that give a brilliant, transparent, and durable finish to most glass, plastic, or acetate surfaces. However, it is important to test plastic surfaces to be sure they are compatible with the paint.

HARDBOARD

Hardboard is a thin board that is made from compressed wood pulp—it is smooth on one side and textured on the other.

HIDE GLUE

This is used as a preparation for gesso, a base for gilding, and as a sealer to stop varnish and water from penetrating the paper.

HOG FITCHES

Good all-purpose brushes, hog fitches can be used for applying paint, glue, waxes, and gilt creams. They are also effective for tamping down metal leaf and painting narrow bands of color.

HOUSEHOLD BRUSHES

Broader and coarser than artist's brushes, household brushes are suitable for painting fairly large surfaces and come in a variety of sizes.

KEY

Rubbing a surface down to make another coat of paint or varnish adhere properly is known as keying. Use fine-grit sandpaper and a tack cloth.

LACQUER

Available in spray or liquid form, lacquer provides a protective varnished surface. Always apply several fine coats, rather than one heavy coat, to avoid runs and a buildup of varnish.

LATEX PAINT

Available in flat or satin finishes, this paint has a tough, plastic, waterproof finish when dry. It can be used as a paint, thinned with water to make a wash, or tinted with acrylic paints, universal stains, or powder pigments to make a range of decorative colors.

LIMING, OR PICKLING, WAX

A rich paste of clear wax and white pigment used to give a pickled-lime effect to wood. It can also be used as a finishing wax. After opening the grain of the wood with a wire brush, apply the paste with fine steel wool or a cloth. Remove the excess with a cloth and then buff with a neutral wax to obtain a sheen.

MEDIUM

A liquid in which pigment is suspended.

METHYLATED SPIRITS

Used as a solvent for latex paint when creating a distressed effect, methylated spirits can also be used as a thinner and a brush cleaner for shellac and French enamel varnish. It can also be used with fine steel wool for cleaning surfaces.

MINERAL SPIRITS

Mineral spirits are used as a thinner for oil-based paint and transparent oil glaze, as well as to clean brushes and to clean or remove splashes and spills of oil-based paint.

OIL-BASED HOUSEHOLD PAINTS

Available in flat, eggshell, and gloss finishes, oil-based paints give a much tougher finish than latex and are particularly useful in light-colored, oil-based glazes. They can be tinted with artist's oil paints or universal stains to create an even more diverse range of colors.

OIL-BASED PRIMER

A slow-drying, durable primer that is useful for surfaces that do not easily accept or grip acrylic primers, such as some metal and plastic surfaces.

OIL-BASED VARNISH

A slow-drying varnish, available in a polyurethane or alkyd formula. It comes in matte, satin, and gloss finishes and is generally more durable and heatproof than water-based varnish, although it does yellow with time. Water-soluble crackle varnish finishes should always be sealed with a protective coat of oil-based varnish.

OIL GLAZE

A medium to which paint is added to suspend the color and delay drying time. Various decorative effects can be achieved while this glaze is wet.

PAINT STRIPPERS

Use paint strippers for varnished or painted surfaces that need to be taken right back to the original wood. Always work with plenty of ventilation and follow the manufacturer's guidelines.

PALETTE KNIFE

Useful for applying filler, mixing paints, or even applying paint, these knives are very flexible and available from most art shops.

PASTE WAX

A blend of several waxes with good resistance to water and fingermarks, suitable for applying to painted furniture. It creates a seal for crackle and peeled-paint techniques, and also enhances the aging effect.

PERMANENT MARKERS

Essential for marking designs on stencil film, these pens are permanent, do not smudge, and create clear outlines.

PLYWOOD

Made from three veneers of wood that are bonded together—birch is usually the outer veneer.

POWDERED PIGMENTS

Natural earth and mineral pigments in powder form can be mixed with other paint colors, acrylic and PVA mediums, and wax.

PRIMER

Usually oil-based but sometimes available as acrylic, primer should be applied to all raw wood or metal surfaces before painting.

Glossary (continued)

PVA & ACRYLIC MEDIUMS

These water-based mediums are white but dry transparent. PVA can be used as a glue or varnish and, when thinned with water, as a paint medium or binder. It can also be mixed with acrylic, gouache, universal stains, or powder pigments to make paints and washes. Artist's acrylic mediums are useful for extending acrylic paints and for mixing with powder pigment to make concentrated color.

RAGGING

This refers to a range of decorative finishes in which a scrunched cloth (ragging) or plastic bag (bagging) are used to make patterns in wet glaze.

ROTTENSTONE

A finely ground, grayish brown limestone powder. It is usually used for polishing but can also be used as a powder pigment, especially for antiquing stains.

RUSTPROOFING PRIMER

An essential base for any piece of metal that is to be coated in a water-based paint or that has been cleaned and sanded of existing rust.

SANDING SEALER

Spirit-based, sanding sealer is useful for sealing new, stripped, dark or heavily knotted wood before paint is applied. It is an excellent sealing base for découpage projects and can be used before waxing to give a good base for the wax sheen.

SANDPAPER

Available in a range of fine-, medium-, or coarse-grit, this paper is used to prepare a surface for decoration, to distress paint, and to smooth paints and varnishes. See also silicone carbide finishing papers.

SEA SPONGES

These sponges have a better absorbency and more varied structure than synthetic sponges, so are ideal for creating attractive decorative patterns.

SHELLAC

The naturally occurring resin of the lac beetle, shellac is mixed with methylated spirits to form a quick-drying varnish. It is traditionally used in furniture restoration and French polishing. Shellac is available in a variety of grades and colors and may be sold under a number of different names. Use clear shellac sanding sealer, white French polish, and white button polish for sealing wood, paper, and paint. Use brown French polish or garnet polish for staining, aging, and sealing. French enamel varnish is transparent shellac with added dye, and is good for aging and sealing wood.

SILICON CARBIDE FINISHING PAPER

Sometimes known as wet and dry paper, this paper is available in much finer grits than regular sandpaper. They are used to give a smooth finish to varnish or distress a painted surface without causing scratches.

SOFTENING

A term used to refer to the "blurring" of paint, color, or glaze edges. Soft brushes or cloths are used to blend the colors and soften the division.

SOFT-HAIRED MOP BRUSHES

These round brushes are often used in gilding because they are ideal for dusting gilding powder onto gold size. A soft squirrel-hair paintbrush can be used as a cheap alternative.

SPONGING

A simple decorative technique involving the application of paint with a sponge. Sponges can also be used to lift wet paint from a surface, creating an attractive, textured effect.

SPRAY PAINT

Ideal for stenciling projects, acrylic spray paints can be used on most surface types, including wood, plaster, and plastic. Spray enamels for metals and glass, including pearlized finishes and polyurethane varnishes, are also available. Apply the paint in several thin coats, rather than one heavy one, to avoid paint buildup and runs.

STEEL WOOL

There are various grades of steel wool, from very fine (0000) to coarse (00). It can be used for cleaning wood, metal, and glass, for applying wax, and for distressing painted surfaces. Fine steel wool does not scratch or mark wood if it is used gently, and can help to create a smooth finish. Soaked in mineral spirits or warm water, it is useful for cleaning wooden furniture. If it is used with varnish and paint removers, always wear protective gloves and cover the surrounding area to catch the fine steel filaments that come away as the wool is rubbed.

STENCILING

The technique of applying a design to a surface using thin film or card, such as card stock, acetate, or stencil film. The design is cut into the stencil material, and then paint is applied through the incisions onto the surface.

STENCIL BRUSHES

Usually made from natural bristles, these are round and firm-bristled, and come in a wide range of sizes for both small and large stencil work. When stenciling with acrylic paint, choose brushes that have a little give in the bristles, rather than the very firm variety. A double-ended stencil brush is particularly useful when using two colors. Special stencil brushes for use on fabrics are also available; these have softer, longer bristles but are not suitable for hard surfaces.

STENCIL FILM

Made from transparent polyester sheeting, stencil film is very flexible and durable.

STENCIL PAINT AND STICKS

Water-based acrylic or oil-based stencil paint can be obtained in small jars. Stencil sticks are oil-based and wrapped in a sealed film. They are very versatile and can be blended to make different shades and colors.

STIPPLING

The term used for lifting on or off very fine speckles of paint.

STIPPLING BRUSHES

Stippling brushes have stiff, dense bristles in a squared-off shape. They are useful for merging paints and removing hard lines and edges.

SWORD LINERS

These long-haired, soft brushes are tapered and angled, and are capable of producing many widths of line simply by varying the pressure applied to the brushstroke.

SACK CLOTHS

These are small, versatile, long-lasting oily cloths that are ideal for cleaning wood, metal, plaster, or any other surface (except glass). They pick up and hold dust and dirt, leaving a completely clean surface.

TRADITIONAL PAINT

Containing natural pigments and chalk, traditional paints dry to a completely matte finish that appears considerably lighter than the color in the can. They can be easily marked and so should be protected with a coat of varnish or wax. The paints can be thinned with water and tinted in the same way as latex paint.

TRANSFER METAL LEAF

Bronze, aluminum, and copper leaf are inexpensive and a good substitute for real gold and silver leaf when adding decorative touches to furniture. Transfer leaf, which is sold in packs of sheets, is available in craft stores. Each sheet consists of very finely beaten metal backed with wax paper. The metal is transferred from the paper onto tacky size. Metal leaf tarnishes in time, so it needs to be sealed with shellac or varnish.

TRANSFER PAPER

Coated with a chalky film, transfer paper is colored red, blue, black, and white. It is placed between the design to be transferred and the surface to be decorated. The outline is then transferred by tracing over it with a pen or pencil.

TWO-PART *CRAQUELURE* VARNISH

This consists of a slow-drying, oil-based varnish and a quick-drying, water-soluble varnish. The water-soluble varnish is brushed over a layer of slightly tacky oil-based varnish. Later, a cracked porcelain effect appears, which is due to the difference in drying times. This becomes clearly visible when artist's oil color is rubbed into the surface and gets caught in the cracks.

UNDERCOAT

A layer of protective paint applied between primer and final surface paint.

UNIVERSAL STAINS

Although universal stains lack the range of subtle colors of oil and latex paints, they will mix with virtually anything, including both water-based and oil-based mediums. They come in liquid form, are extremely strong, and are cheap to obtain.

VARNISH REMOVERS

A number of varnish removers are available, although most paint strippers can also be used on varnished surfaces.

VERDIGRIS

A bluish-green patina that forms on copper, bronze, or brass with age. The effect is associated with historic spires and domes, but can be imitated with paint and gilding cream.

WATER-BASED VARNISH

Water-based acrylic varnishes are now widely available in gloss, satin, matte, and flat finishes. Although they are milky in appearance, these varnishes dry to a clear finish and are nonyellowing. However, the matte and flat versions contain chalk, which gives them a cloudy appearance when a number of coats are applied. This means they are unsuitable to use for the many layers that are required in découpage. These finishes are also softer and less durable than satin or gloss varnish.

WAXES

Clear furniture wax is an effective resist (that is, it creates a block, preventing paint from reaching a surface), when creating an aged appearance on furniture. It can be used over paint or wood to prevent a new layer of paint from adhering to the surface. Clear liquid wax is particularly good for this and is obtainable from special suppliers. Clear wax is also used as a protective finishing wax over paint or matte varnish; it can be colored with rottenstone and other pigments.

There is also a large variety of brown or antiquing furniture waxes that can be used for staining wood. Walnut shades are good for aging all colors of paint, but the antiquing waxes are generally yellowing and are not suitable on blue paint. However, they give a wonderful glow to many shades of yellow and green paint.

WET AND DRY PAPER

See silicon carbide finishing paper.

WIRE BRUSHES

These are used to open up the grain on wood before liming and to remove flaking paint and rust.

WOOD FILLER

Special wood fillers tend to be better for wooden surfaces than ordinary, multipurpose fillers. Water-based varieties are particularly easy to use and come in a number of wood color finishes. They can be used to fill small holes, dents, and cracks, as well as seal around bad joints in wood.

Index